D0026018

Visual Culture Studies

Visual Culture Studies

Marquard Smith

Los Angeles • London • New Delhi • Singapore

First published 2008

SAGE Publications Ltd
1 Oliver's Yard
55 City Road
London EC1Y 1SP

SAGE Publications Inc.
2455 Teller Road
Thousand Oaks, California 91320

SAGE Publications India Pvt Ltd
B 1/I 1 Mohan Cooperative Industrial Area
Mathura Road
New Delhi 110 044

SAGE Publications Asia-Pacific Pte Ltd
33 Pekin Street #02-01
Far East Square
Singapore 048763

Library of Congress Control Number: 2007934349

British Library Cataloguing in Publication data
A catalogue record for this book is available from the British Library

ISBN 978-1-4129-2369-9
ISBN 978-1-4129-2370-5 (pbk)

Typeset by Cepha Imaging Pvt Ltd, Bangalore, India

Printed on paper from sustainable resources

CONTENTS

PREFACE AND ACKNOWLEDGEMENTS

This book introduces readers to a series of deliberations on Visual Culture Studies as an academic field of inter-disciplinary inquiry, and the key debates shaping and determining the study of visual cultures. The Introduction alone offers several interwoven 'accounts' of its inter-disciplinary genealogy, as well as including a consideration of the ways in which visual culture practice itself has led to new ways of seeing, knowing, and understanding the visual and its study.

Following its Introduction, *Visual Culture Studies* comprises thirteen engaging and insightful interviews with influential European and North American intellectuals from across the Arts, Humanities, and Social Sciences working today within a university context and necessarily beyond its ivory towers. As academics, scholars, researchers, teachers, and practitioners with an interest in questions of vision, the visual, and visuality, they have all contributed in provocative ways to disturbing the parameters of more traditional areas of study – such as History, Literature, Art History, Sociology, Religious Studies, Government, and Communication Studies – and in so doing have played a significant part in the possibility of establishing the discipline or inter-discipline variously known as Visual Studies, Visual Culture, or, as I'm calling it here, Visual Culture Studies.[1]

Each interview, in turn, draws out the interests and commitments of the interviewees in order to interrogate critically the past, present, and future possibilities of Visual Culture Studies, the study of visual culture, and visual culture itself. In so doing, and in beginning from an attention to the specific concerns of a unique individual's body of research, writings, and practice, the Introduction and the interviews concentrate on three broad areas of deliberation: (1) the intellectual and institutional status and potential of Visual Culture Studies; (2) the histories, genealogies, and archaeologies of visual culture and its study; and (3) the diverse ways in which the experiences of vision, or the visual, can be articulated and mobilized to political, aesthetic, and ethical ends.

The Intellectual and Institutional Status of Visual Culture Studies

What is visual culture or visual studies? Is it an emergent discipline, a passing moment of inter-disciplinary turbulence, a research topic, a field or subfield of cultural studies, media

> studies, rhetoric and communication, art history, or aesthetics? Does it have a specific object of research, or is it a grab-bag of problems left over from respectable, well-established disciplines? If it is a field, what are its boundaries and limiting definitions? Should it be institutionalized as an academic structure, made into a department or given programmatic status, with all the appurtenances of syllabi, textbooks, prerequisites, requirements, and degrees? How should it be taught? What would it mean to profess visual culture in a way that is more than improvisatory?
>
> W.J.T. Mitchell (2002: 165–66)

W.J.T. Mitchell's quotation, above, taken from an article entitled 'Showing Seeing: A Critique of Visual Culture' and published in the *Journal of Visual Culture* in 2002 raises a series of questions in order to point out, confront, and begin to critique the current intellectual and institutional status of Visual Culture Studies. As Mitchell goes on to outline in that article, even though the field of inquiry is still in its infancy, it has already become complacent. The questions he raises begin an important examination of some of the ways in which this is the case. His interrogation raises many of the issues that must be addressed in any deliberation on the subject of Visual Culture Studies, for they are questions of definition, of disciplinarity, and of the 'object' of visual culture, as well as questions for academic institutions and for pedagogy. These questions in turn lead to others: what is Visual Culture Studies? Is this field of inquiry a discipline, a sub-discipline, an inter-discipline, or something else? Why are the bonds between Visual Culture Studies and its intersecting fields of inquiry, the very fields that inform it, so tense? What is the purview or object domain of Visual Culture Studies, or, rather, what is the 'object' of study of Visual Culture Studies? What objects or artefacts or media or environments are 'appropriate' for or particular to this field of inquiry? Has the 'object' of visual culture found a faithful interpreter in the scholar of Visual Culture Studies? What role does the intellectual play in interrogating our visual cultures, and, in so doing, in shaping Visual Culture Studies? And finally, what does it mean for Visual Culture Studies to be taught, and how should this teaching take place? These are some of the questions with which we struggle in *Visual Culture Studies* as the interviewees and I seek to delineate the intellectual and institutional status and possibilities of this field of inquiry.

There are many more questions here than there are answers. As we shall go on to discover, this is one of the troubles, as well as one of the pleasures, of Visual Culture Studies.[2] With this in mind, this book will propose multi-faceted ways of engaging with these often quite seemingly straightforward and yet deeply intricate questions which have enormous implications for those of us concerned with the study of the past, present, and future of our visual cultures.

The Histories, Genealogies, and Archaeologies of Visual Culture and its Study

Already in its short lifetime, Visual Culture Studies has been accused of ahistoricsm. That is to say, historians and theorists of the study of visual culture are said to often concentrate their attentions on the objects, artefacts, media, and environments of recent and contemporary visual culture: photography, film, video, and the internet, as well as other visual spectacles of entertainment, information, and commodity circulation. The positive 'take' on this accusation – and this is certainly the case – is that Visual Culture Studies has played a key role in exploring and explaining our contemporary visual culture *as it takes place* in an ever-changing global context. With its attention to transnational media and the global public sphere, Visual Culture Studies, we can say with confidence, evidences a cultural genealogy of the emergence of globalization. The negative 'take' on the accusation of ahistoricism in Visual Culture Studies is that with its over-attention to the present, its present-ism, it is said to spotlight mediated and re-mediated encounters with such recent communication technologies at the expense of the historical and critical interrogation of earlier forms of visual culture and their study. Similarly, Visual Culture Studies' over-interest in 'theoretical' ways of seeing and practices of looking, knowing and understanding, visual and scopic regimes and technologies of vision, makes it further open to and guilty of charges of ahistoricism. In these and other ways, critics say that Visual Culture Studies has contributed to an anthropological turn, a turn away from history and the lessons of history, and towards a synchronic study of culture.[3]

While this can certainly be said to be true in some cases, it is then ironic that two of the founding texts of Visual Culture Studies, Michael Baxandall's *Painting and Experience in Fifteenth-Century Italy*, a social history of style and the period eye, and Svetlana Alpers' *The Art of Describing: Dutch Art in the Seventeenth Century*, a study of seventeenth century Dutch description, representation, images, appearance, cartography, and visuality are decidedly *not* contemporary – at least as far as their subject matter is concerned.[4] (In addition developments in the 1960s, 1970s, and 1980s, in, say, Marxist art history, feminist film theory, postcolonial considerations of the politics of representation, and gay and lesbian studies into the identity politics of visibility and invisibility, are testament to an ongoing commitment to interrogate the histories of visual cultures.)

With this in mind, the Introduction and the interviews collected for *Visual Culture Studies* question the perceived crisis in/of history that Visual Culture Studies seems to both signal and to which it draws attention. In putting in place some of the histories, genealogies, and archaeologies of visual culture and its study, the book ponders the place of philosophies of history from Kant and Hegel onwards for Visual Culture Studies, asking how in turn the field of inquiry might affect such models. The considerations in these interviews, then, begin from the premise that while Visual Culture Studies as an academic, professional, and bureaucratic area of study may have emerged only recently, the *study* of visual culture, to say nothing of visual culture itself of course, has a much longer history.

Experiences of Vision or the Visual

In light of this, the interviews in *Visual Culture Studies* attend to historical and conceptual specificity, and they do so by concentrating on experiences of vision, the visual, and visuality. They ask for instance: how do cultural histories of vision reveal to us the different ways in which earlier historical moments, as well as our own, bustle with, to quote Svetlana Alpers (1996), their own 'notions about vision [...,] on image making devices [...,] and on visual skills [...] as cultural resources'? How, similarly, can distinct ways of seeing and practices of looking embedded in the experiences of the past – from the art of describing to the optical unconscious, from scopic regimes to phenomenological perception, glances, glazes, spectacles, for example – be understood in subsequent moments through archival, historical, material, conceptual, and interpretive means? And how do such understandings of the past shed light on the present in order to further engage contemporary visual culture, and its futures?

In all of this, the interviews here are caught up in considering critically the pitfalls and possibilities of Visual Culture Studies; the very historical and contemporary experiences of vision or the visual as they are comprehended by those drawn to, seeking to outline, and encourage the study of visual culture.

At the same time, the interviews probe into how and why intellectuals are stimulated or provoked or enraged by, worry over, and feel vulnerable when faced by certain kinds of political issues, cultural debates, and visual culture practices. There is in evidence here a healthy anxiety that intellectuals feel in characterizing Visual Culture Studies – or what some of them call Visual Culture or Visual Studies – as there should be amongst those participating in any emerging field of inquiry. This is the case because Visual Culture Studies is well aware of itself – as newer, and indeed more established disciplines need to be – *as a living methodology*. It is a living methodology whose very ground is transformed continuously as new political situations, ethical dilemmas, historical documents, conceptual turns, and the new objects, artefacts, media, and environments of visual culture, and questions posed of and by visual culture, impress themselves upon our fields of vision. In fact, as a living methodology, rather than a discipline, a sub-discipline, a field of study, a tactic, or a movement we may end up discovering, following Michael Ann Holly, something we might have known all along: that Visual Culture Studies is in fact 'an intellectual attitude'. It is a sensibility. It names a problematic. Bursting with intellectual attitude, the intellectuals interviewed in *Visual Culture Studies* offer historical and conceptual accounts of their decisions as researchers, scholars, teachers, critics, curators, and practitioners as they seek to engage, speak with, and mobilize this problematic: Visual Culture Studies as a living methodology.

The Medium of the Interview

Visual Culture Studies engages directly with the debates outlined above in order to: interrogate the status of Visual Culture Studies as a discipline, or field of study; consider its diverse genealogies; and reflect upon the ways in which it has transformed and continues to transform our means of knowing, our practices of looking, and our ways of seeing and doing. It does this both in its Introduction, and by way of the interviews. The book presents a series of conversations with intellectuals from across the Arts, Humanities, and Social Sciences who have made key contributions – historically and/or conceptually – to the formation of Visual Culture Studies, and our abilities to think visual culture in all its fascinating, fractious, and often contradictory complexities.

In proposing that Visual Culture Studies is both *a living methodology* and *an intellectual attitude*, the medium of the interview, an invention of nineteenth century journalism, reveals itself to be a most ideal format. Interviews, then, form the basis of this book for a number of reasons.[5]

First, interviews foreground the *figure of the intellectual* as a scholar, a researcher, a teacher, a contributor to the formation of Visual Culture Studies and visual culture itself. All of the intellectuals interviewed here inhabit positions in the university and its contexts of academic and professional life *and* in the public sphere where their activities contribute profoundly to the wider civic community. (There may or may not be contradictions and conflicts of interest in such dual inhabiting.) They are cultural forces. They care about ideas, and the urgency of ideas. They are committed to participation. They take their responsibilities seriously, but not always too seriously. They are not afraid to learn in public. The intellectual, writes Edward Said in 1994, is an individual 'endowed with a faculty for representing, embodying, articulating a message, a view, an attitude, philosophy, or opinion to, as well as for, a public'.[6] I believe this is true of the individuals interviewed in *Visual Culture Studies*.

Second, the medium of the interview offers affable, personal insights into the research, writings, and activities of these particular individuals, and the drives and agendas that motivate their thought, as well as a focus on their own intellectual development. The interviews published here – and this is something articulated well by Peter Osborne in his book of interviews entitled *A Critical Sense: Interviews with Intellectuals* – are 'intended to provide contextual elaborations, more accessible formulations, and extensions of the theoretical and political views of their authors – as a way into, rather than a substitute for, their other writings'.[7]

Third, as an encounter, the interview presents what I'd call *thoughts-in-formation*. It is a snapshot of current thinking for Visual Culture Studies. In conducting interviews with intellectuals based in and thinking across the fields of History, Cultural Studies, Sociology, Literature, Film Studies, Art History, Media Studies, Performance Studies, Government, Disability Studies, Communication Studies, and the Visual Arts, we get a real sense of current thinking across the Arts, Humanities, and Social Sciences. The interview gives interviewees the opportunity to contemplate their previous, current, and imminent research, the limitations and possibilities of Visual Culture Studies *as it takes place*, and an engagement with the conceptualization and mobilization of their aesthetic, political, and ethical encounters with the objects, subjects, media, and environments of visual culture itself – as well as their studies of it. Because of this, there is often a wonderfully informal and dialogical quality to the interview. The outcome of conversation is not pre-determined. Speculating – carefully, wildly, and elliptically – about the future of Visual Culture Studies is a must. For me, this is in keeping with the sensibility of Visual Culture Studies and its studies of visual culture: as a living methodology. Things are not determined in advance. Rather, transformations in Visual Culture Studies – as well as the transformative potential of studies of visual culture – are enacted in encounters such as this. This is how new things yet to suggest themselves, that belong to no one, can take shape, come into view, come into being.

Fourth, the interview is *live*, or at least performs live-ness. In the main the interviews in this book took place face-to-face in England and the US, in hotel rooms and hotel bars, in cafes, around people's kitchen tables and around my own. Coffee, food, and alcohol were often a welcome accompaniment. There is something extraordinary about the immediacy of conversation: a series of genuine acts in real time; the apparent naturalness and veracity of improvized exchange; the sound and materiality of the voice, its resonance, its cadence, its unhurried qualities, and its urgency; pauses, the noises we make as we formulate our thoughts before we're ready to put things into words, over-speaking. And yet, this live-ness is not reproducible. Given the fleeting ephemerality of even powerful words, there is thus sometimes a need to preserve them.

Some of the interviews did, though, take place in a more technologically mediated fashion, either via telephone or email. While they offer the interviewee more time to ponder, we have endeavored to retain a 'sense' of live-ness, to take on the characteristics of live-ness. Whether live or mediated, I affirm the medium of the interview as a format in which conversations can take place *over time*, since serious ideas and pressing thoughts *need* time to unfold. (Of course I am not trying to fool anyone: the raw material, the conversations, whether face-to-face, via the telephone, or email, are subject to editorial mediation too: they are transcribed and edited and re-edited, and sometimes 'liveness' is 'injected' into them after the fact. Some interviewees for instance decided to leave in the sound of their laughter, to pearl out from the page, while others decided against it.)

Fifth, by way of conversation and exchange the medium of the interview builds community. As the individuals interviewed here will attest, no one person is capable on their own of constructing and developing an emerging field of inquiry such as Visual Culture Studies. Nor would they want to be. Collaborative building projects such as this need many hands, many voices, many ongoing conversations between individuals, institutions, organizations, and cultural practices. Whether we agree with one another is not the point. Better in fact if, sometimes, we don't agree. Conversations can be all the more productive because of this. For me such conversations are the basis of community. In my understanding of community, I follow Bill Readings (1996) in his still prescient book *The University in Ruins*. Here community is not based on unity and consensus but rather on a network of intellectual obligations, on the chance to think incomplete thoughts together, on occasions when we can raise the very question of '*being-together*', and, in so doing, picture the possibility of 'the notion of community otherwise' (1996, 20). This is how communities are made: between comradeship and conversation, debate and disagreement, hard work and will, hindsight and foresight, realism and utopianism. *Sous les pavés, la plage!*

Such are the ambitions of the medium of the interview. They are all in keeping with the etymology of the word 'interview' itself, which comes from the French *entre vue*, to 'see between'. I hope that *Visual Culture Studies* gives its readers the chance to do just that.

Acknowledgements

I cannot thank enough the contributors to *Visual Culture Studies*. I'm enamored by their generosity, their thought, their willingness to contribute to a project such as this; and to be speculative, to embrace the interview format, the conversation, in this way. It's been a humbling process, and there's something terribly precious about all of this for me, and for that I'm enormously grateful.

I'd like to express my appreciation to Julia Hall, my Commissioning Editor at Sage Publications. Julia has been behind this project from the beginning, and is also the personal responsible for commissioning – the person with the insight to want to commission – *Journal of Visual Culture*. In having recently left Sage after 15 or so years to pursue other publishing and non-publishing dreams, I wish her the best in all aspects of her new life.

Thanks also go to the anonymous referees at Sage for their supportive and constructively critical comments on the initial proposal for this book. Useful comments one and all.

Thanks to friends and colleagues for input of various kinds along the way: Jennifer Crisp, Anna Everett, Coco Fusco, Raiford Guins, Stuart Hall, Juliette Kristensen, Mark Little, Kobena Mercer, Laura Mulvey, Simon Ofield, Vivian Rehberg, Mila Steele, Rob Stone, Margi Thomas-Tanner, and to all my colleagues in the School of Art and Design History and the wider Faculty of Art, Design and Architecture at Kingston University, London. And of course a special thanks to Joanne Morra who has read this book, in parts, as it took shape, more times than I care to remember. She's still sceptical of Visual Culture Studies, but that's art historians for you.

Dedications are strange things. How many times in our lifetime do we have the chance to dedicate something to someone in public? To acknowledge them, to proclaim our debt, to express our obligation, to say thanks. The nature of this project demands that I dedicate this book not to a person but to two educational milieu.

The first is the BA(Hons) programme in History of Modern Art, Design and Film at Newcastle Polytechnic, now Northumbria University at Newcastle. As an 18-year-old living in London, planning to go to college, I knew that I wanted to travel 300 miles to the North East of England for this programme. I didn't know Newcastle, which I came quickly to love, or what a polytechnic was, or what a properly inter-disciplinary degree would be, or could do, but I must have known some of these things without realizing. I see now that same thing in my own undergraduate students, those who come to Kingston to study for degrees in Art, Architecture, and Film or Visual and Material Culture or Museum and Gallery Studies. They are doing it for the same reason: because even if they can't quite articulate it when they arrive, as I couldn't, they already have a sense that they necessarily begin their thinking and looking and experiencing from the truly *inter*; the inter-sensory, the inter-medial, and the inter-disciplinary. I'd like to thank everyone that was involved in making my time in Newcastle so stimulating, so surprising, so challenging, so rewarding. Whether they like it or not, it's in large part because of them that I'm doing what I do. The undergraduate programme at Northumbria has been going for more that 30 years now, here's to the next 30!

The second dedication is to the Department of Fine Art (now the School of Fine Art, History of Art & Cultural Studies) at University of Leeds. The Department housed the Centre for Cultural Studies, newly created as I arrived in Leeds for my MA in Cultural Studies. And it is where I continued my postgraduate studies. The Department has a long and illustrious history: it is synonymous with the formation of the social history of art. T.J. Clark set up a graduate programme there in 1976, and was canny enough to employ Griselda Pollock, Fred Orton, and Terry Atkinson (a founding member of Art & Language). Others such as Janet Wolff and John Tagg have taught there, before moving on to the US. During my MA at Leeds, and my PhD studies, I had the chance to work with an incredibly rich and diverse range of scholars from Art History/Visual Culture Studies (Griselda, Fred, and Adrian Rifkin, then head of the department), Cultural Studies (Barbara Engh), French Studies (Max Silverman and David Macey), Adult Education (Tom Steele), and History of the Philosophy of Science (John Christie). The intellectual life that these people brought to their Departments, to the University as a whole, was in itself a lesson in community.

A book such as *Visual Culture Studies* would not exist without communities – networks of individuals and institutions and organizations – such as these. For me, Visual Culture Studies is an intellectual project, a way of thinking, and a way of teaching and learning – both in the classroom and in public. To an extent our intellectual preoccupations – and the very possibility of wanting to or being able to do intellectual labour – are down to our educational trajectory. This pedagogical formation often has as much if not more to do with good fortune and serendipity as it does with good judgement. I am glad of that.

Notes

1 There are extensive ongoing debates concerning the designation of the field of study under consideration. See, for instance *October's* 'Visual Culture Questionnaire' (1996); John A. Walker and Sarah Chaplin, *Visual Culture: An Introduction* (1997); Nicholas Mirzoeff (1998, 2002); Nicholas Mirzoeff (1999); Marita Sturken and Lisa Cartwright, *Practices of Looking* (2001); James Elkins, *Visual Studies* (2002); Hal Foster, *Design and Crime (and Other Diatribes)* (2002). For the purposes of this publication 'Visual Culture Studies' – rather than 'Visual Culture' or 'Visual Studies' – names the field of study while 'visual culture' designates the objects, subjects, media, and environments of study. The reasons for this will be discussed in my Introduction.

2 In this, I distinguish fundamentally this book from Margaret Dikovitskaya (2005) that announces on its dust jacket how it will offer 'an overview of this new area of study in order to reconcile its diverse theoretical positions'.

3 See for instance 'Visual Culture Questionnaire', *October*, 77 (1996) and Hal Foster (2002).

4 Michael Baxandall (1972) and Svetlana Alpers (1983). Since then there have been numerous books and collections that continue to interrogate the visual culture of diverse historical periods, such as Claire Farago (1995); Pamela Selwyn and Valentine Groebner (2004); and Vanessa Schwartz and Jeannene Przyblyski (2004). Jonathan Crary's research (1990) remains exemplary in this regard.

5 For important collections of interviews, in which the interview format itself is foregrounded, see Peter Osborne (1996), Paul Bowman (2003), and Dikovitskaya (2005). The first is situated firmly within Continental Philosophy while the second is within Cultural Studies, and neither collection is concerned with Visual Culture Studies, questions of vision, the visual, and visuality except in passing. Margaret Dikovitskaya's collection concentrates its attentions on the recent development of 'Visual Studies' programmes in US universities. Also on interviews see Jacques Derrida (1995); Derrida and Bernard Stiegler (2002 [1996]); Gayatri Spivak (1990); and Raymond Williams (1979). On the artist interview, see the themed issue of *Art Journal* (Fall 2005); a recent

themed issue of *Dialogue*, an online arts magazine (July 2006–January 2007 – accessed 10.03.07); and the 24-hour marathon interview organized by curator Hans-Ulrich Obrist and architect Rem Koolhaas at The Serpentine Gallery in 2006.

6 See Said (1994). On intellectuals, and intellectuals and interviews, see Peter Osborne, 'Introduction: Philosophy and the Role of Intellectuals' (1996). See also Paul A. Bové (1986); Michel Foucault (1977 [1972]); Bill Readings (1996); Bruce Robbins (1993); and Bruce Robbins (1996).

7 Peter Osborne, *A Critical Sense: Interviews with Intellectuals*, xxiii, London: Routledge.

References

Alpers, Svetlana (1983) *The Art of Describing: Dutch Art in the Seventeenth Century*. Chicago: The University of Chicago Press.

Alpers, Svetlana (1996) 'Visual Culture Questionnaire', *October*, 77 (Summer): 25–70.

Art Journal (2005) vol. 64, no. 3, Fall.

Baxandall, Michael (1972) *Painting and Experience in Fifteenth-Century Italy*. Oxford: Oxford University Press.

Bové, Paul A. (1986) *Intellectuals in Power: A Genealogy of Critical Humanism*. New York: Columbia University Press.

Bowman, Paul (ed.) (2003) *Interrogating Cultural Studies: Theory, Politics and Practice*. London: Pluto Press.

Crary, Jonathan (1990) *Techniques of the Observer: On Vision and Modernity in the Nineteenth Century*. Cambridge, MA: The MIT Press.

Derrida, Jacques (1995) *Points ... Interviews, 1974–1994*. (Peggy Kamuf et al., *trans.*). Stanford: Stanford University Press.

Derrida, Jacques and Stiegler, Bernard (2002 [1996]) *Echographies of Television: Filmed Interviews*. (J. Bajorek, *trans.*). Cambridge: Polity Press.

Dialogue, 'Inside the Interview: explaining the workings of the artist interview' (July 2006–January 2007) at http://www.axisweb.org/dlIssue.aspx?ISID=5 (accessed 10.03.06)

Dikovitskaya, Margaret (2005) *Visual Culture: The Study of the Visual after the Cultural Turn*. Cambridge, MA: The MIT Press.

Elkins, James (2002) *Visual Studies: A Skeptical Introduction*. London: Routledge.

Farago, Claire (ed.) (1995) *Reframing the Renaissance: Visual Culture in Europe and Latin America: 1450–1650*. New Haven: Yale University Press.

Foster, Hal (2002) *Design and Crime (and Other Diatribes)*. London: Verso.

Foucault, Michel (1977 [1972]) 'Intellectuals and Power: A Conversation Between Michel Foucault and Gilles Deleuze' [1972], in Michel Foucault, *Language, Counter-Memory, Practice: Selected Essays and Interviews* (ed. Donald F. Bouchard). Ithaca: Cornell University Press.

Jones, Amelia (ed.) (2003) *Visual Culture and Feminism*. London: Routledge.

Mirzoeff, Nicholas (ed.) (1998/2002) *The Visual Culture Reader*. London: Routledge.

Mirzoeff, Nicholas (1999) *An Introduction to Visual Culture*. London: Routledge.

Mitchell, W.J.T. (2002) 'Showing Seeing: A Critique of Visual Culture', *Journal of Visual Culture*, 1(2): 165–81.

Osborne, Peter (1996) *A Critical Sense: Interviews with Intellectuals*. London: Routledge.
Readings, Bill (1996) *The University in Ruins*. Cambridge, MA: Harvard University Press.
Robbins, Bruce (1996) *Secular Vocations: Intellectuals, Professionalism, Culture*. London: Verso.
Robbins, Bruce (1993) 'Introduction: The Phantom Public Sphere', in Bruce Robbins (ed.) *The Phantom Public Sphere*. Minnesota: University of Minnesota Press.
Said, Edward (1994) *Representations of the Intellectual: The 1993 Reith Lectures*. London: Vintage.
Schwartz, Vanessa and Przyblyski, Jeannene (eds.) (2004) *The Nineteenth Century Visual Culture Reader*. London: Routledge.
Selwyn, Pamela and Groebner, Valentine (eds.) (2004) *Defaced: The Visual Culture of Violence in the Late Middle Ages*. New York: Zone Books.
Spivak, Gayatri (1990) *The Post-Colonial Critic: Interviews, Dialogues, Strategies* (ed. Sarah Harasym). London: Routledge.
Sturken, Marita and Cartwright, Lisa (2001) *Practices of Looking*. Oxford: Oxford University Press.
'Visual Culture Questionnaire' (1996) *October*, *77* (Summer): 25–70.
Walker, John A. and Chaplin, Sarah (1997) *Visual Culture: An Introduction*. Manchester: Manchester University Press.
Williams, Raymond (1979) *Politics and Letters: Interviews with 'New Left Review'*. London: Verso.

THE EDITOR

Marquard Smith is a founder and the editor-in-chief of the *Journal of Visual Culture* (Sage Publications). He is course director of the MA in Art and Design History in the School of Art and Design History, Kingston University, London, where he is Reader in Visual and Material Culture. Marq is the editor and co-editor of over a dozen volumes and themed issues of journals, including *Cultural Studies and Philosophy* (1996) *Translating Algeria* (Taylor & Francis, 1998), *The Reinterpretation of Dreams* (Taylor & Francis, 2000), *The Limits of Death* (Manchester University Press, 2000), and *The Prosthetic Aesthetic* (Lawrence & Wishart, 2002). Most recent publications include: *Stelarc: The Monograph* (edited, The MIT Press, 2006), *The Prosthetic Impulse: From a Posthuman Present to a Biocultural Future* (co-edited, The MIT Press, 2005), and *Visual Culture: Critical Concepts in Media and Cultural Studies*, a four volume co-edited Major Works project for Routledge (2006), He is currently writing two books, *Moving Bodies ... Mostly Human* and *The Erotic Doll: A Tale of Artificial Love*.

NOTES ON CONTRIBUTORS

Mieke Bal, a well-known cultural critic and theorist, is Royal Dutch Academy of Science Professor, Professor of the Theory of Literature at the University of Amsterdam, and A.D. White Professor-at-Large at Cornell University. A co-founder of the Visual and Cultural Studies programme at Rochester, among Bal's many books are: *A Mieke Bal Reader* (2006), *Travelling Concepts in the Humanities* (2002), *Louise Bourgeois' Spider: The Architecture of Art-Writing* (University of Chicago Press, 2002), *Looking In: The Art of Viewing* (G&B Arts International, 2001), and *Quoting Caravaggio: Contemporary Art, Preposterous History* (University of Chicago Press, 1999).

Giuliana Bruno is Professor of Visual and Environmental Studies at Harvard University. She is the author of *Streetwalking on a Ruined Map* (Princeton, 1992) and *Atlas of Emotion: Journeys in Art Architecture, and Film* (Verso, 2002), and her latest books are *Jane and Louise Wilson: A Free and Anonymous Monument* (Film and Video Umbrella/The Baltic Centre for Contemporary Art, 2004) and *Public Intimacy: Architecture and the Visual Arts* (The MIT Press, 2007).

Susan Buck-Morss is Professor of Government at Cornell University, and author of *The Origins of Negative Dialectics* (The Free Press, 1977), *The Dialectics of Seeing* (MIT, 1989), *Dreamworld and Catastrophe: The Passing of Mass Utopia in East and West* (MIT, 2000), and *Thinking Past Terror: Islamism and Critical Theory on the Left* (Verso, 2003).

Lisa Cartwright is Associate Professor in the Department of Communication and the Graduate Science Studies Program at the University of California at San Diego. She is co-author of *Practices of Looking* (Oxford 2001), author of *Screening the Body: Tracing Medicine's Visual Culture* (Routledge, 1995), co-editor of *The Visible Woman* (NYU Press, 1998), and author of *Moral Spectatorship* and *Images of Waiting Children: The Visual Culture of Transnational Adoption* (both forthcoming, Duke University Press).

Mark A. Cheetham is Professor of Art History in the Department of History of Art at University of Toronto. His books include: *Abstract Art Against Autonomy* (Cambridge University Press, 2006); *Kant, Art, and Art History: Monuments of Discipline* (Cambridge University Press, 2001); and *The Rhetoric of Purity* (Cambridge University Press, 1991), and co-editor of *The Subjects of Art History* (Cambridge University Press, 1998) and *Theory Between the Disciplines* (University of Michigan Press, 1990).

Lennard J. Davis is Professor of English, Disability Studies, and Medical Education, as well as Director of Project Biocultures at University of Illinois at Chicago. His recent publications include: *Enforcing Normalcy: Disability, Deafness, and the Body* (Verso, 1995, reprinted 2000), *Disability Studies Reader* (edited, Routledge, 1997, reprinted 2007), *My Sense of Silence* (University of Illinois Press, 2000), and *Bending over Backwards: Essays on Disability and Disability Culture* (NYU Press, 2001). He has a book forthcoming on obsession with The University of Chicago Press.

Hal Foster is Townsend Martin, Class of 1917, Professor of Art and Archaeology at Princeton University. Internationally regarded for his provocative writings on twentieth century art practice, and as an editor of the journal *October*, Professor Foster is the author of *Prosthetic Gods* (The MIT Press, 2004), on the relation between modernism and psychoanalysis, *Design and Crime (and Other Diatribes)* (Verso, 2002), *The Return of the Real* (The MIT Press, 1996), *Compulsive Beauty* (The MIT Press, 1993), *Recodings: Art, Spectacle, Cultural Politics* (Bay Press, 1985), and editor of the defining *The Anti-Aesthetic: Essays on Postmodern Culture* (Pluto Press, 1983), among other books. Recent and forthcoming books include *Art Since 1900*, a co-authored textbook on twentieth-century art, as well as a survey of Pop Art.

Paul Gilroy is a cultural practitioner and critic, a DJ, and, after a stint as Professor of Sociology and African American Studies at Yale University, is back in England as Professor of Sociology in the Department of Sociology at the London School of Economics. Along with numerous key articles on Black British, European, and American visual, acoustic, and cultural studies, he is the author of *After Empire: Multiculture or Postcolonial Melancholia* (Routledge, 2003), *Against Race: Imaging Political Culture Beyond the Color Line* (Harvard, 2000), *The Black Atlantic: Modernity and Double Consciousness* (Harvard, 1993), *Small Acts: Thoughts on the Politics of Black Cultures* (Serpent's Tail, 1993), and *There Ain't No Black in the Union Jack: The Cultural Politics of Race and Nation* (Hutchinson, 1987).

Michael Ann Holly is Director of Research and Academic Program at the Sterling and Francine Clark Art Institute, Massachusetts, and was previously Director of the Visual and Cultural Studies Program at Rochester, of which she was the co-founder. She is the author of *Panofsky and the Foundations of Art History* (Cornell University Press, 1985), *Past Looking: Historical Imagination and the Rhetoric of the Image* (Cornell University Press, 1996), and co-editor of a series of key collections in the development of Visual Culture Studies such as *Visual Theory: Painting and Interpretation* (Polity Press, 1990), *Visual Culture: Images and Interpretations* (Wesleyan University Press, 1994), *The Subjects of Art History* (Cambridge University Press, 1998), and *Art History, Aesthetics, and Visual Studies* (Clark, 2003).

Martin Jay is Sidney Hellman Ehrman Professor of History at the University of California, Berkeley. Co-editor of *Vision in Context* (Routledge, 1996), his books include *Permanent Exiles: Essays on the Intellectual Migration from Germany to America* (Columbia University Press, 1990), *The Dialectical Imagination: A History of the Frankfurt School and the Institute of Social Research, 1923-1950* (University of California Press, 1976), *Adorno* (Harvard University Press, 1984), *Marxism and Totality: The Adventures of a Concept from Lukács to Habermas*; *Downcast Eyes: The Denigration of Vision in Twentieth-Century French Thought* (University of California Press, 1993), *Cultural Semantics: Keywords of Our Time* (University of Massachusetts Press, 1998), *Refractions of Violence* (Routledge, 2003), and *Songs of Experience: Modern American and European Variations on a Universal Theme* (Berkeley: University of California Press, 2005).

Nicholas Mirzoeff is Professor in the Department of Art and its Professions, New York University. He is author of *Silent Poetry: Deafness, Silence, and Visual Culture in Modern France* (Princeton, 1995), *Bodyscape: Art, Modernity, and the Ideal Figure* (Routledge, 1995), *An Introduction to Visual Culture* (Routledge, 1999), and *Visions of Babylon: Watching the War in Iraq* (Routledge, 2004), and editor of *Diaspora and Visual Culture* (Routledge, 1999), and the *Visual Culture Reader* (1998 [2nd edition, 2002]).

W.J.T. Mitchell is Gaylord Donnelley Distinguished Service Professor for English and Art History, The University of Chicago. Editor of *Critical Inquiry*, among his many books he is the author of *The Last Dinosaur Book* (University of Chicago Press, 1998), *Picture Theory* (University of Chicago Press, 1994), *Iconology: Image, Text, Ideology* (University of Chicago Press, 1986), and *What Do Pictures Want?* (University of Chicago Press, 2005.)

Keith Moxey is Ann Whitney Olin Professor of Art History at Barnard College and Columbia University in New York City. He is the author of books on the historiography and philosophy of art history, and his publications include *The Practice of Persuasion: Politics and Paradox in Art History* (Cornell University Press, 2001), *The Practice of Theory: Poststructuralism, Cultural Politics and Art*

History (Cornell University Press, 1994), and *Peasants, Warriors, and Wives: Popular Imagery in the Reformation* (University of Chicago Press, 1989). He is the co-editor of a series of key collections in the development of Visual Culture Studies such as *Visual Theory: Painting and Interpretation* (Polity Press, 1990), *Visual Culture: Images and Interpretations* (Wesleyan University Press, 1994), *The Subjects of Art History* (Cambridge University Press, 1998), and *Art History, Aesthetics, and Visual Studies* (Clark, 2003).

Peggy Phelan is the Ann O'Day Maples Chair in the Arts at Stanford University, having worked in the Department of Performance Studies, Tisch School of the Arts, New York University, from 1985 to 2002. She is the author of *Unmarked: The Politics of Performance* (Routledge, 1993), *Mourning Sex: Performing Public Memories* (Routledge, 1997), and the forthcoming *Death Rehearsals: The Performances of Andy Warhol and Ronald Reagan*, as well as survey essays for the art catalogues *Art and Feminism* (Phaidon, 2001) and *Pipilotti Rist* (Phaidon, 2001). She is co-editor with the late Lynda Hart of *Acting Out: Feminist Performances* (University of Michigan Press, 1993) and with Jill Lane of *The Ends of Performance* (New York University Press, 1998). Professor Phelan has also written plays and performances, and has exhibited her visual art.

Vivian Sobchack is Professor Emeritus in the Department of Film, Television and Digital Media, UCLA. She was the first elected woman President of the Society for Cinema and Media Studies, and is on the Board of Directors of the American Film Institute. Her essays have appeared in journals such as *Quarterly Review of Film and Video*, *Artforum International*, *camera obscura*, *Film Quarterly*, and *Representations*, and she has edited two anthologies: *Meta-Morphing: Visual Transformation and the Culture of Quick-Change;* and *The Persistence of History: Cinema, Television, and the Modern Event.* Her own books include *Screening Space: The American Science Fiction Film*, *The Address of the Eye: A Phenomenology of Film Experience*, and *Carnal Thoughts: Embodiment and Moving Image Culture*.

INTRODUCTION
Visual Culture Studies: History, Theory, Practice[1]

What is Visual Culture Studies?

Visual Culture Studies is the discipline or sub-discipline or field of inquiry that studies visual culture.

If we go to our university or college library, to a local bookshop or to any website that sells printed matter, we will encounter numerous books with 'visual' and 'culture' in the title. When they are not in a section of their own – which rarely happens – Visual Culture Studies books are shelved throughout the library or bookshop in sections that are in keeping with the categorizing systems of these places and the programmed drifting of the potential lender or purchaser. Depending on the type of library or bookshop you're in, these books appear in sections as diverse as Art History or Art Theory or Aesthetics or Critical Theory or Philosophy or Film and Media Studies or Women's Studies or Black Studies or Theatre and Drama or Architecture or Queer Theory or Anthropology or Sociology. No one quite knows where to put 'Visual Culture Studies' books and no one quite knows where to look for them. Neither authors, publishers, retailers, nor customers are entirely clear as to what a Visual Culture Studies book should do or where it should be placed.[2]

Why is this? Because books with 'visual' and 'culture' in the title come in all shapes and sizes, they provide an almost infinite diversity of texts that seem to want to address all historical periods, explore any and every geographical location, conceive of all manner of thematic, and recommend an encyclopaedia of accompanying methodological tools and practices. So, for example, some books are gathered together diachronically, marking a broad historical timeframe from the Middle Ages to the present, while others amass synchronically across diverse territories from Wales to Latin America. Books that set themselves apart by identifying their frames of reference in these two ways include *Defaced: The Visual Culture of Violence in the Late Middle Ages* (Selwyn and Groebner, 2004); *Reframing the Renaissance: Visual Culture in Europe and Latin America: 1450–1650* (Farago, 1995); *The Visual Culture of Wales* (Lord, 1998–); and *The Visual Culture of American Religions* (Morgan and Promey, 2001). Others cut across a variety of themes or subject matter such as race, class, gender, and sexuality that have been at the heart of debates in the Humanities for three decades, and thus central to the emergence of Visual Culture Studies as a political and ethical field of study. These include *Diaspora and Visual Culture* (Mirzoeff, 1999); *Displacement and Difference: Contemporary Arab Visual Culture in the Diaspora* (Lloyd, 2001); *The Feminism and Visual Culture Reader* (Jones, 2003); and *Outlooks: Lesbian and Gay Sexualities and Visual Culture* (Horne and Lewis, 1996).

Ultimately, we find that the majority of books with 'visual' and 'culture' in their titles are introductions to readers or textbooks, often edited collections, frequently written for pedagogical purposes – for students – and sometimes concerned with pedagogical matters themselves. In the main, these books are what we might call methodological inquiries, cabinets of curiosity, since they offer a variety of interpretive ways of engaging with our past and present visual cultures – including semiotics, Marxism, Feminism, historiography, social history, psychoanalysis, queer theory, deconstruction, postcolonial theory, ethnography, and museology. In addition to being concerned with the production, circulation, and consumption of images and the changing nature of subjectivity, they are also preoccupied with what Rogoff (1998) has called 'viewing apparatuses' which include our ways of seeing and practices of looking, and knowing, and doing, and even sometimes with our misunderstandings and unsettling curiosity in imagining the as-yet un-thought. Examples here include *The Visual Culture Reader* (Mirzoeff, 1998/2002); *The Block Reader in Visual Culture: An Introduction* (*Block* Editorial Board and Stafford, 1996); and *Practices of Looking: An Introduction to Visual Culture* (Sturken and Cartwright, 2001).

The diversity of books addressing 'visual culture' is certainly testament to the potential historical range and geographical diversity of the study of visual culture, the array of themes Visual Culture Studies is willing to address, that comprise it even, and the multiple methodological practices it is able to put forward in order to engage with the objects and subjects and media and environments included in and thus composing its purview. It is also worth pointing out that these books consider all manner of visual culture – from high culture to popular, mass, and sub culture; from the elite to the everyday; from the marginal to the mainstream; from the ordinary to the extraordinary – and that the objects and subjects and media and environments embraced by Visual Culture Studies can include anything from painting, sculpture, installation and video art, to photography, film (terrestrial, cable, satellite) television, the internet, and mobile screenic devices; fashion; to medical and scientific imaging; to the graphic and print culture of newspapers, magazines, and advertising; to the architectural and social spaces of museums, galleries, exhibitions, and other private and public environments of the everyday.

Interestingly, these books recognize most acutely the points where images and objects and subjects and environments overlap, blur, converge, and mediate one another. They argue for instance, that interacting with newspapers or the internet always involves a coming together of text and image, of reading and looking simultaneously; that cinema always comprises sight and sound, viewing and hearing at once; that video phones necessitate a confluence of text (texting), image (photographing/videoing), sound (ringtones), and touch (the haptic or tactile bond between the user and his or her unit) (see Cooley, 2004). These books recognize, then, that every encounter taking place between a viewer, participant, or user *and* her or his visual (and multi- or inter-sensory) culture makes it possible to imagine a distinct new starting point for thinking about or doing Visual Culture Studies, as well as a new 'object' of visual culture.

In addition, as I have already mentioned, these books present us with an almost inexhaustible diversity of critical tools, models and methods, and mechanisms and techniques, as well as tropes, figures, modalities, and morphologies. They do so both to engage with the objects and subjects and media and environments of visual culture themselves *and* to facilitate our doing so by providing us with the meanings by which to grasp, understand, and navigate the numerous historical, conceptual, and contemporary ways of seeing, practices of looking, scopic regimes, and visual metaphors that are crucial to our encounters with visual culture and our studies of it.[3]

At the same time, the huge number of books tells us that the phrase 'visual culture' is becoming ubiquitous, omnipresent, that it can and is being used to signify works or artefacts or spaces from *any* historical period, geographical location, thematic concern, or combination of methodological practices.[4] Because of this, the phrase 'visual culture' conveys little that is specific to our past or present visual culture *per se*. It seems that 'visual culture' is everywhere, and thus nowhere, wholly over-determined and almost meaningless simultaneously.

So where does this leave us with regard to the question with which we began this section: 'What is Visual Culture Studies?' As has become obvious in this brief trawl through books with 'visual' and 'culture' in their titles, the phrase seems to be wholly pervasive, indicating that Visual Culture Studies is fast becoming a prevailing field of inquiry in the Humanities and beyond, and yet is also ubiquitous, an unhelpful indicator of both what it is and what it does. What is astonishing about all these books, and somehow not unexpected, is that there is no real common consensus as to what the term 'visual culture' actually signifies. The answers to this question very much depend on the specific nature of the inquiry undertaken in each book. Sometimes 'visual culture' is employed to characterize a historical period or geographical location such as the visual culture of the Renaissance or Aboriginal visual culture, or as Svetlana Alpers (1996) has put it in her discussion of Dutch visual culture, a culture that is bustling with a plethora of 'notions about vision (the mechanisms of the eye), on image making devices (the microscope, the camera obscura), and on visual skills (map making, but also experimenting) as cultural resources'.[5] Sometimes 'visual culture' is used to designate a set of thematic individual or community-based concerns around the ways in which politically motivated images are produced, circulated, and consumed to both construct and reinforce, *and* resist and overthrow articulations of sexual or racial ontologies, identities, and subjectivities – such as black visual culture or feminist visual culture or lesbian and gay visual culture. Sometimes 'visual culture' marks a theoretical or methodological problematic that can be caught up in epistemological debates, or discussions of knowledge, of what determines our looking, seeing, or viewing practices, and how we can articulate this in terms of questions of disciplinarity, pedagogy, and what constitutes an 'object' of visual culture.

All in all, then, it's not in fact true, as it often seems, that Visual Culture Studies simply includes anything and everything that is visual – although it's certainly the case that the field of inquiry is preoccupied with the problem of visuality.[6] Rather, the phrase 'visual culture' is always used in particular ways for specific ends – and if this doesn't seem to be the case, it may well be that an author is using the phrase in a number of ways simultaneously. So, this is why asking the question 'What is Visual Culture Studies?' *in any given instance* is always more valuable than finding a single answer to the question.

Disciplines, Inter-disciplines, Indisciplines

In this section, we need to concentrate on the question of the status of Visual Culture Studies as a field of inquiry: is Visual Culture Studies a discipline, in the sense that Philosophy or History are disciplines? Is it a sub-discipline, a component or an offshoot of a more established discipline such as Art History or Anthropology – or even of a newer discipline such as Film Studies or Media Studies? Is it, like Cultural Studies, what we might call an inter-discipline – something that exists between disciplines and emerges from within this grey area so that Visual Culture Studies operates between visual cultural practices and ways of thinking? Is it indeed the spark itself created by either the sympathetic or the hostile friction of disciplines rubbing together? Or is it something else altogether? Entertaining these questions of disciplinarity reveals that there are a number of interwoven accounts of the genealogy or the emergence of Visual Culture Studies as a discursive formation.[7]

1 *The search for origins*. Some accounts of Visual Culture Studies do their best to locate the origins of the area of study as specifically as possible, trying, for instance, to identify the person who first used the phrase 'visual culture', and in so doing identify the founding moment of the discipline. The two often cited winners of this contest are Michael Baxandall for *Painting and Experience in Fifteenth-Century Italy*, a social history of style and the period eye, and Svetlana Alpers for *The Art of Describing: Dutch Art in the Seventeenth Century*, a study of seventeenth-century Dutch description, representation, images, appearance, cartography, and visuality.[8] I would argue,

though, that this quest for beginnings is a red herring – at best it gives us an 'official' starting point, although I'm not sure what the purpose of this would be, and at worst it wilfully misleads by intimating that the 'naming' of a field of inquiry necessarily pinpoints the first time a certain kind of interrogation has taken place. This is simply not the case: analyses of visual culture were being carried out long before 'Visual Culture' or 'Visual Studies' or 'Visual Culture Studies' emerged as academic fields of inquiry, and similarly universities in the UK, such as Middlesex and Northumbria, have been delivering undergraduate degrees in Visual Culture Studies – without being named as such – for over twenty-five years.

2 *The return of the 'forefathers'*. What is more useful to my mind is not to isolate individuals using the phrase 'visual culture' reasonably recently but rather to follow researchers and academics who have begun to excavate the Humanities and visual arts for the writings of earlier generations of scholars and practitioners working in and against a variety of disciplines that has led to the emergence of the study of visual culture as a truly interdisciplinary project. Such Visual Culture Studies scholars *avant la lettre* might include Aby Warburg and Erwin Panofsky, Sigfried Kracauer, Walter Benjamin, André Malraux, Roland Barthes, Raymond Williams, John Berger, and Gerhard Richter. Calling these scholars 'forefathers' is meant to be a little facetious. At the same time, it must be noted that they offer the most important and fascinating earlier prototypical models or visual cultural practices that form part of the genealogy of Visual Culture Studies and a series of methodological techniques that are 'proper' to its interdisciplinary nature, its criticality, its sensibility, and its often awkward arrangement of images, objects, and environments of study. See, for example, Warburg's *Mnemosyne Altas* (c. 1925–29), Benjamin's *Passagenwerk* (1927–40), Malraux's *The Voices of Silence* (c. 1950), or Richter's *Atlas* (1961–present).

3 *The practices of pedagogy*. One more useful account of the emergence of Visual Culture Studies as a field of inquiry charts its historical development back to the 1970s and 1980s in the university, former polytechnic, adult education, and art and design school sector of the British education system. Here, Art History and Design History and studio staff worked towards equipping practice-based as well as academic-stream students with the inter-disciplinary tools necessary for their craft: to introduce social history, context, and criticality into a consideration of art history and fine art practice; to present students with a history of (not just fine art) images; to furnish them with the resource of a diverse visual archive; and to mobilize practice itself. As a history of Visual Culture Studies that emerges specifically from pedagogical and practice-based imperatives, in the main this was a push to encourage students to think outside of or past the tenets of formalism within the discourse of Modernism.

4 *The limits of disciplinarity*. Concomitant with this account, another suggests that Visual Culture Studies as a reasonably distinct series of interdisciplinary

intellectual practices surfaced around the same time, and that it was brought on by feelings of discontent experienced by academics struggling within Art History, Design History, Comparative Literature, and other disciplines in the Humanities to become more self-reflexive about their own disciplinary practices. Individuals, clusters of academics, and in some cases whole departments frustrated by what they felt were the limitations of their own discipline: what subjects and objects can they include in their purview? What range of critical tools do they have at their disposal, and do they have the wherewithal to wield them? How best to motivate their students in a critical analysis of the historical, conceptual, and aesthetic nature of an ever-changing visual culture? Needing to converse with new visual, tactile, sonic objects of convergence, as well as other spaces and environments – how, for instance, would the discipline of Art History deal fully with the intricate and inter-sensory multivalences of performance art or video art or installation art or site-specific art? – they were driven by an impulse if not to break down then certainly to *question* established disciplines and to *pressure* existing disciplinary boundaries.[9]

5 *Theorizing between disciplines*. Allied to this is the impact of 'theory'. As well as attending to new forms of visual arts practice, along with the emergence of the Marxist and feminist 'New Art History' in the late 1960s and early 1970s, exemplified by the work of T.J. Clark, Linda Nochlin, and Michael Baxandall, scholars began to pay close attention to allied developments in Film Studies, in particular to semiotics and psychoanalysis. At the same time, they began to integrate the interests of Cultural Studies – just as Cultural Studies had drawn on Anthropology. For while questions of class, gender, and race had already been integral to the development of the New Art History, Cultural Studies offered a means of addressing analogous concerns focusing more on the ordinary, the everyday, and the popular and on the politics of representation, difference, and power in ways that reminded us how *cultural practices themselves do make a difference*. Thus emerged what we might call a visual 'take' on Cultural Studies. Here Visual Culture Studies, like Cultural Studies before it, begins to function as an inter-discipline, drawing from existing disciplines and ways of thought, and because of it finding techniques to articulate the objects of visual culture differently.

6 *Conferences and programmes*. Still another flashpoint in the development of Visual Culture Studies is the period 1988–89 in which two events took place. The first was a conference on Vision and Visuality held in 1988 at the Dia Art Foundation in New York. Participants included Norman Bryson, Jonathan Crary, Hal Foster, Martin Jay, Rosalind Krauss, and Jacqueline Rose. The proceeds of this event went on to appear as the influential collection *Vision and Visuality*, edited by Foster (1988). Of this collection, Martin Jay (2002: 268) has recently remarked that its publication 'may be seen as

> the moment when the visual turn ... really showed signs of turning into the academic juggernaut it was to become in the 1990s [because] a critical mass beg[a]n to come together around the question of the cultural determinants of visual experience in the broadest sense'. The second event was the establishment in 1989 of the first US-based graduate programme in Visual and Cultural Studies at the University of Rochester, which gave a certain academic and institutional legitimation to Visual Culture Studies. (Founding staff in the programme included Mieke Bal, Bryson, Lisa Cartwright, and Michael Ann Holly.)

Offering this account of the genealogies of Visual Culture Studies is part of the process of legitimizing it as an academic field of inquiry, a discipline in its own right, or at least as a discursive formation, a site of inter-disciplinary activity, a 'tactic' or a 'movement'.[10] This is necessary because the question of the disciplinary status of Visual Culture Studies matters, and it matters for two reasons in particular. First, because introducing such accounts of the emergence of Visual Culture Studies as a potentially legitimate discipline, as I have done here, makes us aware of the fact that it *does* have its own distinct, albeit interwoven, histories that need to be acknowledged and articulated. For a field of inquiry that is so often accused of ahistoricism, as I mentioned in the Preface, it is imperative to recognize that Visual Culture Studies did not simply appear from nowhere, as if by magic, at some point in, say, the late 1980s but does in fact have a series of much longer divergent and interconnecting genealogies. The status of Visual Culture Studies continues to be hotly contested, and everyone has a different story to tell about its origins. Second, the question of the disciplinary status of Visual Culture Studies matters because it offers new ways of thinking, and of thinking about objects, such that it *is* a distinct field of inquiry.

As Martin Jay points out, Visual Culture Studies *did* become an academic, intellectual, and publishing juggernaut in the 1990s – the number and range of books I listed above testifies to this. On the whole the 1990s and the early years of the first decade of the twenty-first century have seen a multitude of triumphant books and journals, conferences, departments, centres, programmes, courses, minors, and modules bearing the name 'Visual Culture' or 'Visual Studies'.[11] If Visual Culture Studies was inaugurated out of frustration in relation to the stifling effects of disciplinary policing and border controls, as a call to look self-reflexively both inwardly towards the limitations of one's own discipline and outwardly to the opportunities made available by others, it can safely be said that it continues to do this, and to productive ends. In working with and against other disciplines and between fields of inquiry, following its counter- or anti-disciplinary impetus it has led to disciplines questioning their own foundations and imperatives, even as it has also displayed outward hostility towards the prospect of its own conditions of possibility. Perhaps even more importantly, it has found its own methodologies and its own objects of study.

It is a true example of what Barthes, paraphrased by Mieke Bal (2003: 7), says of inter-disciplinary study, that it 'consists of *creating* a new object *that belongs to no one*'. I shall return to this assertion in a moment.

Finally, in bringing this section to a close, I would like to offer a word of caution: in its ongoing and ever-more successful search for legitimation, Visual Culture Studies has the potential to become too self-assured, and its devotees too confident. In so doing, it can all too easily lose sight of its drive to worry or problematize other disciplines. It must remember to continue plotting a fractious course between disciplines, learning from them and teaching them lessons in return; and to continue engendering new objects or mobilizing more established things in new ways, by carrying on *doing* the work that it does. Visual Culture Studies should be careful not to lose, as W.J.T. Mitchell (1995) puts it, its 'turbulence', its 'incoherence', its 'chaos', or its 'wonder' as an *in*discipline: the 'anarchist' moment of 'breakage or rupture' when 'a way of doing things ... compulsively performs a revelation of its own inadequacy'.[12]

What's in a Name: Visual Culture or Visual Studies or Visual Culture Studies?

Mitchell's conception of Visual Culture Studies as an *in*discipline is very appealing.[13] Here, the chance to consider attending to the field of inquiry as 'a way of doing things' is fascinating, as is gesturing towards the extent to which studies of visual culture have the potential, indeed must make evident their own limitations as a necessary part of their capacity and willingness to comprehend and perform these new 'way[s] of doing things'. But does this challenge of Visual Culture Studies as an *in*discipline allow us to settle another question: what do we in fact call this field of inquiry itself, Visual Culture or Visual Studies or Visual Culture Studies?

When writing on or from within this new discipline, inter-discipline, indiscipline, discursive formation, or movement, some scholars are happy to use the phrases 'Visual Culture' and 'Visual Studies' interchangeably to designate the field of study. But there are plenty of reasons not to do this: 'Visual Culture' and 'Visual Studies' are not the same thing after all. Mitchell, for instance, makes this clear when he distinguishes between 'Visual Studies' and 'visual culture' as, respectively, 'the field of study and the object or target of study'. He goes on to write, 'Visual Studies is the study of visual culture' (Mitchell, 2002: 166).

We won't find a clearer definition of the two terms anywhere, or a better explanation of the difference between them. The reasons Mitchell gives for making this distinction are good ones: he says he wants to 'avoid the ambiguity that plagues subjects like history, in which the field and the things covered by the field bear the same name' (Mitchell, 2002: 166). That is, he wants us to avoid confusing 'Visual Culture' as an area of inquiry with the subjects, objects, media, and environments of 'visual culture' themselves, so that these things are not sacrificed to the study of them.

To add to this concern, Visual *Studies* does sound overly bureaucratic, and perhaps this isn't surprising for a field of study that is so inordinately concerned with definitions, delineations, naming, historiography, methodology, tropologies, and paradigm shifts, as it tries to establish, account for, and validate itself by way of these very concerns. It is also interesting to note that 'Visual Studies' should be so caught up in these questions of knowledge, these epistemological concerns, at a time when, as it is often said, we live in a post-epistemological age.[14] Actually, ironically, many of the most aggressive critiques of Visual Studies or Visual Culture have been launched at the field of inquiry from exactly this angle, accusing it of ahistoricism, as I have already noted on a couple of occasions. Such claims are best exemplified in – perhaps they even began with – the first question asked in the 'Visual Culture Questionnaire', compiled by the prominent arts journal *October* in 1996:

> It has been suggested that the inter-disciplinary project of 'visual culture' is *no longer organized on the model of history* (as were the disciplines of art history, architectural history, film history, etc.) but on the model of anthropology. Hence it is argued by some that visual culture is in an eccentric (even, at times, antagonistic) position with regard to the 'new art history' with its social-historical and semiotic imperatives of 'models' and 'text'.[15]

More recently, in 2002, Hal Foster, one of the editors of *October* responsible for the 'Visual Culture Questionnaire', returned to this issue in order to further elaborate. In his book *Design and Crime (and Other Diatribes)* he suggests that Visual Culture is or is seen to be the '"visual wing" of cultural studies' (p. 90), and he goes on to say that:

> As an academic subject ... 'visual culture' is ... maybe as oxymoronic as 'art history'. Certainly its two terms repel each other with equal force, for if art history is sustained between the autonomy implied in 'art' and the imbrication implied in 'history', then visual culture is stretched between the virtuality implied in 'visual' and the materiality implied in 'culture.' (p. 90)

Foster continues:

> Its [visual studies'] ethnographic model might also have this unintended consequence: it might be encouraged to move horizontally from subject to subject across social space, more so than vertically along the historical lines of particular form, genre or problematic. In this way visual studies might privilege the present excessively, and so might support rather than stem the posthistorical attitude that has become the default position of so much artistic, critical, and curatorial practice today. (p. 91)

While flipping backwards and forwards at will between 'Visual Culture' and 'Visual Studies', here *October* and Foster do highlight importantly both what is for many a crucial feature dividing Art History from Visual Culture *and* a key criticism of Visual Culture: its potential ahistoricism. Foster's argument here is that the attention 'Visual Studies' or 'Visual Culture' lavishes on the contemporary, and on particular contemporary forms of visual culture – the spectacle of visual commodities, technologies, information, and entertainment – is both born of and leads to subjective, interpretive, and ethnographic practices – from psychoanalysis and anthropology – that are themselves in effect dematerializing and dehistoricizing. (In their attention to the visual, they dematerialize art. In their attention to culture, they dehistoricize history.) This is the case, he says, because '[j]ust as social imperative and anthropological assumptions have governed the shift from "history" to "culture" so technological imperatives and psychoanalytic assumptions have governed the shift from "art" to the "visual"' (2002: 92). While I have never been quite sure why *in principle* 'the visual' is open to accusations of de-materialization or why 'the cultural' is charged with a will to de-historicize, Foster's argument is nonetheless a precise account of why Visual Studies or Visual Culture as a field of inquiry needs, if it does not do so already, to attend to history, and historical formation as well as consider the present.

But what kind of 'history'? The matter of history in general, and the supposed *a*historical impulse of Visual Culture or Visual Studies is imperative, and the fact that the word 'history' does not appear in either nomenclature is a point worth making. It does imply that the field of inquiry does not have a commitment to 'history' in the same way as does, say, Art History or Film History. And this is of course the point: not that Visual Culture or Visual Studies might be modelled on the practices of Anthropology, as the *October* Questionnaire intimates, but that it is *no longer organized* on the model of history as it was conceived of *at the advent* of the discipline of Art History in the nineteenth century or even Film History in the twentieth century. Rather, Visual Culture or Visual Studies may well be organized on a *different* model of history, to use *October*'s phrase, that has to confront and struggle with the very question of 'history' as a question in our post-epistemological age – or with what Foster refers to above as a posthistorical attitude.[16] To adopt a posthistorical attitude is not to concentrate simply on the present at the expense of the past but to take account of the problem of the state of 'history' in the present, which is all we can ever do, and that will of course have implications for how we then 'speak with' the past. Similarly, neither Visual Culture nor Visual Studies necessarily intrinsically imply an over-attention to the present at the expense of the past – instead it may well be committed to an effort to focus on how the past can only be glimpsed through the distorting prism of the present. (This is nothing new for Art History.)[17]

This tells us that Foster is right in principle to warn those involved in Visual Culture or Visual Studies of the need to attend to 'history', and we can respond to this challenge by reaffirming that the problem of 'history' should always be very much in view. Visual Culture or Visual Studies has to respond to this perceived ahistoricism, and in particular to the perceived lack of attention it might pay in its analyses to the historicity of the objects, subjects, media, and environments under consideration, to make sure they are not stripped of their own history. This is the reason why I have taken the time here to consider both the genealogies of Visual Culture or Visual Studies *and* 'history', specifically in relation to discussions of the naming of this field of inquiry: it is in taking account of the question of 'history' that we see why a choice of names has to be made. For if it is problematic to use the term 'Visual Studies' to designate this emerging field of inquiry, as we have already indicated, so too is it a problem to use the term 'Visual Culture': to do so is to conflate the name of the field of inquiry ('Visual Culture') with the objects, subjects, media, and environments analysed therein ('visual culture'), and in the moment of this conflation the danger is that the historical and material character of these things in their specificity gives way to the analysis of them.

Because there are problems with the nomenclature of both 'Visual Culture' and 'Visual Studies', following. Walker and Chaplin's *Visual Culture: An Introduction* (1997: 1) I prefer to use the phrase Visual Culture Studies, a phrase that does not designate a discipline so much as 'a hybrid, an inter- or multi-disciplinary enterprise formed as a consequence of a convergence of, or borrowing from, a variety of disciplines and methodologies'. Using 'Visual Culture Studies' allows us to consider what in *Feminism and Visual Culture* Amelia Jones (2003: 2) has called 'the formation of new interdisciplinary strategies of interpretation'.

In fact, it is at this point that one comes to realize it is not its disciplinary status that is of interest so much as the prospect that Visual Culture Studies might be a whole new *strategy* for doing research, of seeing and knowing, of outlining our encounters with visual culture, and mining them for meaning, constituting its own objects and subjects and media and environments of study that belong to no one, as Barthes would have it, *and* that can only come into existence, be made, and made sense of as 'a way of doing things' that is particular to Visual Culture Studies. It is in this way that the 'object' of visual culture, and the question of the 'object' in Visual Culture Studies, comes into view.

What is the 'Object' of Visual Culture Studies?

Given the work that Visual Culture Studies *does*, with what objects does it engage, and how are they constituted?

Some academics are happy simply for Visual Culture Studies to include an expanded field of vision, an expanded purview, an expanded object domain, to include all things 'visual'. (Of course some would say that in certain quarters the discipline of Art History has already been doing this for years.[18]) Other scholars are more attentive to its particular character. In writing of and on Visual Culture Studies they have returned, explicitly and implicitly, to mull over meticulously the full implications of Roland Barthes's remarks on interdisciplinarity mentioned earlier. Rogoff (1998: 15) for instance, like Bal, has drawn on Barthes' ideas in thinking of Visual Culture Studies, and its inter-disciplinarity, as 'the constitution of a new object of knowledge'. Bal (2003: 23) has recently made similar comments, pointing out that '[i]f the tasks of visual culture studies must be derived from its object, then, in a similar way, the methods most suitable for performing these tasks must be derived from those same tasks, and the derivation made explicit'. Likewise in suggesting that this field of inquiry has the potential to be an example of inter-disciplinarity in an 'interesting' sense, James Elkins (2002: 30) has suggested that it 'does not know its subjects but finds them through its preoccupations'. All of this is to say that, whether we are discussing objects or subjects or media or environments or ways of seeing and practices of looking, the visual or visuality, Visual Culture Studies as an inter-disciplinary field of inquiry has the potential *to create new objects of study*, and it does so specifically by *not determining them in advance*.

What does this actually mean? It means that Visual Culture Studies is not simply 'theory' or even 'visual theory' in any conventional sense, and it does not simply 'apply' theory or visual theory to objects of study. It is not the study of images, based on the casual premise that our contemporary culture is an image culture.[19] Rather, it is the case that between (1) finding ways of attending to the historical, conceptual, and material specificity of things (2) taking account of 'viewing apparatuses' and (3) our critical encounters with them, the 'object' of Visual Culture Studies is born, emerges, is discernible, shows itself, becomes visible. In these moments of friction, the 'object' of Visual Culture Studies comes into view, engendering its own way of being, of being meaningful, of being understood, and even of not being understood. It is not a matter of *which* 'objects' are 'appropriate' or 'inappropriate' for Visual Culture Studies, but of how beginning from the specifics of our visual culture, our preoccupations and encounters with it, and the acts that take place in and by way of visual culture, *none of which are determined in advance*, make it possible for us to focus, as José Esteban Muñoz (1996: 12) has written, 'on what acts and objects do ... rather that [sic] what they might possibly mean'.

Notes

1 An earlier version of this introduction appeared as Smith (2005a).

2 There are of course many other books on the topic of 'visual culture' that don't include the phrase itself in their title, including books on visual studies (a phrase often used interchangeably with visual culture). Some of the most important books and edited collections in the development of the area of inquiry include neither, such as Buck-Morss (1989),

Crary (1990), and Martin Jay (1993). And there are also the accompanying journals, and journal articles, as well as conferences, departments, programmes, and courses that have both spawned and been spawned by visual culture. In the English context, it is often said that the first avowedly visual culture journal is *Block*, fifteen issues of which were produced by academics based at Middlesex University — then Middlesex Polytechnic — between 1979 and 1989.

3 On scopic regimes see Jay (1993).

4 There is a concern, of course, within discussions of Visual Culture Studies that the phrase can be applied in such undifferentiated and homogenizing ways.

5 Alpers (1996) p. 26. See also Alpers (1983) and Jay (1993).

6 Visuality has been defined by Jessica Evans and Stuart Hall (1999, p. 41) as 'the visual register in which the image and visual meaning operate', and more clearly by Amelia Jones (2003, p. xx) who speaks of visuality as 'the condition of how we see and make meaning of what we see'.

7 In noting Stuart Hall's insistence that Cultural Studies is a '"discursive formation" rather than a discipline', Amelia Jones (2003, p. 2) makes it possible for us to imagine also characterizing Visual Culture Studies in the same way.

8 Evans and Hall (1999) comment that Alpers is the first to use the phrase 'visual culture' in her *The Art of Describing* (Alpers, 1983, p. xxv), but Alpers herself in that book attributes the phrase to Michael Baxandall (Baxandall, 1972, p. xxv). It is worth noting that those mentioned (Alpers and Baxandall) are firmly established within the discipline of Art History. (Incidentally, for all the emphasis that Visual Culture Studies is said by its detractors to place on analyses of the contemporary, it is well worth noting that these so called earliest instances of visual culture analysis are of fifteenth-century Italian and seventeenth-century Dutch culture.) Walker and Chaplin (1997, p. 6, footnote 2) say that to the best of their knowledge, the first book to use the term 'visual culture' is in fact Caleb Gattegno's *Towards a Visual Culture: Educating through Television* (1969). Dikovitskaya (2005) also affirms this. To my knowledge, no one writing on the development of Visual Culture Studies from within Art History has noticed that in 1964 Marshall McLuhan used the phrase 'visual culture' in *Understanding Media*. It needed a scholar with a background in Film and Media Studies to spot this, Raiford Guins (in conversation).

9 For more on issues raised in points 3 and 4 see Walker and Chaplin (1997, pp. 35–50).

10 Mirzoeff (1998, p. 5) refers to Visual Culture as a 'tactic'. Recently Mieke Bal (2003, p. 6) has referred to it as a 'movement'.

11 *October*'s 'Visual Culture Questionnaire' (1996) continues to be a most engaging critique of Visual Culture Studies. In particular, the questions posed by the Editors of the 'Questionnaire' rather than the answers to it accuse Visual Culture Studies of *a*historicism (an over-attention to analyses of the contemporary) and of dematerializing the image. On this question of ahistoricism, it is well worth mentioning that Art History, along with many other disciplines in the Humanities, including Visual Culture Studies, is no stranger to questions of historiography. From their inception, such questions necessarily plague, challenge, and offer ways forward for disciplines themselves. *October* is well aware of this. While the 'Questionnaire' has been a huge bone of contention in subsequent discussions of Visual Culture Studies, a clear, extended elaboration of its underlying assertions written by one of its originators can be found here in the interview with Foster and in Foster (2002).

12 Mitchell (1995, p. 541). It is here that Mitchell first uses the wonderfully damning phrase 'safe default interdisiciplinarity' to characterize a particularly prevalent but ineffectual form of inter-disciplinary study. It is a phrase that parallels Stephen Melville's (1996, pp. 52–4) comment in the *October* Questionnaire. Carlo Ginzburg (1995, pp. 51–3) has also reasonably reminded us, albeit not in reference to Visual Culture Studies, that 'there is nothing intrinsically innovative or subversive in an interdisciplinary approach to knowledge'.

13 In this section, I will be using the terms Visual Culture and Visual Studies as they are employed in Mitchell's argument rather than how they are used in the rest of this Introduction.

14 See for instance Cheetham, Holly and Moxey (1998, p. 2) 'Introduction'.

15 'Visual Culture Questionnaire' (p. 25); my italics. In addition to accusations of ahistoriciam, the *October* questionnaire – the questions posed by the editors of the journal, rather than the answers to it – accuses Visual Culture or Visual Studies of anthropologism and of a dematerialization of the image.

16 Here I want to distinguish very strongly between the interesting if thorny challenge of the question of our post-epistemological age and of its post-historical attitude, *and* the neo-conservativist discussions of the end of history by the likes of Francis Fukayama (1992).

17 It is of course well worth mentioning that Art History, along with many other disciplines in the Humanities, is no stranger to questions of historiography. From their inception, such questions necessarily plague, challenge, and offer ways forward for disciplines themselves. *October* is well aware of this.

18 See Donald Preziosi, 'Introduction' (1999) where he offers an astute account of Art History's efforts to expand its object domain, its willingness and ability to extend its purview.

19 Manghani, Piper and Simons (2006). For a critique of this image culture, see Sobchack (2004, p. 181) who writes: 'Our contemporary image culture (as well as our contemporary theory) has increasingly reified our bodies as manageable matter. We have become fixated on the appearance and objectivity of the visible – and, as a consequence, both images and bodies have lost their other dimensions and values'.

References

Alpers, Svetlana (1983) *The Art of Describing: Dutch Art in the Seventeenth Century*. Chicago: The University of Chicago Press.

Alpers, Svetlana (1996) 'Visual Culture Questionnaire', *October*, 77 (Summer): 25–70.

Bal, Mieke (2003) 'Visual essentialism and the object of visual culture', *Journal of Visual Culture*, 2(1): 5–32.

Barthes, Roland (1986) *The Rustle of Language*. New York: Hill & Wang.

Baxandall, Michael (1972) *Painting and Experience in Fifteenth-Century Italy*. Oxford: Oxford University Press.

Benjamin, Walter (no date) *Passagen-Werk* (unpublished) published as *Walter Benjamin: The Arcades Project* (2002) (edited by Rolf Tiedemann) (Howard Eiland and Kevin McLaughlin, *trans.*). New York: Belknap Press.

Block Editorial Board and Stafford, S. (eds.) (1996) *The Block Reader in Visual Culture*. London: Routledge.

Brennan, Teresa and Martin, Jay (eds.) (1996) *Vision in Context: Historical and Contemporary Perspectives on Sight*. London: Routledge.
Buck-Morss, Susan (1989) *The Dialectics of Seeing: Walter Benjamin and the Arcades Project*. Cambridge, MA.: MIT Press.
Cheetham, Mark, Holly, Michael Ann and Moxey, Keith (eds.) (1998) *The Subjects of Art History: Historical Objects in Contemporary Perspectives*. Cambridge: Cambridge University Press.
Cooley, H.R. (2004) 'It's all about the *Fit*: The Hand, the Mobile Screenic Device and Tactile Vision', *Journal of Visual Culture*, 3(2): 133–51.
Crary, Jonathan (1990) *Techniques of the Observer: On Vision and Modernity in the Nineteenth Century*. Cambridge, MA.: MIT Press.
Crimp, Douglas (1999) 'Getting the Warhol we Deserve', *Social Text*, 59 (n. 17): 49–66.
Doy, Gen (2000) *Black Visual Culture*. London: I.B. Tauris.
Elkins, James (2002) *Visual Studies: A Skeptical Introduction*. London: Routledge.
Evans, Jessica and Hall, Stuart (eds.) (1999) *Visual Culture: The Reader*. London: Sage.
Farago, Claire (ed.) (1995) *Reframing the Renaissance: Visual Culture in Europe and Latin America: 1450–1650*. New Haven: Yale University Press.
Foster, Hal (ed.) (1988) *Vision and Visuality*. Seattle: Bay Press.
Foster, Hal (2002) *Design and Crime (and Other Diatribes)*. London: Verso.
Fukuyama, Francis (1992) *The End of History and the Last Man*. New York. Free Press.
Ginzburg, Carlo (1995) 'Viteos and Compatibilities, *Art Bulletin*, 77(4): 51–3.
Horne, Peter and Lewis, Reina (eds.) (1996) *Outlooks: Lesbian and Gay Sexualities and Visual Culture*. London: Routledge.
Jay, Martin (1988) 'Scopic Regimes of Modernity', in H. Foster (ed.), *Vision and Visuality*. Seattle: Bay Press, pp. 3–27.
Jay, Martin (1993) *Downcast Eyes: The Denigration of Vision in Twentieth-Century French Thought*. Berkeley: University of California Press.
Jay, Martin (2002) 'Cultural relativism and the Visual Turn', *Journal of Visual Culture*, 1 (3): 267–78.
Jones, Amelia (ed.) (2003) *The Feminism and Visual Culture Reader*. London: Routledge.
Levin, D.M. (1997) *Sites of Vision: The Discursive Construction of Sight in the History of Philosophy*. Cambridge, MA.: The MIT Press.
Lloyd, F. (ed.) (2001) *Displacement and Difference: Contemporary Arab Visual Culture in the Diaspora*. London: Saffron Books.
Lord, Peter (1998–) *The Visual Culture of Wales* (4 volumes). Cardiff: University of Wales Press.
Malraux, André (1953 [1951]) *The Voices of Silence*. New York. Doubleday & Company, Inc.
Manghani, S., Piper, A. and Simons, J. (2006) *Images: A Reader*. London: Sage Publications.
McLuhan, Marshall (1964/1987) *Understanding Media*. London: Routledge.
Melville, Stephen and Readings, Bill. (eds.) (1995) *Vision and Textuality*. London: Macmillan Press.
Melville, Stephen (1996) 'Visual Culture Questionnaire'. *October* 77: 52–4.
Mirzoeff, Nicholas (ed.) (1998/2002) *Visual Culture Reader*. London: Routledge.
Mirzoeff, Nicholas (ed.) (1999) *Diaspora and Visual Culture: Representing Africans and Jews*. London: Routledge.
Mitchell, W.J.T. (1995) 'Interdisciplinarity and Visual Culture', *Art Bulletin*, 77(4): 540–4.

Mitchell, W.J.T. (2002) 'Showing Seeing; A Critique of Visual Culture', *Journal of Visual Culture*, 1 (2): 165–81.

Morgan, David and Promey, Sally (eds.) (2001) *The Visual Culture of American Religions*. Berkeley: University of California Press.

Muñoz, José Esteban (1996) 'Ephemera as Evidence: Introductory Notes to Queer Acts', *Woman & Performance: A Journal of Feminist Theory*, 8(2): 5–16.

October (1996), 77, 'Visual Culture Questionnaire'.

Preziosi, Donald (ed.) (1999) *The Art of Art History*. Oxford: Oxford University Press.

Rogoff, Irit (1998) 'Studying Visual Culture', in N.Mirzoeff (ed.) *Visual Cultural Reader*. London: Routledge, pp. 14–26.

Selwyn, Pamela and Groebner, Valentine (2004) *Defaced: The Visual Culture of Violence in the Late Middle Ages*. New York: Zone Books.

Smith, Marquard (2005a) 'Visual Culture Studies: Questions of History, Theory, and Practice', in Amelia Jones (ed.) *A Companion to Contemporary Art since 1945*. Oxford: Blackwell, pp. 470–89.

Smith, Marquard (2005b) 'Visual Studies, or the Ossification of Thought', in Martin Jay (ed.) 'The State of Visual Culture Studies', *Journal of Visual Culture*, 4(2): 237–56.

Smith, Marquard and Morra, Joanne (eds.) (2006) *Visual Culture: Critical Concepts in Media and Cultural Studies* (4 volumes). London: Routledge.

Sobchack, Vivian (2004) *Carnal Thoughts: Embodiment and Moving Image Culture*. Berkeley: California University Press.

Sturken, Marita and Cartwright, Lisa (2001) *Practices of Looking: An Introduction to Visual Culture*. Oxford: Oxford University Press.

Walker, John and Chaplin, Sarah (1997) *Visual Culture: An Introduction*. Manchester: Manchester University Press.

Warburg. Aby. *Mnemosyne-Atlas*. Unpublished.

Wollen, Peter and Cooke, Lynne (eds.) (1999) *Visual Display: Culture Beyond Appearances*. New York: The New Press.

1

VISUAL CULTURE, EVERYDAY LIFE, DIFFERENCE, AND VISUAL LITERACY

Interview with Nicholas Mirzoeff

Introduction

Nicholas Mirzoeff is Professor in The Steinhardt School of Education, New York University. He is author of *Silent Poetry: Deafness, Silence, and Visual Culture in Modern France* (1995), *Bodyscape: Art, Modernity, and the Ideal Figure* (1995), *An Introduction to Visual Culture* (1999), *Watching Babylon: The War in Iraq* (2005) and forthcoming books on Visual Literacy and on Seinfeld. He is also the editor of the landmark *Visual Culture Reader* (1998 [2002]). This interview draws out a number of threads central to Mirzoeff's recent and forthcoming intellectual projects. Some of these threads cluster around reoccurring issues central to the study of visual culture such as historicity, pedagogy, studio practice, academic labour and the knowledge economy, the politics and ethics of the visual, visual literacy, and how visual subjectivity and identity impact upon questions of disability, racialized difference, and queer politics. Other threads tangle around the subject of the power of images in global culture and why the visual is so central to Western capitalism. In so doing, the interview stresses what it means to live in what Giorgio Agamben has called a 'state of exception', and the consequent need to engage critically with the spectacle of late capitalism.

Visual Culture Studies, Visual Culture, and visual culture: Then and Now

Marquard Smith (MS): After the first edition of the edited collection *The Visual Culture Reader* (1998) and *An Introduction to Visual Culture* (1999), your name became synonymous with Visual Culture Studies or at least with certain ways of thinking about the study of visual culture. What have been the effects of this?

Nicholas Mirzoeff (NM): The idea of creating the two books was that it would make it possible for someone who wanted to teach a class in the field to do so and to give them the necessary evidence to prove to a dean or a curriculum committee that a field such as this existed. For that matter, I think the books make a material difference in convincing students that visual culture is an academic discipline. So, by the way, when some people have said that the *Reader* is nothing more than a packet of photocopies in bound form, I think they missed the importance of the materiality of books in general and books that advance a new claim in particular. Returning to the strategy of the books, it seems that the goal of enabling new courses has been achieved, so much so that they are now the target of a certain form of institutional critique, at least within Anglo-American universities.

So much for what was intended: the interesting things have been the unintended consequences. Perhaps the most striking thing to me about the way the *Reader* in particular has been used was that it was adopted first by studio art programmes, even as art historians informed us that visual culture was anti-art and so on. That dialogue between visual culture and contemporary art has been extremely interesting and important to me personally, given that I now teach in a studio department, and to the field in general. I'm thinking here of the Visual Cultures programme at Goldsmiths College, which has developed this interface in very exciting ways. Of course at the same time, being embraced by a fashion-conscious milieu like the art world has the inevitable consequence of becoming unfashionable, sooner or later. We've already seen some artists who were originally contributors to the *Reader* decide that visual culture is old hat, which indeed it is in a certain sense, very old. At the same time, the relationship between the Interventionist art practice of theory and visual culture's theory of practice remains very significant.

Finally, I think one of the most significant things the books did was simply to circulate globally. Anecdotally, I've heard about people using them in Tajikistan, Argentina, Turkey, India and many other places where Anglophone academic books aren't always used. My hope is this is the first step in a continuing exchange that has already begun with the publication of volumes like Jeanne Van Eeden and Amanda du Preez's (2005) collection *South African Visual Culture*.

MS: I'm sure that *The Visual Culture Reader* is the most influential and successful Visual Culture Studies book of all time. Its first edition appeared in 1998, and the second edition appeared in 2002. You and I have spoken in the past about the role of the editor, the intricate intellectual (as well as pragmatic) processes and practices involved in this role, and the ways in which these activities are often underestimated. With this in mind, I'd like to ask you about the two editions of *The Visual Culture Reader*. In the transition from the first to the second edition, you've introduced a number of differences: as well as a new design, you also decided to rewrite your introductory sections, add a couple of new introductory articles, some contributions have been dropped while others have been added. What most interests me, though, is the overall conceptual/structural changes to the *Reader*, and what they mean to you.

That's to say, the first edition had sections (appearing in the following order) entitled: 'A Genealogy of Visual Culture: From Art to Culture'; 'Visual Culture and Everyday Life'; 'Virtuality: Virtual Bodies, Virtual Spaces'; 'Race and Identity in Colonial and Postcolonial Culture'; 'Gender and Sexuality'; and 'Pornography'. The sections in the second edition are entitled: 'Plug-in theory'; 'Global/Digital' – which has subsections on 'Imagining globalization' and 'The space of the digital'; 'Spectacle and Display', with subsections on 'Spectacle, display, surveillance', and 'Cinema after film, television after networks'; 'Visual Colonialism/Visual Transculture', with subsections on 'Visual colonialism' and 'Identity and transculture'; and 'The Gaze, the Body and Sexuality' with subsections on 'The gaze and sexuality' and 'Technobodies/Technofeminism'.

All of which is to say, between 1998 and 2002 you made a series of significant structural changes to the *Reader* that for me indicates a shift in your thinking about the field of Visual Culture Studies, the pedagogical purposes and priorities of the *Reader* as it pertains to this area of inquiry, and even the conceptualization of visual culture itself. Is this the case?

NM: Editing is to my mind a dialogic art. In producing the first edition of the *Reader*, I had discussions with real and imaginary potential users of the book as to what they felt was necessary in such a book and how they might use it. So the notion of a 'genealogy of visual culture' was intended to make a case of the necessity and existence of the field. I chose to demonstrate that idea with examples from art history because that was my training but you could have made the case with other areas, as Jessica Evans and Stuart Hall (1999) later did with semiotics in their *Reader* for Sage.

By the time it became clear that the *Reader* was getting dated in 2000 – having been devised for the most part in 1996 – a number of changes were self-evident. On the one hand, while people still debated what visual culture could and should be, there was enough acceptance that an issue, or a debate, or a field (depending on your perspective) did exist that one could make space for new material by setting the genealogical material aside. I also assumed that people who might use the new *Reader* had the old one and could still reference or assign that and other sections we cut.

The next obvious issue was the question of digital culture that had been referenced in the first edition mostly in relation to the question of virtual reality. If you remember, in 1995 when we first discussed doing the *Reader*, the Internet was still seen as a geeky sideshow, even by people like Bill Gates. So by 2002 we were wildly offbeat in not having proper coverage of the importance of new media and their relationship to globalization.

In drawing up the second edition, I also had the benefit of a good deal of feedback from people who were actually using the book. So the section of theoretical excerpts was a response to something a number of people had asked for in these surveys to give them another teaching tool. I had always envisaged people using the book as the basis of a network of readings, viewings, and other activity and that's true for many people. In other situations, people needed to be able to use the book by itself and I think it benefits from that change of perspective.

But the changes were more than taxonomic. In the first edition, I was looking back to see where visual culture had come from. In the second edition, I wanted to try and ask where it was going. So in addition to the introductory pieces, I sought out new work from people whose work impressed me, like Jonathan Beller, Lisa Nakamura, Wendy Hui Kyong Chun, Tara McDonald, Olu Oguibe, Lisa Parks, and Jill Casid. Second, I made a consistent self-conscious effort to make sure that the second edition was more diverse in every sense: for example, that the authors are more diverse by age and ethnicity; that there's better geographic range; and that art has been displaced as the central reference point to one means of visual representation among others. Here I am in many ways just following the ways in which what is being made, taught, and seen as 'contemporary art' has shifted and expanded in response to new media and globalization.

MS: I have a question about *An Introduction to Visual Culture*. Do you regret beginning that book with the sentence: 'Modern life takes place onscreen' (p. 1). I know it's a bit of a cheeky question, but it's not intended to be disingenuous. Rather, it's about the contemporaneity of Visual Culture Studies. That is, do you believe that Visual Culture Studies and/or the study of visual cultures is necessarily a concern with or an attention to the contemporary – to what you'd called modern life? As someone who's written a book set in the eighteenth and nineteenth centuries, your *Silent Poetry: Deafness, Sign and Visual Culture in Modern France* (1995), I know you're attentive to matters of history. (It's also worth mentioning, as I noted in the previous question, that a section of the first edition of your *Reader* is entitled 'A Genealogy of Visual Culture', and throughout your writings you do endeavour to acknowledge histories and genealogies of visual culture.) I suppose it's also worth mentioning that in part my question is asked as a way of giving you a chance to respond to accusations made by both supporters and detractors alike that Visual Culture Studies is often dangerously ahistorical.

NM: This seems to me two distinct questions. As to the opening of the *Introduction*, when I wrote it, I was an obscure assistant professor. My hope was people might ask themselves what was meant by 'the modern': beginning where, involving whom, in what space or spaces? and what kind of screen was imagined: television, film, pictorial or psychoanalytic? If that sentence helped grab people's attention to the book, which I think it did, then it would be silly to repudiate it now. And it did express a certain sense of the period, the late 1990s, in which technology seemed in and of itself to be emancipatory and confining at once, as [the film] *The Matrix* visualized so effectively. In general, I think that I decided to write the *Introduction* in bold face, as it were, meaning that I enhanced and sharpened the rhetorical stakes with the hope of provoking debate and reaction. It was never intended to be a 'textbook', even if it gets used that way, because there was no agreed field to be introduced at that time. It is rather an *Introduction* to a series of questions, debates and issues that might be taken as constituting the possibility of a field.

As to the second question, it's always seemed odd to me that visual culture has been characterized as ahistorical, whether dangerously or not. It was Svetlana Alpers's *The Art of Describing* (1983), a study of seventeenth century Dutch art, that put the term into the field of art history, for instance. And scholars like Michael Ann Holly and Keith Moxey are not only historians but historiographers. Then you might look at someone like Susan Buck-Morss whose historical interrogation of philosophy is exemplary. In my own case, you really don't have to look into the back catalogue to see this. As much as the Introduction to *An Introduction to Visual Culture* gets referenced, I sometimes feel that the rest of the book is overlooked. The first chapter deals with questions of perspective in the seventeenth century, for instance, and the transcultural approach of the second half ranges widely in historical time. I think the chapter on the Congo is perhaps most indicative in this regard because, like many other sections, it introduces new research and concepts rather than summarizing a given body of existing work. I think the allegation that visual culture is ahistorical needs to be thought through in relation to the concept of danger that you introduced. Dangerous to whom or to what? Presumably to a mode of politically-engaged intellectual practice that has served under the slogan 'always historicize' for some time now. It's true of course that my version of visual culture doesn't fit well with Jameson's vision of totalizing history. But its engagement with a form of politics is central, beginning with the question of how one might have a politics of the visual, why the visual is so central to Western capitalism, and what the political response to that could or should be.

The Everyday and Identity, Globalization, and the Media

MS: To be more charitable, I do know what you mean by the statement that modern life takes place onscreen. Really, you're simply drawing our attention to the fact that our lives, experiences, and knowledges are mediated and re-mediated by way of the televisual, the cinematic, and other kinds of vision and forms of visual media: that we're under constant surveillance; that there's an increase in the wealth and diversity of our visual encounters; and that this, in part, has to do with the legacy of living in a post-modern culture dominated by the flowing, the circulating, the enlivening, distracting, enervating force of images.

I think this interest in the experience of being in modern life, of becoming through modern life, has to do in some way with your efforts to bring together the concerns and benefits of Art History with Cultural Studies: a converging and contextualizing of the history of images – and their modes of making and modalities of meaning – with a political and ethical impulse. And a preoccupation with everyday life. You say this explicitly in a number of different ways in the *Reader*, and in *An Introduction to Visual Culture* where you make the following statements:

> Visual culture directs our attention away from structured, formal viewing settings like the cinema and art gallery to the centrality of visual experience in everyday life. (p. 7)
>
> Just as cultural studies has sought to understand the ways in which people create meaning from the consumption of mass culture, so does visual culture prioritize the everyday experience of the visual from the snapshot to the VCR and even the blockbuster art exhibition. (p. 7)
>
> Visual culture seeks to blend the historical perspective of art history and film studies with the case-specific, intellectually engaged approach characteristic of cultural studies. (p. 12–13)
>
> The transcultural experience of the visual in everyday life is, then, the territory of visual culture. (p. 41)

My question, then, is this: what place does the everyday have in your thinking, research, and writing?

NM: There's no question that the everyday has been the boundary against which I have tried to think out the practices and possibilities of the visual. What I have meant by that has changed quite considerably over the past decade. I did my PhD at Warwick University at a time when cultural studies work was generating a community of interest there (although it tended to be called 'theory' then). Then and later, I was enormously influenced by the work of Stuart Hall and the Birmingham group, who seemed to have a means of interfacing the academic with the political that was full of potential. I remember seeing Stuart do a political meeting on a wet night in North London to a handful of people in some union hall and being quite brilliant and inspiring. So I have always wanted visual culture to call itself that, rather than say visual studies, in order to emphasize the engagement with the politics of the everyday.

In the 1990s that seemed to me and many others to be about moving away from formal spaces of viewing created in the era of mechanical reproduction, like cinemas and art galleries, to the personal interface with the visual, ranging from face-to-face encounters, the drift of Western city life with its signage and display, the spread of ambient media (like TVs in airports and post offices) and the sheer proliferation of channels, whether on television or the Internet, that placed a premium on 'capturing eyeballs'. If, as de Certeau had argued in *The Practice of Everyday Life*, walking, cooking and shopping could be seen as tactics of negotiating with disciplinary power, it seemed that such everyday looking might be added to that list as a means of engaging the spectacle of late capital. Add to that the proliferation of digital media, in which consumers were enabled to become producers and which tended to create challenges to centralized authority because 'information wants to be free', and one had the sense that the possibilities of visual culture were quite striking at that time.

Now of course many of these tactical sites are also locations of surveillance and of the generation of statistical and other records. Walking is, in many American suburbs and cities, a potentially suspect activity in and of itself. At the same time, the digital has become the agent and locus of capital's free mobility, rather than of 'freedom' in an emancipatory sense, and the web is less free in the sense of being without charge. Once again but from a different optic, I feel the force of the Situationist protest against 'the colonization of everyday life'. The agent of that colonization is a networked intersection of the resurgent militarized state and transnational capital that has been named *Empire* by Hardt and Negri (2001). The everyday is, then, no longer necessarily a place of resistance in the sense made common by cultural studies, so much as the locus of an elusive trace of that resistance to be reconstituted by political action, or more precisely, by the reconnection of the general intellect with praxis. That action takes place in the context of what Giorgio Agamben (2005) has called the 'state of exception', that is to say, a moment in which the government claims that it needs to suspend the laws in order to preserve the rule of law. Everyday life in the state of exception is, as Tom Mitchell has pointed out, nothing less than the experience of fascism (which is not quite to say Nazism, and does not necessarily imply extermination camps). This neo-fascism, as Paulo Virno calls it, does not aestheticize politics in the famous phrase of Walter Benjamin, so much as cast a pall of invisibility over that which is done in the name of the state of exception. What we have had to learn is that simply making things visible, as in the exemplary case of the 'Abu Ghraib' photographs (taken to mean all those depictions of lawless violence undertaken in the current global civil war), has not had the consequences one might have expected. It seems that as long as people accept the rhetorical framing of such spectacles as necessitated by the current emergency, their contents remain, in a certain sense, invisible: not that there was not revulsion but no significant political consequences followed from the Abu Ghraib scandal. Bush, Howard, and Blair were all re-elected and no person of seniority has been disciplined, let alone jailed. At the same time, the anti-war protests of February 15 represented, as the Retort group has argued, a moment in which the multitude – that is to say, the mass of humanity, as opposed to the 'people' predicated by the neo-liberal State, as in the endless reiteration of the war as being for 'the people of Iraq' – became visible to itself, even as it soon experienced defeat.

MS: You return to these issues of everyday life in the opening pages of your recent book *Watching Babylon* (2005): The war in Iraq and global visual culture where, in the context of discussions of globalization and visual culture, you also speak of 'vernacular watching' (p. 13, pp. 30–1). *Watching Babylon* is, overall, about how such everyday experiences of 'watching' are caught up in and take place by way of what you characterize as the 'digital and global culture of hegemonic capitalism' (p. 13). This is about the power of images in global culture, the saturation of our field of vision, and what you call the visual event. You go on to speak of watching as 'all the things we do when we watch television: looking, not looking, listening, not listening, eating, making a phone call, working, doing laundry, child care, reading and so on'. You speak of 'vernacular watching' which 'tak[es] everyday life as its domain'. Watching, you say, 'needs to be thought of as an activity that is necessarily intersected and implicates both other forms of watching and other activities altogether' (p. 13). Could you tell us some more about this lovely turn of phrase 'vernacular watching'?

NM: Thanks, I'm very glad that you like the term. It owes a debt to the emergent field of vernacular photography – photographs taken by non-specialists – in general and Geoffrey Batchen's championing of the idea in his book *Each Wild Idea* (2001) in particular. W.J.T. Mitchell (2002) also used a similar term in his 'Showing Seeing' essay and, like everyone in the field, I'm always in debt to his work and his generosity. I was also thinking of Anna McCarthy's book *Ambient Television* (2001) which talks about TV 'out of place', whether in bars, airports, post offices or other such places. The phrase resulted from an experience in a gym in Long Island where I found myself watching the bombing of Baghdad as a man dressed in military-style work out clothes celebrated each and every bomb and I could not find words to deflate his ardour. Watching was clearly not resistance here. It is a means, then, of trying to encapsulate the oddities of vernacular experience in the state of exception. I also wanted to try and suggest by this what I have always intended, namely that watching is not the performance of a disembodied eye – what Duchamp called the retinal – but a performative constellation of certain modes of habit, domesticity, leisure, and work. If, as Jonathan Beller (1994) has put it, 'to look is to labour', watching is an uneasy meditation on the place of the intellect in the everyday and in the production of value, rather than a passive consumption of media. In this regard, I also wanted to evoke the importance for visual culture of the experiences of watching and being watched that are not mediated by technology (while granting that all phenomenal experience is shaped and understood by means of the age of the world picture). At the same time, many people do spend more and more time watching screens on static and portable media as their work and as their play. While they perform this work or play, they are often subject to certain modes of being watched themselves, whether by a webcam monitoring child-care, a computer noting the number of keystrokes performed in a given time, or an observer in the classroom checking for faculty 'bias'. The visual event is, then, a place of complex intersection that we resolve to ourselves as 'watching', knowing that watching is also being watched, that vision is not an isolated perceptual event but a compound one and that there is nothing banal about the quotidian.

MS: In *Silent Poetry* (1995), *Bodyscape: Art, Modernity and the Ideal Figure* (1995), and the edited collection *Diaspora and Visual Culture: Representing Africans and Jews* (1999), as well as elsewhere, you've written extensively about identity, identity politics, identity formation, and what, in *Watching Babylon*, you call 'visual subjectivity'. I'd like to ask you a couple of questions about the matter of identity – which is so often a question of representation – and its place in Visual Culture Studies.

In both *Silent Poetry* and *Bodyscape*, you pay close attention to blindness and deafness. In fact I think it's fair to say that of all the scholars working between Art History and Cultural Studies, in Visual Culture Studies, you're the one with the most unmistakable commitment to Disability Studies, and the questions that Disability Studies raise for vision and visuality. That's to say, in your writings, blindness and deafness, for instance, don't simply crop up as ways to engage with the non-visual but, rather, demonstrate how differently-abled bodies, identities, and subjectivities are constituted by, with, and against more hegemonic regimes of vision and visuality. (Actually, it strikes me that you also do something similar with matters of race, nation, diaspora, and so on: you use them as a dialectical counterpoint, a lens through which to both see these matters themselves and also see differently the hegemonic projects and prejudices to which they are tied, imbricated, embedded, caught up in one another's concerns – in this case racism, nationalism, xenophobia.) Can you tell us more about this way of looking, seeing, knowing?

NM: To me disability studies has opened up crucial new modes of thinking about specific identities within a collective framework. To argue, as Lenny Davis puts it, that we have all been 'disabled' (as infants) and that some form of disability attends all those who live into 'senior citizen' status is to reframe identities as contingent and flexible, while also being collective. By the same token, thinking about necessary disability is to put pressure on the very abstract notions of sensory perception that dominate the academic discussion on such matters. Georgina Kleege (2001), for example, has written about how the sighted expect the blind to have no visual perception whatsoever, rather than the complexly variegated forms of visual perception that pass under the rubric blindness. I think here of Borges's essay on yellow, the only colour that his eyesight would latterly let him perceive, in which he displays not a bitterness of loss but a remarkable meditation on his monochrome world. By the same token, I am what the deaf call 'hard-of-hearing', a person with very restricted hearing that nonetheless lives as a hearing person. So I tend to become impatient with arguments that all visual materials are also audio materials because sound is such a problem for me. So whereas the regime of normality insists that sight either is or is not available ('referee, are you blind?' meaning that only a person without sight could not see), it also claims that hearing must always be available ('he can hear if he wants to' is the vernacular version of this). So I would say that the 'normal' is constituted by its own formation of what 'disability' must mean and the insistence that the 'normal' is synaesthetic. It's striking that, in the US, the same authorities that are prepared to grant the administration ever wider powers to exceed and evade the norm under the rubric of the state of exception are at the same time restricting what the state can be expected to do for people with disabilities and expanding the reach of the normal so as to exclude people from disability benefits. One can't help but be reminded of the Catch-22 whereby anyone with any apparent African descent is African-American because there is no perceived advantage to that status, whereas anyone wanting to be called Native American has to go through a rather rigorous process of certification because of the perceived benefits that accrue. Such interfaces of the collective and the particular within sensory and legal regimes of normality seem to me to epitomize what visual culture might do.

By extension, I have always felt that by the very engagement with 'culture', with all its attendant baggage from the eighteenth century on, requires visual culture to make questions of difference a first-order priority (I recall here being put down by a grand British academic a few years ago when I mentioned identity politics: 'We don't say "identity", we speak of "difference"', itself of course a claim of superior 'European' identity to the backward 'American'). However, these issues are often now dismissed as 'so 1990s', as if they had been resolved at that time. One of the reasons that the aftermath of Hurricane Katrina and the Asian tsunami were so shocking to many was that here one could not ignore the interface of racialized difference, class, neocolonial state policy, and human suffering. However, the effects of this shock in the US have been very short term and quickly passed over. But there is an emergent critical response that seeks to connect questions of 'race', sexuality, nationality, and Empire, such as Roderick Ferguson's queer of colour politics and the recent special issue of *Social Text*, edited by David L. Eng, José Muñoz, and Judith Halberstam (2005) on queer politics and theory. The latter has caused quite a stir for its critique of white middle-class gay male practice in academia. It is becoming obvious that the state of exception has caused a revival of racialized sentiment and politics in the Anglophone Iraq war coalition of the US, Britain, and Australia, even as the effects of the globalized neoliberal economy are producing similar results in Europe. With the recent provocation of the Danish cartoons of Mohammed causing a worldwide uproar, it's clear that visual culture needs to engage with the politics of global difference as a matter of urgency. It's been salutary, for instance, to see how the remarkable effort of Okwui Enwezor's *Documenta XI* has had so little effect on the corporate globalized art world with its non-stop art fairs, biennales, and new museums. Once again, in a somewhat different context, the sheer quantity and scope of the market is able to absorb and neutralize any challenge so that it can take an active effort to remember it, even as we are surrounded by constant memorialization.

MS: My second question on identity is a short one. Early on in *Watching Babylon* you say that you watched the war in Iraq with a Western viewpoint, as a European based in the United States and watching by way of US television, but that you want to 'disidentify' with this viewpoint. Why? Can you?

NM: Here I wanted to use José Muñoz's (1999) idea of disidentification to suggest a mid-point between a meaningless denial of my complicity with the Western viewpoint – because clearly I have no other – and a refusal to identify with it. The book strategises precisely on this point: how might one make the naturalized 'American' viewpoint seem strange or open to question? As an American immigrant, I arrived in Los Angeles in 1990 only to find it was always already intensely familiar as the scenery and imaginary of film and television, just as a certain New York is known worldwide. Now it is of course the case that as Mike Davis and others have shown, there's another Los Angeles that is not that of the mediascape. In *Watching Babylon*, I wanted to frame the American viewpoint in an environment where it is experienced as local and to which it is addressed, that is to say, the American suburb. Unlike many European cities, American suburbs are increasingly independent of the cities of which they are in theory the outlying areas. So in this case, the town of Babylon on Long Island, New York, from where I watched the war on Iraq (or at least the active invasion up until the capture of Saddam Hussein) was a place from which one could ask what it means to watch war. This is a place of outsize cars buying products from superstores to stock their gigantic McMansions and in which to watch outsize TV, all the while haunted by the suspicion that the constant exhortion to 'move on, there's nothing to see' is concealing something terrible. It's not by coincidence that the town of Babylon includes Amityville, site of the events that generated *The Amityville Horror*, first made in 1978 and remade in 2004. So, without repeating the argument of the book at length, it was exactly my intent to explore and negotiate the presumed normality of the West, rather than claim an affiliation with – for example – a viewer in Baghdad whose experience is to all intents and purposes unknown to me, blogs, al-Jazeera, and all other mediation notwithstanding.

The University, Visual Rights, Visual Literacy

MS: On the issue of Visual Culture Studies as a challenge for the university, disciplinarity, and thinking in general, in *An Introduction to Visual Culture* you write:

> To some, visual culture may seem to claim too broad a scope to be of practical use. It is true that visual culture will not sit comfortably in already existing university structures. It is part of an emerging body of postdisciplinary academic endeavours from cultural studies, gay and lesbian studies, to African-American studies, and so on, whose focus crosses the borders of traditional academic disciplines at will. In this sense, visual culture is a tactic, not an academic discipline. It is a fluid interpretive structure, centred on understanding the response to visual media of both individuals and groups. Its definition comes from the questions it asks and issues it seeks to raise. Like the other approaches mentioned above, it hopes to reach beyond the traditional confines of the university to interact with peoples' everyday lives. (pp. 4–5)

A few years down the line, with Visual Culture Studies more established, and with you in a new institution, and specifically in a practice-based visual arts context, what do you think about this whole issue now?

NM: The question of the academic institution and academic labour has certainly changed but not in the way that I had hoped. I had a rather utopian belief that the information revolution would transform university practice by making the simple provision of information available to all and thereby both compelling and enabling universities to become the site of critical practice. I envisaged a transformed humanities sector in which the nineteenth-century division of labour into highly specialized subfields would be required to change in line with contemporary labour practice into a fluid and open field of work. It is of course somewhat the case that the Internet has made information of a certain sort more widely available, but there's no quality control, as a quick glance at the Wikipedia entry for visual culture will testify.

So what actually happened was a dispersal of academic labour into the marginalized border zones of intellectual production, once known as the knowledge economy. The new university is a place of part-time labour on a per-course basis. This question about working in a practice-based environment is hard to answer, because the universities are now so driven by revenue and labour questions. As much as I continue to think that visual culture is the theory of practice and the practice of theory, the room for such equivalence has been driven out by the continuing issue of the academic workplace. At New York University, where I now teach as you mention, according to the Adjuncts' Union, some 75 per cent of all courses are taught either by such staff or graduate students. The quality of their work is usually excellent so the reduction in salary and benefits is invisible to students. But the disparity between undergraduate fees of around $35,000 a year and adjunct stipends that average $3500 a course is egregious. The graduate students at NYU organized and won union recognition, despite intense opposition from the administration, in 2001. However, the Bush administration overturned the ruling of the National Labor Review Board by which graduate students were recognized as workers and consequently universities are no longer required to recognize unions. In August 2005, NYU arbitrarily ended its contract with the student union, Local 2110 of the United Auto Workers (a union that represents many clerical and administrative staff, including graduate students at the University of California and the staff at the Museum of Modern Art). A bitter and divisive strike has ensued with the university penalizing students on strike in January 2006 of two semesters' (a full academic year) stipend, even though they had by then been on strike for only nine weeks. The university claims that even though the students teach standalone classes and are indispensable to the functioning of the institution, they are not workers but students and therefore all grievances must be resolved by the officers of the university not by 'outsiders'. Without getting lost in the arcana of the dispute, the university presents itself as in a permanent state of exception, caused by apparent financial shortfall, to justify its literally autocratic decisions. The NYU case is typical of the move by US universities to institutions characterized by a highly centralized adminstration, a reduced and demoralized full-time faculty and staff being asked to perform ever greater duties, and an ever-expanding part-time workforce. Reversing viewpoints, Virno (2004) has raised the intriguing prospect that such conditions could become voluntary, a defection from the search for tenure and promotion and professional advancement that might lead to a politics of post-Fordism.

MS: I'd like to bring our 'conversation' to a close in this final section by asking you to speak a little about your long term attention to matters of emancipation, justice, equality, democracy, utopian thinking, even. In our exchanges over the last few months, you've mentioned in passing a series of interests that emerge out of such commitments. They include 'the expanded field of cultural work', the 'Experimental University', and 'visual rights' or the 'rights to visual literacy'. While not new to your thinking and writing *per se*, these interests seem to be coming to the fore with more insistence. I think speaking about these things would be a nice way to end: to showcase your current and upcoming research projects, and to conclude with a note or two of optimism and hopefulness.

NM: I do think it's important to try and be optimistic in the spirit of the 'pessimism of the intellect, optimism of the will'. On the one hand, sheer pessimism leaves you with the Dick Cheney world-view in which evil is active and all means are justified to combat it. On the other, a Frankfurt-school view in which the sheer domination of the culture industry is such that all resistance is futile is a recipe for revolutionary rhetoric in the seminar -room and a social conservatism in practice as one waits for the revolution that never comes. So in

Watching Babylon, I ended each chapter on an utopian or weak messianic note as a counter to the difficult and depressing material.

More recently, I have been working on a project that I call 'Visual Rights' that draws together all my different interests into an extended statement. It's motivated by the awareness that we have no visual rights and yet we live in a renewed society of the spectacle in which the visible and the invisible are of great political moment. (Just as a footnote, the so-called 'Multi-cultural art in America' book that Routledge advertise on Amazon was never more than an idea that they have somehow decided to announce as forthcoming: it never will so don't pre-order!). This book makes a claim for visual rights, even though they do not yet exist. What does exist, and has made the case for visual rights, is a right to look, as Derrida once termed it. The right to look is exercised in the contemporary, which is understood here to mean the living together with others that has been Anglophone experience since the term was coined in the seventeenth century. Consequently, 'the right to look' is 'the invention of that other' (Derrida). The look is a sideways one between those of minority status (the enslaved, Jews, women, children, and all those excluded from majoritarian legal subjectivity) and is always in tension with the law of the gaze. The place of the right to look is therefore the 'South', in tension with the 'North' represented by the gaze. The book offers a historical and theoretical genealogy of minority and the right to look, theorized in terms of deconstruction, psychoanalytic culture criticism and the fragmentary method of Walter Benjamin and postcolonial theory. Minority was a strategy of forming transnational collectivity that existed in counterpoint with the universal claims of Enlightenment and revolution until the division of Western society into the 'normal' and distinct minorities made such transverse links impossible by the early twentieth century. I concentrate here on the related Atlantic world figures of the enslaved African and the transcultural Jewish ragpicker known as the *Smouse* from the seventeenth century to Oscar Wilde's London. However, far from being an object of antiquarian curiosity, minority has again become a feature of the globalization of our time. The numerical majority finds itself in the position of Minority, unable to influence the key practices of security, finance, and ecology that determine their conditions of existence. This new Minority requires a new claim to rights, especially visual rights, because so much of globalization is conducted as a form of invisibility, in which the citizen has no right to look but is asked to 'move on, there's nothing to see'. Minority is, then, a means of imagining the multitude in a way that insists that the collective is constituted by difference and deferral.

How these ideas might move into play in the general attempt to challenge the state of exception and reassert the possibilities of Minority is perhaps too presumptive a question for me to answer. My hope is simply that in making certain performative claims about the rights in relation to the global spectacle that some friction might be introduced into the seemingly relentless process by which scandal and crisis recedes into oblivion as the endless cascade of mediatized information inundates any given object. The performance of rights would be first a claim to that which one does not have as if one does, which Rancière (2004) has called 'dissensus', that is to say, a breaking of the conservative consensus. Second, it would mobilize the process of surrogation that is the sibling of memory and performance as Joseph Roach has taught us, in that any right is a surrogation of difference that does not erase the difference so much as put it into play. By asserting the hold of right in the flows of transnational neo-liberal intellectual capital, one would also emphasize the placing of law as right over law as force, remembering Derrida's meditation on *droit* in 'Force of Law' (1990). Here, following Benjamin, Derrida places the law's capacity to enforce and hence conserve itself in tension with the right [*droit*] to strike, a violence that founds and creates. Visuality was Thomas Carlyle's 1840 word for what Chartism was not: that is to say, he opposed Chartism's vision of non-representative democracy (that is, a democracy that does not delegate its governing function to others) with his idea of the Hero, a single all-powerful figure. In 1906, Georges Sorel and Rosa Luxemburg would come to understand the general strike as a means to create 'groups of images' assembled into a picture of what socialism might achieve, like Benjamin's famous dialectical image that resulted from his interface of his reading of Sorel with the Arcades project that he began two years later. In claiming the right to strike, or to what Virno calls general civil disobedience, one thus tries to visualize, or create a dialectical image of, the 'general intellect' other than it is, without erasing difference into a Hegelian subject.

References

Alpers, Svetlana (1983) *The Art of Describing: Dutch Art in the Seventeenth Century*. Chicago: University of Chicago Press.

Agamben, Giorgio (2005) *State of Exception* (Kevin Attell, *trans.*). Chicago: University of Chicago Press.

Batchen, Geoffrey (2001) *Each Wild Idea*, Cambridge: The MIT Press.

Beller, Jonathan (1994) Cinema, Capital of the Twentieth Century. *Postmorden Culture*, 4(3), (May 1994) (Unpaginated).

de Certeau, Michael (1984 [1980]) *The Practice of Everyday Life* (Steven Rendall, *trans.*). Berkeley: University of California Press.

Derrida, Jacques (1990) 'The Force of Law', *Cardozo Law Review* 11: 919–1045.

Eng, David. L. Muñoz, José and Halberstam, Judith (eds.) (2005) 'What's Queer about Queer Studies Now?' *Social Text*, 23(3–4/84–85): 1–310.

Evans, Jessica and Hall, Stuart (eds.) (1999) *Visual Culture: The Reader*. London: Sage Publications.

Hardt, Michael and Negri, Antonio (2001) *Empire*. Cambridge, MA: Harvard University Press.

Kleege, Georgina (2001) *Sight Unseen*, New Haven, CT: Yale University Press.
McCarthy, Anna (2001) *Ambient Television: Visual Culture and Public Space*. Durham, NC: Duke University Press.
Mirzoeff, Nicholas (1995) *Silent Poetry: Deafness, Sign, and Visual Culture in Modern France*. Princeton: Princeton University Press.
Mirzoeff, Nicholas (1995) *Bodyscape: Art, Modernity and the Ideal Figure*. New York: Routledge.
Mirzoeff, Nicholas (1998) *The Visual Culture Reader*. New York: Routledge.
Mirzoeff, Nicholas (1999) *An Introduction to Visual Culture*. New York. Routledge.
Mirzoeff, Nicholas (1999) *Diaspora and Visual Culture: Representing Africans and Jews*. New York: Routledge.
Mirzoeff, Nicholas (2005) *Watching Babylon: The War in Iraq and Global Visual Culture*. New York: Routledge.
Mitchell W.J.T. (2002) 'Showing Seeing': A critique of visual culture, *Journal of Visual Culture*, 1(2): 165–81.
Muñoz, José Esteban (1999) *Disidentifications: Queers of Colour and the Performance of Politics*, Minneapolis: University of Minnesota Press.
Rancière, Jacques (2004) 'Who is the Subject of the Rights of Man?' *South Atlantic Quarterly*, 103(2/3): pp. 277–310.
Van Eeden, Jeanne and du Preez, Amanda (eds.) (2005) *South African Visual Culture*. South Africa: Van Schaik Uitgewers Publishers.
Virno, Paolo (2004) *A Grammar of the Multitude*. Los Angeles, CA: Semiotext(e).

2

MIXING IT UP: THE MEDIA, THE SENSES, AND GLOBAL POLITICS

Interview with W.J.T. Mitchell

Introduction

W.J.T. Mitchell is Gaylord Donnelley Distinguished Service Professor for English and Art History, The University of Chicago. Editor of *Critical Inquiry*, he is the author of many books including *The Language of Images* (1980); *Iconology: Image, Text, Ideology* (1986); *Picture Theory* (1994); *The Last Dinosaur Book* (1998); and *What Do Pictures Want?* (2005b). Here Mitchell raises a series of questions that are key to any historical, political, and institutional consideration of Visual Culture Studies and to the ontology, epistemology, ethics, and aesthetics of the visual. He also addresses carefully the relations between language and visuality, between vision and the other senses, and between different media. (Hence in part his recent shift from Visual Culture Studies to Media Studies.) Towards the end of the interview, as part of a discussion on the politics of landscape – landscape for Mitchell being the 'ground' for his work in visual and media studies – he struggles with how the question of space, place, and landscape intersects with the discourse on globalization.

The Field, the Discipline, the University

Marquard Smith (MS): I'm going to begin by quoting you back to yourself:

> What is visual culture or visual studies? Is it an emergent discipline, a passing moment of interdisciplinary turbulence, a research topic, a field or subfield of cultural studies, media studies, rhetoric and communication, art history, or aesthetics? Does it have a specific object of research, or is it a grab-bag of problems left over from respectable, well-established disciplines? If it is a field, what are its boundaries and limiting definitions? Should it be institutionalized as an academic structure, made into a department or given programmatic status, with all the appurtenances of syllabi, textbooks, prerequisites, requirements, and degrees? How should it be taught? What would it mean to profess visual culture in a way that is more than improvisatory?[1]

As you'll recognize, that is a quotation from your article 'Showing seeing: A critique of visual culture', published in 2002 in the *Journal of Visual Culture*. I often use this quote when I'm teaching my own students about Visual Culture Studies, or when I'm invited to lead workshops on the topic at institutions other than my own; and I've even used it a couple of times in my own published writings (2005, 2006). For me, it raises a wonderful series of questions that are key to any historical, political, and institutional consideration of Visual Culture Studies. From the start, it raises questions of definition, of disciplinarity, and of the 'object' of visual culture, as well as questions for the institution and for pedagogy. I'm interested to know if you think that, a few years down the line, some of the questions that you raise here have become less pressing, redundant even, and further questions, un-thought at that point, have come to the fore?

W.J.T. Mitchell (W.J.T.M): It is always disconcerting, if not terrifying, to have your words quoted back to you in this way. It presents two equally irresistible temptations: (1) to stand pat, repeat what you said the first time, and refuse to change a thing; (2) to quibble, equivocate, re-define, retract, and (worst of all) to rewrite. I will give in to the first by saying that I still think these questions are useful because they set up the set of choices, the 'garden of forking paths' that faces anyone who enters the field of visual culture. I will give in to the second by suggesting a substitution for the shortest word in the whole statement, and that is 'or'. Suppose the questions were not posed as 'either/or', but as a series of 'both/ands'? Suppose that an 'emergent discipline' was *also* 'a passing moment'? Suppose disciplines themselves vacillated between having well-defined objects and 'grab bags of problems'? After all, Marshall Sahlins now believes that anthropology is a dying discipline, killed by its recent abandonment of its key theoretical object, namely culture. The philosopher Leonard Linsky once told me that 'analytic philosophy is dead', and he suggested that its death could be precisely dated to the moment of the appearance of Wittgenstein's *Philosophical Investigations*. Even the most powerful and enduring disciplines, even 'philosophy' itself, may have 'come to an end' to be replaced by literature if Richard Rorty (1979) is correct. Slavoj Zizek has said that all the proper philosophical questions were asked (and answered) between Kant and Hegel. In the mid-1990s Derrida (1994) commented that, like Marxism, deconstruction was dying. But he added that it was dying much more conspicuously in the US than in France, where it had been declared finally dead a long time ago.

My point here is not just that disciplines, like other human inventions, all have a limited life-span. Longevity is surely not the only criterion, but a certain quality of life. How long did phrenology last? And is astrology, an extraordinarily long-lived tradition of hermeneutic practices, a discipline at all? Do we really know what a discipline is? Is it something that has disciples? Or a well-defined object of research? Is it a social phenomenon or a conceptual system? A profession or a set of principles? A department with a secretary and a letterhead? Or (and you will note the return of this fateful word) is it a question of 'either/or' in the first place, or of 'both/ands'? A question of choices or chances, free will or fate? My categorical, unequivocal answer to your question, then, is that I will stand by the words you have quoted, on the condition that every key term (discipline, field, institution, object, profess, programme) – and most especially the little words, the non-terms such as 'or' – will be themselves put into question again and again.

Our fate, Marq, is to have participated in the collective working out of many of these questions. Of course we hope that this work has been, in some sense, 'disciplined' and responsible, not merely wool-gathering. We hope it is more like astronomy than astrology, and that it is not (as Tom Crow has warned us) a kind of New Age fad like 'Mental Culture' (1996: 34). (But I am always reminded of a magnificent and transient programme that never achieved or perhaps even sought disciplinary status, the 'History of Consciousness' at University California, Santa Cruz). Visual culture is clearly more of a discipline than the history of consciousness. It has made considerable headway on both sides of the 'ors' and 'ands' that identify it as a coherent research project and/or an extended family quarrel.

So in answer to your question about issues that have become less pressing: yes, I think the questions of institutionalization and pedagogy are not nearly so open or urgent as they once were. I think visual studies has achieved a relatively secure place among the disciplines, fields, or areas of the humanities, and in some places it even has a bureaucratic existence within the academy. I also think the question of the object or concept of visual studies has been answered affirmatively, and we now have a strong idea of 'visuality' that is foundational to the work of many researchers. By a 'strong' idea, I mean one that can be shown to 'have legs' in both a philosophical sense (the ontology, epistemology, ethics, and aesthetics of the visual) and in a historical sense (an idea, as Nicholas Mirzoeff (2006) has shown in his recent article 'On Visuality' in the pages of *Journal of Visual Culture*) that reveals complex, multi-dimensional genealogies.

As to the new questions that have come to the fore: I'm sure we are going to touch upon many of them in the conversation to come. What is the relation of vision to the other senses? What are the boundaries of the visual? What place does blindness, the unseen, or the unseeable, even the unimaginable play in the study of the visual? What is the relation of visual studies to comparable 'emergences' in the study of culture such as media studies and material culture? I also remain fascinated by the question of the relation of visual culture to 'image culture' and iconology. I don't see them as simply the same thing at all. So as you can see, if I was happy to see visual culture as a 'dangerous supplement' to art history and aesthetics, a kind of necessary inside/outside breaching of their disciplinary boundaries, as I go on to say in the article published in *Journal of Visual Culture* that you've mentioned, I am equally happy to look for the dangerous supplements to visual culture itself. This is the necessary fate of the 'indisciplinary' scholar, the epistemological anarchist. Consider the most recent case in the 'scandals of the visible': the caricature of Mohammed as a suicide bomber that appeared in the Danish newspaper *Jyllands*. To a scholar of visual culture, the thing that has to jump out at us is that no one had to actually *see* the cartoon. To *hear* about it was enough to be offended. This is in sharp distinction from other recent scandals of the visible. The Abu Ghraib photographs would have had no effect if they had not been circulated widely, made literally visible. By contrast, the key issue with the Mohammed caricature as with images such as Andre Serrano's 'Piss Christ', or Chris Ofili's 'dung Madonna', from a 'visual studies' standpoint is what they can be made to say, what can be said about them. No one needs to see them to be offended by the mere fact of their existence.

I suspect that the most interesting new questions for visual studies, then, will be located at the frontiers of visuality, the places where seeing approaches a limit and is faced with its own negation, or with some other perceptual modality or medium. That is probably why, in my own 'general' teaching, I have shifted from visual culture to media studies. It's not because I have given up on visual studies, but because the problem of mediation opens the visual onto different phenomenological frontiers (stillness and motion; audition, tactility, and embodiment) as well as technologies and regimes of the visible. This leads me to ask what the digitization of the visible field means, and to press for answers that would take us beyond the received ideas, e.g. the 'loss of the real' posited by so many theorists, from Jean Baudrillard to my namesake, William J. Mitchell. I am about to publish an essay on 'Realism and the Digital Image' that will argue, contra Mitchell, that digitization actually enables the production of 'supercopies' and 'optimizations' of the reality effect as well as the referential claims of visual images.[2] And these sorts of technical issues should, in my view, be seen as indissolubly linked to political and ideological matters. The current revival of Guy Debord's concept of the 'spectacle' as a tool for diagnosing the war on terror (see *Afflicted Powers: Capital and Spectacle in a New Age of War* the Retort collective) strikes me as deeply flawed in its hostility to technical considerations, and its recourse to iconoclastic remedies for political maladies. If visual studies is going to engage capitalism, politics, and war through the medium of the spectacle, it is going to require analysis and historical investigation of the spectacular concept itself. It will require something more than expressions of distaste for consumer society, mass culture, and kitsch coupled with horror at the alienation-effects of modernity, commodification, and standardization.

MS: I'm intrigued to hear more about your ambivalent relationship to Visual Culture Studies. Let me give you an example of what I perceive to be this ambivalence. In an interview conducted by Orrin N.C. Wang in 2001, speaking about yourself in the third person you say

> He [Mitchell] continues to think that something called 'visual culture' has a future as an area of research and reflection, and he hopes that someday a book entitled *What Do Pictures*

> *Want?* will lay down its basic principles. This will be a book that will finally get down to the irreducible core of representation, explain to what extent there can (and cannot) be something like a 'linguistics of the visual field'.

Well, *What do Pictures Want? The Lives and Loves of Images* is now out (2005; see also 1996). And I'll be asking you some questions about it in a while. For the moment, I'm interested in how a remark like this might appear to be in contradiction with comments made in another interview, this time in the journal *Mosaic*, where you say:

> I don't want to be a member of a visual culture department. I want to teach visual culture as a kind of dedisciplinary or indisciplinary effort and exercise, but I want to do it in the context of work that is connected with the past in a very firm and discipline way – with cinema studies and philosophy, for instance. (2000)[3]

Is this simply a distinction between what's engaging about 'visual culture' as 'an area of research and reflection' and what might be less engaging about teaching 'visual culture' in a department of the same name, or is there something else going on here? For instance, an acknowledgement that 'visual culture' isn't a discipline but rather a tool used to prod more established disciplines? Or, something about the perceived ahistorical nature of Visual Culture Studies?

W.J.T.M: Well, as for the contradiction between my hopes for a discipline of visual culture complete with a 'linguistics of the visual field', and my own reluctance to be a member of a visual culture department: this was motivated first by my wish to see visual studies develop deliberately and reflectively, rather than rush into premature institutionalization, especially at the expense of traditional disciplines, or as part of a downsizing, speed-up tactic originating in an administrative office. Most important, I wanted to prolong the moment of wonder that is the foundation of every interesting discipline, most notably of philosophy. There was also no doubt a concrete, institutional basis for my ambivalence in my location at the University of Chicago, a place that encourages interdisciplinary collaboration as a matter of principle, and has done so since its founding over a hundred years ago. If I had been located in a different institution, perhaps I would have been in a greater hurry to secure a departmental, programmatic beachhead.

The question of history is, to me, one of the most complex and difficult issues that is faced by Visual Culture Studies. So let me simplify it in the most radical terms as another either/or choice: is there a 'history of vision' or not? Is visual perception, the process by which human beings apprehend the world around them through their eyes, subject to drastic changes that correspond in some way to changes in technology, culture, aesthetics, style, etc.? Walter Benjamin famously argued that 'during long periods of human history, the mode of human sense perception changes with humanity's entire mode of existence. The manner in which human sense perception is organized, the medium in which it is accomplished, is determined not only by nature but by historical circumstances as well' (1969 [1936]). Benjamin was echoing the conclusion of the Vienna School of art history (Riegl and Wickhoff), and his views were re-echoed by Marshall McLuhan's account of media as 'extensions' of man that reshaped the 'sensory ratios' by which we organize perception.

I take these claims to be fundamental doctrines of visual studies today, and to the extent that they are repeated without question, I suspect that the imperative to 'always historicize' has become a dangerous dogma. For one thing, note that Benjamin leaves open the underlying role of something called 'nature' in determining 'the manner in which human sense perception is organized'. At the very least he is allowing for another, presumably ahistorical framework of determination. For another thing, all the interesting questions are begged if one starts from the premise that 'vision has a history'. One needs to hesitate, in my view, and ask what the evidence would be for such a claim, and (more important) what could count as evidence against it. Would one use the history of picture-making and image-processing as a guide to the history of seeing? This immediately leads to a number of absurdities. Did people start seeing the world like a Cubist painting around 1913? Did they have to wait until the invention (really a rediscovery, by the way) of perspective to start seeing the world in depth and three dimensions? And why is there such a noticeable conservative tendency in new digital imaging technologies, a compulsion to seek out greater realism and illusionism? Why does the analog, as Brian Massumi notes, always finally triumph over the digital? (Massumi, 2002) Why do the newest video games try to simulate live-action cinema? And why has film animation now merged with live action in feature length narrative films with recognizable stars? Why is it that the diminishing number of people who have never seen film, television, or photography can so quickly acquire the cognitive skills required to perceive images in these media?

So I want to resist the automatic or default historicism that is invoked in relation to visual studies, either by way of urging it to become a 'serious' (i.e., historical) discipline as fast as possible, or complaining bitterly about its ahistorical tendencies. Both automatisms are toxic to critical thinking about the question of history and vision. To raise the question of history seriously, one would have to specify quite precisely what level of visual experience is being historicized: is it the content of what we see? The medial frameworks through which we see? The inter-medial relations to other senses? And what are the relations – including the *disconnections* – between the history of visual images and the history of seeing? In short, I want to recommend that visual studies not be content with the mandate to 'always historicize', but that it insist as well on an imperative to 'always anachronize' its field of investigation.

MS: To keep going with this discussion of history ... I'm not sure what the etiquette is in this situation, but I'd like to ask you two questions that have been asked of you previously. Without wanting to make you repeat yourself, or asking your readers to reread things they've heard you say in the past, for me it's imperative to do this because the answers to these questions are important in this context for readers of this collection. And of course your answers may also have changed! Both questions were asked to you by Margaret Dikovitskaya (2005) in her interview with you published in *Visual Culture: The Study of the Visual after the Cultural Turn*. The first is this: 'What does visual culture 'want' (to paraphrase the title of your article published in *October* in 1996) and what does it lack?' The second is this: 'Why is art history not enough by itself for the study of the visual? In your article 'Interdisciplinarity and Visual Culture' (1996), you wrote that visual culture is an 'inside-out' phenomenon in its relation to art history. Would you expand on that thought?' Another way of asking these questions would be: isn't Art History in an expanded field more than capable of taking on all the objects, and subjects, and media, and environments, as well as the problems, the challenges, and the possibilities of vision, visuality, and the field of vision?

W.J.T.M: I think I'll take you up on your offer, and simply repeat myself. In answer to the first question, as I said to Margaret,

> the *October* essay originally posed this question in relation to pictures, not to visual culture as such. I raised the question of what pictures 'want' in the sense of what they lack, and suggested a number of answers that are part of both vernacular and systematic theorizing. One of the things that pictures are said to lack is the ability to negate or say 'no'. (There is a classic essay by Sol Worth, entitled *Pictures Can't Say Ain't*, that spells out this claim in detail.) The argument is that pictures can only represent some state of affairs affirmatively. The 'no smoking' sign has a picture of a cigarette (which immediately awakens my desire to smoke, as you well know, Marq) and it has to interdict the positive message of the image with a bar, signifying negation. Magritte's well-known picture *This IS Not a Pipe* puts the negative inscription under the image of the pipe as a way of interdicting or negating the positive message of the image – 'this is a pipe'. Magritte is playing on the idea that the picture lacks what it represents. It does not *have* what it *shows*; it offers a presence and insists on an absence in the same gesture.
>
> If we take this question more generally as addressing visual culture and what it 'wants', my first answer would be that it lacks a great many things which are attributed to language. I don't know, ultimately, whether it actually lacks them in some metaphysical sense; I am interested rather in the prejudices that are built into people's attitudes about visual culture, imaging, visual experience, and so forth. One factor to consider here is that visual culture as an emergent discipline or field lacks (at least so far) the kind of scientific, systematic character that, for instance, linguistics has. The concept of visual culture as a discipline or field is quite comparable to linguistics. Linguistics is the science of language, of all languages; more narrowly, linguistics is the science that deals with the structures of language that underlie any particular speech act or textual formation. The aims of visual culture as a discipline are somewhat analogous. It has the same relation to works of visual art, as linguistics has

to literature; visual art is to literature, painting to poetry (a very traditional comparison) as visual culture is to language in general.

What visual culture – the visual process of seeing the worlds as well as making visual representation – 'lacks', then, is a structural, scientific, systematic methodology. This is no Chomsky or Saussure for visual culture (unless you think of Panofsky and the Warburg school as aiming in this direction, toward a '*bildwissenschaft*', a science of images.) And this lack of a scientific theory of visual culture may be the result of a fundamental difference between visual perception, imaging and picturing on the one hand, and linguistic expression on the other. Language is based on a system (syntax, grammar, phonology) that can be scientifically described; pictures and visual experience may not have a grammar in this sense. Bishop Berkeley argued in the eighteenth century that vision *is* in fact a kind of language, doubly articulated between ideas of sight and touch, but if it is a language, it is one that has so far eluded the net of linguistics. There is some kind of excess, of density, and plenitude in visual culture that escapes formalization – which is not to rule out the possibility that some genius will come along and produce such a theory.

My own intuition is that this excess of the visual, the 'surplus' of images, is an intractable feature of visual culture, and it would be better not to aim at formalizing it within the straightjacket of linguistics. (Nelson Goodman's (1976) argument that images are dense, analog symbol systems, in contrast to the differentiated, articulated schemes of language – an argument that I discuss in *Iconology* [1986] – is relevant here. The infinitely nuanced variability of the analog sign, the lack of finite differentiation between characters, as in an ungraduated thermometer, puts limits on our ability to formalize the rules of pictorial representation). Indeed, some theorists have argued that language itself is not completely formalizable without a reduction that loses all the life of words, and that linguistics is not really a science at all. I remain agnostic on that debate. (Dikovitskaya, 2005: 238–40)

My response to the second question is as follows: Art History is not sufficient because it is focused – quite appropriately – on the history of art. It is concerned with works of visual art as certified and legitimated by some aesthetic tradition or institutional practice – sculpture, painting, photography, the museums, collections, galleries that house works of art – i.e., the fine arts, and visual representation. Visual culture addresses a much broader field, just as linguistics claims to occupy a broader field than literature in the realm of language, so visual art is just one area of visual culture.

Art History – at least in its traditional formations (and this is changing today) – is not enough by itself for the study of visual culture because it is grounded in a distinction between (for instance) mass media, mass culture, kitsch, commercial art, and 'fine art' proper. Art History is not concerned with ordinary everyday practices of seeing, what I call 'vernacular visuality', all the social constructions of the visual field that lie outside image-making, and artistic image-making. Before people make images, much less works of art, they look at each other and look at the world. Visual culture, I think, is the study of that aspect as well as the visual arts; so the latter (art history) clearly does not determine the boundary of the field, although visual art can certainly have an impact on visual culture by exploring novel ways of seeing and representing the world.

In the early stages of the development of art history, it was closer to being what I call visual culture, as can be seen in the work of Riegl, Panofksy, and Aby Warburg. The Warburg school of art history was interested in general iconography and in non-artistic modes of visual representation. Panofsky also made it clear that in order to study iconography one has to go beyond the masterpieces and engage with vernacular forms of visual representation like cinema. Gombrich was a pioneer of visual culture in his resolute insistence on studying 'everyday seeing' and the psychology of visual perception. So visual culture in some ways comes directly out of a certain tendency in art history – many departments of art history in the US are now adding 'visual culture' to their names. Many of the more ambitious art historians have always been interested in areas beyond the traditional boundaries of the fine arts. There has been interest in vernacular modes and spectacle, and space, and performance, especially if you include architectural history as part of art history. Architectural history has always been involved with visual culture because it takes a broader view. To me it seems paradoxical that architectural history is seen as a subfield of art history, since in fact most works of art – sculptures, paintings – are located in architectural spaces. It seems to me that architecture is the master art in that it is the study of the whole spatial environment where all the other kinds of works appear.

Media, the Senses, and Mixing

MS: The very subtitles of *Iconology: Image, Text, Ideology* (1986) and *Picture Theory: Essays on Visual and Verbal Representations* (1994) tell us that for you there is always already a relationship, a co-mingling, between image and text, between the visual and the verbal. This is an interest that goes back to at least your earliest book *Blake's Composite Art* (1977) on text design in William Blake's illustrated poetry, and persists in your recent article 'There Are No Visual Media' (2005a), and your latest book, *What do Pictures Want? Essays on the Lives and Loves of Images* (2005b). (And you are of course Professor of English and Art History, working across and between the Department of English Language & Literature and the Department of Art History at the University of Chicago.) As someone who has always worked across and between books and poetry and the visual arts, and old and new media, what is it that is particularly engaging and pressing for you – historically, conceptually – in this inter-medial mixing? Does it tell us something about our recent critical activities, or simply draw our attention to what was already going on?

And what about the inter-sensory? You've always maintained that part of the reason to speak about the visual, to study visual culture, is because it encourages us to confront the matter of the mixing of the senses – the sometimes self-evident, sometimes obscure, sometimes fraught relations between visual, audio, textual, tactile, aural cultures ...

W.J.T.M: You are certainly right that the dialectic between language and visuality, word and image, has always been foundational for my work. I see it as doubly articulated at the levels of senses (ear versus eye) and signs (symbolic versus iconic), so I will treat your questions about the inter-sensory and the inter-semiotic together. What is it about this intermedial mixing that is so fascinating? I suppose it is partly a matter of a kind of stubborn realism built into my conviction that the human world itself is constructed out of the interweaving of signs and symbols, and it is the heterogeneity of these mediations that makes this a *living* world rather than a static system or stable picture. In other words, I think of 'word and image' first as a kind of epistemological principle, the name of a 'seam' or 'difference' (or is it a Derridean *difference*?) in the structure of knowledge and the knowable. But it is also an aesthetic and phenomenological principle, a seam in the structure of appearance and experience, and ultimately, an ethical and political issue when we approach the boundaries of the unspeakable and the unimaginable. James Agee noted that the verbal-visual dialectics of his collaborative photographic essay with Walker Evans were not aimed at representing the 'whole truth' about the sharecroppers of Alabama, but at producing a dynamic relationship with the reader/beholder: 'who are you who will read these words and study these photographs ... and by what right, and what will you do about it?' (Agee and Evans, 1939: 9). It was the mutually constitutive and mutually deconstructive labour of the composite art form that made the 'work' of the artists into a labour for the reader/beholder in Agee and Evans' book so fascinating to me. And I suppose that is why I have always loved 'composite' verbal-visual forms, from illuminated manuscripts to comic books to films, and why my chronic perversion has been to look at pictures with a reader's ear, and to read texts with a painter's eye.

But of course any perversion worth the name has to turn on itself and seek its own moment of ascesis and refusal. Hence my fascination with 'purity' and 'specificity' in media, the utopian search for the pure opticality of abstract painting, the pure babble of language in Joyce or Blake, the pure scribble of writing and drawing in C.S. Peirce and Robert Morris. And needless to say, the double movements of purification and contamination, specificity and hybridity, have been amply represented in theoretical accounts of media, from Aristotle's division of dramatic art into lexis, melos, and opsis, to the Peircean triad of symbol, index, and icon, to the Lacanian registers of the symbolic, real, and imaginary. What Foucault called the 'seeable and sayable' are always distinct strata of a discourse, but are also always interarticulated and mutually dependent. 'Word and image' is simply a shorthand for this fundamental dialectic, always constituted by a necessary thirdness – the 'and' (or 'or') that links/divides the word and image – the 'bar' or 'slash' that indicates the (non)relation of signifier and signified. This is why I am always insisting that the 'word/image' problem is to be found *inside* language as well as *between* language and visuality;

or why I want to argue that 'there are no visual media' in the sense of some purely optical form of transparency.

MS: Following on from this, I have a quick question about *Critical Inquiry*: to what extent was it a self-conscious decision by the editors for the journal to act as a home, a site, a forum, for critical inquiries in and across diverse disciplines, media, and senses? To what extent do you – all of you – have this mixing in mind? Because of course there are ways in which these things just happen ...

W.J.T.M: On *Critical Inquiry*'s role as an interdisciplinary journal: we have always thought of it under several rubrics: (1) as a space for high-level criticism and theory that would be of potential importance across multiple disciplines; (2) as a site for debate over the crucial issues of the day in the humanities; (3) as a place for the mixing of genres, especially the conjoining of the literary essay with the scholarly article; (4) as a home for critical writing that would be accessible to and interesting for scholars across different fields, and (at times) beyond the boundaries of academic writing.

Global Politics, Landscape, and the Media

MS: Please tell us more about The Chicago School of Media Theory, the research collective of which you are a part at University of Chicago, and the Dead Media Project, the web-based archive of obsolete and archaic media.

W.J.T.M: The Chicago School of Media Theory is a collective of students that formed around my courses in Theories of Media in 2003 and 2004. It spawned a variety of projects that can be seen on the collective's website: (http://www.chicagoschoolmediatheory.net/home.htm).

Among these are: (1) the Glossary of Keywords in Media Theory, a very useful online reference tool written by several generations of University of Chicago students; (2) the Media HyperAtlas, a project that received a $25,000 grant from the University's Advanced Technology Initiative to produce a virtual reality interface for the mapping specific mediascapes or (ultimately) the entire 'mediaverse'. This project is now in its pre-Mercator stage. To see a record of its first steps, look at the 'Media Taxonomy Models' that were produced by the original founders of the project; (3) 'About Face', a project for studying the human face as a medium, including research into racial stereotyping and profiling, the history of expressive codes, and the development of facial recognition software. This project also has a philosophical dimension concerned with the phenomenology of facial recognition, and the ethical/political issues surround 'faciality' in Levinas and Deleuze.

All this work stems from my irrepressible (if mainly non-technical) fascination with what is called 'New Media', and the use of cyberspace as a realm of intellectual exploration and aesthetic invention. The emergence of web-assisted teaching has been especially important to me, because it has such terrific potential for reconfiguring the classroom as a democratic space in which students are writing for and learning from each other. I think my students are writing much more and much better prose in my classes now, simply because of features like the 'Discussion Board' which allow them to interact outside of class sessions. My current seminar on space, place, and landscape is exploring the nature of cyberspace right alongside inquiries into national landscapes, the Enclosure Movement, and the picturesque. It seems clear to me that the 'commons' of cyberspace is in real danger from a new virtual Enclosure Movement that will privatize vast sectors of this space. I am therefore on the side of the poachers and hackers.

MS: From your book on Blake (1977) to your edited collection *Landscape and Power* (1994), and your teaching on modules such as 'Space, Place and Landscape', to say nothing of your trips to and activities in Israel, Palestine, and the Far East, you've paid attention to landscape, and in particular to the politics of landscape. Can you speak a little about this long term commitment to the politics of landscape, which is a political commitment to issues of nationalism, imperialism, place, cultural identity, and so on. I'm interested also to hear how, over the last thirty years or so, the challenge of the question of landscape has for you been recast by shifting conceptualizations of globalization.

W.J.T.M: The study of landscape has indeed been of enduring concern for me. I think of it as the 'ground' for my work in visual and media studies, as opposed to the 'figures' that appear against that ground – the distinct icons, tropes, motifs, images, inscriptions, etc. I think of the landscape as the empty white space on which something might be written or drawn. It is just this blankness and emptiness that fascinates me, because of course it is never actually blank or empty, but is rather a kind of plenitude of possibilities. I'm sure this fascination with space grows out of my Wordsworthian childhood, growing up in the Sierra Nevada mountains, spending long days roaming in the foothills alone with my dog, listening to Western crooners sing 'Don't Fence Me In' on the radio. And of course the landscape or space as 'ground' is capable of turning into a figure in the blink of any eye, which is the fundamental lesson of the multistable image.

I am currently struggling with precisely the question you raise: How does the question of space, place, and landscape intersect with the discourse on globalization? I've just finished an essay entitled 'Regional Imaginaries'[4] that attempts to get at one aspect of this question, namely the inter-, intra-, and trans-national entities that loosely govern the flows of things and persons around the world, and most especially, the contested 'border regions' that sometimes become substantial places in themselves – demilitarized zones, occupied territory, no man's land, terra incognita. This has grown out of a piece entitled 'Gilo's Wall and Christo's Gates' (2006), a photo essay on a security wall in Israel/Palestine and the Central Park Gates of February, 2005.

On globalization more specifically, I have in mind an essay on 'World Pictures'[5] that would take on a curious paradox in our sense of the picturability of the world. Since Heidegger's essay on this topic – the world 'as picture' – we have been accustomed to thinking that modernity has made the world all too picturable (this may also be a motive in the demonizing of the Spectacle in Situationist discourse). But the strange thing is, despite our ability to map the world completely with Global Positioning Systems and Virtual Reality atlases, the world system itself has become increasingly invisible and inscrutable. Fredric Jameson's call for a global 'cognitive mapping' has always appealed to me at the same time that I find it perfectly baffling. I think we need a comprehensive analysis and historical accounting of the concept of the *Weltbild* or *Weltanschauung* today, one that would help us to experience and understand the peculiar difficulty we have in portraying totality – globalization or mondialization – at this moment. Crucial to this effort would be some account of the incredibly rapid and accelerating flow of global images and information, the steady flow of commodities (which as Alan Sekula (2003) notes, takes about as long today as it did in 1900), and the increasing restrictions on the flow of human bodies, the erection of security barriers, border fences, and innumerable checkpoints, and legal obstructions to immigration.

MS: Coming out of this question about landscape, I'm wanting to ask you about some of your current thoughts on terrorism and cloning, of course both topics very much driven by matters of territory, belonging, ownership, rights, as well as the threat, the actualities, of biotechnological warfare.

You're currently working on three book projects: *Totemism, Fetishism, Idolatry*, the second is *Medium Theory*, and finally, *Cloning Terror: The War of Images, September 11 to the Abu Ghraib Photographs*. I believe that the first two projects emerge directly out of your teaching activities, prime examples of teaching-led research. (And sections of all three, the seeds, appear in *What do Pictures Want?*) The third project is, as its title might indicate, an ongoing engagement with the convergence of the figure of the clone (from Dolly the Sheep onwards) with our current climate of 'terror', of what you call 'a New World Order defined by terrorism' (p. 12). Following on from 'Vital Signs, Cloning Terror', your introductory remarks in *What do Pictures Want?* I'd like to hear more about this convergence, and its implications for our futures ...

W.J.T.M: The programme essay for this project, 'Cloning Terror: The War of Images, 9–11 to Abu Ghraib', should be out in *After Beauty* edited by Diarmud

Costello and Dominic Willsdon, from Tate Publishing by the time this interview appears. The basic goal is simple: to produce an 'iconology of the present', that would examine the images, and the underlying logic of image production and construction, that animate the war on terror. My argument is that one cannot grasp the specificity of this historical moment without attending to two linked developments: (1) the mutation in the arts of war into a 'war on terror' composed predominantly of images and fantasies; (2) the mutation in the production of images implied by the genetic revolution, and exemplified most dramatically by the figure of the clone, the uncanny literalizing of the ancient dream (and taboo) on the creation of a 'living image'. I think we need to update the concept of a 'pictorial turn' in the twenty-first century to acknowledge a new development that I want to call the 'biopictorial turn', the production of copies, simulations, or reproductions of living organisms and organs, and along with this, a resurgence of ancient fears about 'doubles', evil twins, and the loss of identity. The coupling of these two mutations produces the strange phenomenon I call 'cloning terror', a phrase which has already become a vernacular shorthand for the fact that the war on terror has had the effect of increasing terror; the fact that military strikes against suspected terrorists has the effect of breeding more terrorists; the fact that much of the heightened security has the effect of increasing the sense of insecurity; the fact that we cannot seem to talk about terrorism without lapsing into biological images of sleeper cells, viruses, cancers, metastases, autoimmune disorders, and plagues.

So my sense is that 'the pictorial turn' has taken on a new kind of meaning since the moment, some twelve years ago, when I first coined the phrase. And that new meaning grows out of what Walter Benjamin would have recognized as a new mode of production and reproduction, the twin revolutions in biology and information science that I call 'biocybernetics'. The clearest symptom of this double revolution is the confident assertion that, on the one hand, we live in the 'digital age', and, on the other, that images – analogue signs, mind you – have now taken on a new and unprecedented power. We will not be able to keep our bearings in the new visual and mediatized worlds that are opening before us unless we grasp firmly at both horns of this dilemma.

Enough! Or too much!

Notes

1 W.J.T. Mitchell (2002), 'Showing seeing: A critique of visual culture', *Journal of Visual Culture* 1(2), pp. 165–81. The article appeared simultaneously in Michael Ann Holly and Keith Moxey (eds.) (2002), pp. 231–50, and Mirzoeff (2002). It has subsequently appeared in Joanne Morra and Marquard Smith, (eds.) (2005), and W.J.T. Mitchell (2005).

2 W.J.T. Mitchell (forthcoming) 'Realism and the Digital Image', in Jan Baetens and Hilde van Gelder (eds.) *Critical Realism and Photography*, Leuven: Leuven University Press. W.J.T. Mitchell, 'The Spectacle Today', is forthcoming in *Public Culture*.
3 For Mitchell's thoughts on Visual Culture Studies, inter-disciplinarity, and in-disciplined thinking, see W.J.T. Mitchell (1996).
4 W.J.T. Mitchell, 'Regional Imaginaries' is unpublished.
5 Delivered as the keynote address to symposium on 'Globalization and Cultural Translation', at Tsinghua University in Beijing, August 10, 2006.

References

Agee, James and Evans, Walker (1939) *Let Us Now Praise Famous Men*. Boston: Houghton Mifflin.

Benjamin, Walter (1969 [1936]) 'The Work of Art in the Age of Mechanical Reproduction', in *Illuminations*. (Intro Hannah Arendt, *trans*. Harry Zohn.) New York: Schocken.

Crow, Tom (1996) 'Visual Culture Questionnaire', *October* 77: 34–36.

Costello, Diarmud, and Dominic Willsdon (forthcoming) *After Beauty*. London: Tate Publishing.

Derrida, Jacques (1994) *Specters of Marx: The State of the Debt, the Work of Mourning & the New International* (Peggy Kamuf, *trans*.). London: Routledge.

Dikovitskaya, Margaret (2005) 'An Interview with W.J.T. Mitchell', *Visual Culture: The Study of the Visual after the Cultural Turn*. Cambridge: The MIT Press, pp. 238–57.

Goodman, Nelson (1976) *The Languages of Art*. Indianapolis: Hackett Publishing.

Heidegger, Martin (1938) 'The Age of the World Picture' (William Lovitt, *trans*.) in *The Question Concerning Technology and Other Essays*. NewYork: Harper & Row, 1977.

Holly, Michael Ann and Keith Moxey, (eds.) (2002) *Art History, Aesthetics, Visual Studies*. Williamstown, Mass: Sterling and Francine Clark Art Institute, pp. 231–50.

Massumi, Brian (2002) *Parables for the Virtual*. Durham, NC: Duke University Press.

Mirzoeff, Nicholas (ed.) (2002) *The Visual Culture Reader*. (2nd ed.) New York: Routledge, 86–101.

Mirzoeff, Nicholas (2006) 'On Visuality', *Journal of Visual Culture*, 5: 1, April, 53–79.

Mitchell, W.J.T. (1977) *Blake's Composite Art: A Study of the Illustrated Poetry*. Princeton: Princeton University Press.

Mitchell, W.J.T. (1986) *Iconology: Image, Text, Ideology*. Chicago: University of Chicago Press.

Mitchell, W.J.T. (1994) *Picture Theory: Essays on Visual and Verbal Representation*. Chicago: University of Chicago Press.

Mitchell, W.J.T. (1994) *Landscape and Power*. Chicago: University of Chicago Press.

Mitchell, W.J.T. (1996) 'What do Pictures Really Want?', *October* 77: (Summer): 71–82.

Mitchell, W.J.T. (1996) 'Interdisciplinarity and Visual Culture', *The Art Bulletin* 77 (4): 540–44.

Mitchell, W.J.T. (1998) *The last dinosaur book: The life and times of a cultural icon*. Chicago: University of Chicago Press.

Mitchell, W.J.T. (2000) 'Essays into the Intertext: An interview with W.J.T. Mitchell', *Mosaic*, p. 10, available at:/www.umanitoba.ca/publications/mosaic/backlist/2000/june/mitc hell.htm.

Mitchell, W.J.T. (2002) 'Showing Seeing: A Critique of Visual Culture', *Journal of Visual Culture*, 1 (2): 165–81.

Mitchell, W.J.T. (2005a) 'There Are No Visual Media', *Journal of Visual Culture*, 4 (2): 257–66.

Mitchell, W.J.T. (2005b) *What Do Pictures Want? The Lives and Loves of Images*. Chicago: The University of Chicago Press.

Mitchell, W.J.T. (2006) 'Gilo's Wall and Christo's Gates', *Critical Inquiry* 32(4): 587–601.

Mitchell, W.J.T. (forthcoming) 'Realism and the Digital Image', in Jan Baetens and Hilde van Gelder (eds.) *Critical Realism and Photography*. Leuven: Leuven University Press.

Mitchell, W.J.T. (forthcoming) 'The Spectacle Today', in *Public Culture*.

Mitchell, W.J.T. (unpublished) 'Regional Imaginaries'.

Morra, Joanne and Marquard, Smith (eds.) (2005) *Visual Culture: Critical Concepts in Media and Cultural Studies*. 4 volumes. London: Routledge, 2005.

Retort (2005) *Afflicted Powers: Capitalism and Spectacle in the New Age of War*. London: Verso.

Rorty, Richard (1979) *Philosophy & the Mirror of Nature*. Princeton: Princeton University Press.

Sekula, Alan (2003) *Fish Story*. Berlin: Richter Verlag.

Smith, Marquard (2006) 'Visual Culture Studies: History, Theory, Practice', in Amelia Jones (ed.) *Companion to Contemporary Art Since 1945*. London: Blackwells, pp. 470–89.

Wang, Orrin N.C. (n.d) 'The Last Formalist, or W.J.T. Mitchell as Romantic Dinosaur', available at http://www.rc.umd.edu/praxis/mitchell/mitch-cover.html

3

GLOBALIZATION, COSMOPOLITANISM, POLITICS, AND THE CITIZEN[1]

Susan Buck-Morss in conversation with Laura Mulvey
and Marquard Smith

Introduction

Professor Susan Buck-Morss is the author of *The Origin of Negative Dialectics* (1977), *The Dialectics of Seeing* (1989), *Dreamworld and Catastrophe: The Passing of Mass Utopia in East and West* (2000), and *Thinking Past Terror: Islamism and Critical Theory on the Left* (2003). Through these and other writings, and as an active and influential political intellectual, her works have had a resounding impact on various fields of inquiry including Visual Culture Studies, Critical Theory, Cultural Studies, and Government and Political Science, on topics including the Frankfurt School, the thinking of Theodor Adorno and Walter Benjamin, theories of mass culture, and cultural histories of globalization. Here, Professor Buck-Morss speaks about these and other matters.

Visual Culture as Living Methodology

Marquard Smith (MS): Towards the beginning of *Dreamworld and Catastrophe* [2000] you say that this recent book is an 'experiment in visual culture'. It attempts, you go on to propose, to use 'images as philosophy' by presenting, both literally and metaphorically, a way of seeing the past that challenges common conceptions as to what this last [the twentieth] century was all about. Would you tell us more about what lies behind this adventurous endeavour? It certainly seems to be a similarly intricate task to the one you set yourself in your previous book, *The Dialectics of Seeing* [1989]. Are such experiments born of a montage mentality, of a Benjaminian mentality, or is there something else going on as well? Is there perhaps something specifically Buck-Morssian about it?

Susan Buck-Morss (SBM): Often I begin simply being fascinated with an image, particularly an image that doesn't seem to fit, or that disturbs conventional understanding. There are 140 images in *Dreamworld and Catastrophe*, and they are from many different genres. Some are paintings, some are photographs or film stills, some are clippings from newspapers – all kinds of visual data. They were the inspiration for the writing of the text, rather than being illustrations of the text, which would not have been written if the images had not been found. That is important to me. It leads to plundering film studies, art history, photography books, and whatever else I can get my hands on. I plunder visual culture for a certain theoretical use.

Benjamin worked that way too, more than we realize. Although he includes very few images in his work, many of his most insightful theoretical contributions are reflections on visual culture. My presentation differs in its dependence on images mounted directly in the text. The juxtaposition of images and text is meant to produce a cognitive experience in readers, who can *see* the theoretical point in a certain way, one that surprises and illuminates. Affect, as much as reason, is mobilized.

MS: *The Dialectics of Seeing* and *Dreamworld and Catastrophe* are incredibly distinct from one another in all kinds of ways. Yet they are almost identical in their desire to start from the difficulty of making sense of the relationship between various images, between images and written texts, between images and their relations to history, philosophy, and aesthetics. Both books somehow manage to realize this in book form.

SBM: One of the most difficult things with the production of *Dreamworld and Catastrophe*, even at MIT Press, was to bring the artwork and the text together in meaningful dialogue. They managed, after a bit of a struggle, to do a very good job. There are distinct points throughout the book when this image–text dialogue takes on particular forms. In chapter two, for instance, a straightforward story unfolds until a point where the text begins to speak about the shattering of the dreamworld of Modernity – about 'history' itself as shattered. At that point the book shatters, the actual presentation changes, so that then you get fragments of text and image, rather than sequential text. That took a lot of back-and-forth, as the art department was used to working separately from the copy editor. In some ways it would have been easier to produce the book on a home computer than at a university press. I still don't understand why it should have been so difficult, or so expensive. For example, I wanted to have the 'hypertext' in chapter one printed in various colours, coded to keywords in the text. Although any modern laptop could have handled multiple colours with no problem, at the press we had to settle for alternate size fonts. That isn't totally satisfactory from a conceptual point of view, because it reestablishes the hierarchical relation between texts that is characteristic of old-time footnotes, rather than the egalitarian relation provided by hypertext links. In other parts of the book, we treated text fragments as material blocks, as if they too were visual objects that could be moved about and altered in scale, and juxtaposed to image-objects. It worked quite well.

This book is an attempt to use visual methods and to use Benjaminian methods. It isn't about Benjamin, or about visual theory so much as an attempt to practice both in a theoretical–historical context, looking back at the twentieth century after the end of the Cold War. It is difficult to have that intent register within the commercial process of book marketing, which segments the reading public in unhelpful ways. There is a desire to make something out of my book that is not there. If you go to bookstores in the United States, you will find it shelved under Political Science – because I am in a Government Department and the book is about the East and West. But there is no real discipline to place it into. And that makes some people in the profession extremely uneasy.

MS: For me, it's very straightforward. It goes in Visual Culture Studies, when and if that exists in a bookstore. And it goes next to books that do similar kinds of things – methodologically, thematically, tropologically – with a huge diversity of different and distinct material. Surely this isn't so much to do with the issue of categorizing books on shelves *per se* as it has to do with the question of sensibility, as a working method, as a series of strategies, a modality even, for dealing with the fraught relations between words and images. And making sense of them. Or failing to do so. There's perhaps something about a Visual Culture Studies sensibility that's different from a Political Science sensibility, or from an historian's sensibility, or an art historian's sensibility even. Maybe that sensibility itself is very much *of* Benjamin?

SBM: When *The Dialectics of Seeing* was published, my emphasis on the visual in Benjamin's thought was seen as 'inaccurate' because although Benjamin did look at images in the Bibliothèque Nationale – and there are a few places in his published works that include images – his piece on Russian toys, for instance – for the most part there are none in his essays. So why do I make so much of the visual in Benjamin? He says at one place in the arcades project [1927-40/1999] that the present surrounds his text like 'invisible ink' – a present that is clearly the material world in which he lived, the places in Paris where he worked, the arcades where he strolled, the metros he rode, and the sidewalk cafes where he wrote on the back of cocktail napkins (some of these are saved in the archives).

When I was doing research on Benjamin's arcades project, I spent time in Paris, but not only in the Bibliothèque Nationale. I made pilgrimages to all the surviving arcades. I would go to the old magazine stores and look at the illustrated magazines from the 1930s to get an idea of what he was seeing, what formed the visual context for his writing. There was a Daumier exhibition and a Grandiville exhibition in Paris in the 1930s – artists who appear importantly in the arcades project. There was a world exposition in Paris in 1937, while he was writing about the first-world expositions of the mid-nineteenth century. All of the figures – the *flâneur*, the prostitute, the collector – were visible to him in Paris, which is why he interpreted them as *urforms* of the present. If I hadn't discovered these visual cues, I would not have gotten anywhere with *The Dialectics of Seeing*. Now that Benjamin's book on the arcades is out in English translation, you hear people saying: 'Oh, it is so fragmentary! It is just a mélange of quotations and commentary, without any coherent order'. But I do think there is a rigour in his way of working that you can only discover if you develop a method that comes out of visual studies or visual culture. Only then can you begin to see that there is more than random interest in Benjamin's choice of texts, and in their arrangement under keywords. Or, the other way around: the struggle of trying to interpret Benjamin's arcades project leads to the development of a visual methodology.

Even we mere mortals who are no Benjamin-type geniuses can learn from him a visual method of theorizing. That's what method is, a set of tools that can be used by other people. It is the strong part of Benjamin's work from a philosophical (as opposed to literary) point of view. If it were purely a case of the genius Benjamin writing wonderful things, then we wouldn't be able to enact and re-enact the methodological possibilities that his work makes available. Benjamin's texts visualize ideas. He is clearly fascinated with images. But the visual metaphors he creates, that so impress us with his literary brilliance, are never simply metaphors. They are also objects in his world.

MS: So, it's a living methodology ...

SBM: Or a materialist praxis, a way of working – a way of thinking. We describe how art moves 'into life' in the early twentieth century. Perhaps the same could be said of a variant of philosophical thought ...

MS: It demands that one pay attention to the visual, the archival, and other material one's working with, and realize that the material itself offers certain ways of engaging one with it. One has to hear the way material presents itself, and respond to it accordingly. It's being sensitive to the sound of its grain – to mix metaphors – that's what tells you how it's possible to write it. And in a sense, and to that extent, it's a methodology which demands that to hear it right is to do it some kind of justice.

SBM: One needs all of one's senses to do justice to material reality. Benjamin speaks about 'fragments of the past'. Now what is a fragment of the past? Is it a piece of text? An image? Proust's taste of the madeleine? A melody remembered? All of these. Everything, even a textual fragment, has a sensory component. Working in the old Bibliothèque Nationale, I took out the books that

Benjamin found there, and looked through them to find the piece of text he pulled out ... it's interesting, never the topic sentence of a paragraph or the lead idea of a chapter but, rather, some obscure fragment that resonates with his own thought, not in an abstract, intellectual way, but sensorily, concretely.

I have had discussions with postmodernists who are content to ignore the archive, who criticize reverence for archival truth as fetishistic. 'Don't bother with the archive', they tell me, 'It is not the source of truth'. And of course they are right, if one treats the archive as the traditional historicist would. The 'archive' of a 'living methodology', as you call it, consists of the material remains of life stored – rescued – in libraries, museums, second-hand stores, flea-markets. Obviously, the fact that only certain material objects survive, even as photographic traces, is part of their 'truth' – from a critical–historical point of view, perhaps the most important part. But I am working as a theorist rather than a historian. And why do I think the historical material matters? It's a good question, if truth is an impossible category, why would material matter?

MS: So why *does* materiality matter for Susan Buck-Morss?

SBM: Because it is an anchor against my own subjective and presentist fantasy. It intervenes as a counter to purely subjective interpretation. And it forces you to curtail speculation for its own sake. It demands a certain rigour.

Critical Archaeologies of Globalization

Laura Mulvey (LM): The question is: what kind of material allows us to rescue the utopian hopes of Modernity – as a Leftist project? You talk about rubble in *Dreamworld and Catastrophe*, which is very much a book about visual culture. So what kind of residue, historical and visual, might we address to take this utopian project seriously?

SBM: The project of the Constructivists, for one example, particularly their quite serious attempts to create 'socialist objects', industrial–aesthetic products that would be 'comrades' of people in their daily life, avoiding the fetish character of bourgeois commodities. Then there is the dreamworld of Soviet cinema. I refer in the book to the movie, *Circus*, directed by Gregorii Alexandrov (who worked with Eisenstein in the 1920s), but I hadn't had a chance to view it until more recently. It is absolutely extraordinary, not only for the Busby Berkeley look-alike musical finale, but for the enlightened way that race is handled, mixed marriages, the whole gamut. It was released in 1936! You don't find racial integration thematized so progressively in the *West* in the mid-thirties.

'Residues' useful for a utopian project in our own time can also be facts that challenge our entrenched Cold-War imaginaries of East versus West, by showing that the cultural connections were more fluid than is generally supposed. In the book I put together a story, a coherent story, from pieces found in disparate places – the fact that US engineers built the factories of Stalin's first Five Year Plan, and the fact that the US public has a National Gallery of Art in Washington DC. How do these facts fit together? Stalin needed hard currency to pay the engineers, and he got it by selling – secretly – European masterpieces from the Hermitage museum to the US Secretary of the Treasury, Andrew Mellon, who, to avoid prosecution for tax evasion, willed to the Government both the paintings and money to build a museum. So the US got 'socialized art' – the National Gallery – and the USSR got capitalist steel mills from the Mellon family fortune! I found the first part of this story in the literature of an extreme Right-wing think tank; I found the second part in the art history library. But no one had put them together. The images for this section include photographs of Magnitogorsk taken by Margaret Bourke White, who traveled to the USSR in the 1930s.

The goal is not to tell a newly definitive history. The pieces can be pulled apart and put together to express another idea. But the constellations are not arbitrary. The ideas they create are not fictional. To move these pieces of the past around is a bit of a gesture of *Der Grübler*, the figure of allegory who tries to piece together what past history has split apart. And the politically utopian interest in these historical fragments comes from the fact that they are all we've got! Where else but to the past can you look if you give up the myth of marching joyously forward, counting on the inevitability of progress? So the rescue of history is not out of nostalgia for the past, but to make the past useful. Really useful. Useful for thinking on the Left today.

The problem with using historical facts is that people want you to weight them in a way that tells history 'as it actually was'. The book has been criticized for not putting enough emphasis on the horrors of the Soviet situation – Stalin's mass murders, or the disasters of peasant collectivization. But remembering the victims is not a sufficient strategy for the Left today, particularly if recollecting these horrors is used as a way of discrediting the tradition of socialism in its entirety. For us, it is the Cold-War telling of history that needs to be brushed against the grain. My strategy is a pragmatics of time that avoids chronology in order to place historical fragments in useful juxtaposition. I really have in mind as a model the method of photomontage, the political photomontages of John Heartfield and others.

MS: So this is the way in which the piece you published in *Critical Inquiry* [2000] on Hegel and Haiti works, for instance?

SBM: Absolutely. It's the same method. Thank you for seeing that. After *Dreamworld and Catastrophe* appeared, people tended to conclude that I 'do' Soviet Studies. But then I tell them I just wrote on Hegel and Haiti, and they protest. 'You're not supposed to hop about like that'. Obviously you can be accused of dilettantism here [laughter]. But the method is the same. In both cases I am putting together fragments of the past with the political intent of transforming our historical imaginaries. With the Hegel and Haiti project, it was a task of restoration, putting the historical facts together to restore a picture that the splicing of the story by different disciplines – Philosophy, Caribbean Studies, French Revolutionary History, Art History, Print Media History – had obscured and made impossible to see.

MS: To clarify, and without wanting to simplify too much, the article on Hegel and Haiti concerns how, historically, Hegel began to develop a particular model of history at a particular historical moment, and how this model, this account, becomes a guiding principle in understanding the emergence of Modernity. But it is more than this, because you shift the story very far away from its more familiar iconographical, historical, cultural, and geographical milieu, and pivot it through *Haiti* to show not only that Hegel's philosophy of history has a concrete historical whereabouts but also that the master–slave dialectic is very much always already a question of and for the postcolonial, as well as a question of class. What part, then, does the Hegel and Haiti configuration play in the beginnings of your new project, a cultural genealogy of globalization?

SBM: *Dreamworld and Catastrophe* is about the end of the modernist landscape of East versus West. The disintegration of this geopolitical map is, let's say, the end of Modernity. So now, if you go back to the beginning of the modern era, you have to think *without* the map that is now destroyed. You're thinking back into the space of the origins of Modernity, without presuming that it is going to end up with the Cold-War map that you know! That frees you for other kinds of intellectual projects. So for me it was absolutely logical to move to Hegel and Haiti, as key to a genealogical mapping of the origins of globalization, and of movements that are resisting it in its present form. Our new reality, unlike Modernity, is not inherently Eurocentric.

Basically, the project hinges on an archival find that I would not have looked for if I hadn't already had a hunch that it must be there. That is, the first mention of the master–slave dialectic by Hegel was in the Jena manuscripts of 1803–05; these notes immediately preceded the writing of the *Phenomenology of Mind*. In 1803 Napoleon arrested Toussaint-Louverture, who had liberated the slaves of Saint-Domingue and forced the French Revolutionary Government to abolish slavery throughout the colonies. In 1804–05, Dessalines took up the struggle in Saint-Domingue, and succeeded in liberating the colony, establishing the 'black Empire' of Haiti. Hegel formulated the master–slave dialectic in precisely these years. So I thought there must be a connection, although academics in the specific disciplines hadn't seen it. Only one scholar, a philosopher from West Africa living in Paris named Franklin-Tavarés, has speculated about a connection.

And it turns out – this was the archival find – that *the* leading political journal in Germany at the time by the name of *Minerva* – which Hegel read, we know that – had in 1803, 1804, and 1805 hundreds of pages on the Haitian revolution, telling the whole story of 10 years of struggle against slavery and colonialism. In fact, every press in Europe was full of the story (except in France, where Napoleon censored the news from the colony). Wordsworth, who was born in the same year as Hegel, wrote a sonnet to Toussaint-Louverture that was published in the *Morning Post* in 1803. The significance of the Haitian revolution for literate Europeans was that 'freedom from slavery', the root metaphor of European political philosophy in Hobbes, Locke, and Rousseau, was suddenly shown to be no longer merely a metaphor, but an actual event in world history, and this is precisely what inspired the young Hegel. The inner-historical approach to political philosophy in Hegel's dialectic of master and slave replaced the 'state of nature' narrative as justification of freedom. Hegel made a note to himself: 'Robinson Crusoe *and* Friday' – in the 'state of nature', the slave was already there, *with* Crusoe. So if you just shift the whole story geographically off-centre, it becomes clear how our disciplinary boundaries and the Eurocentrism underlying them have made that original connection, evident to everyone at the time, impossible for *us* to see.

Now, that's where visual culture comes in. The presence of blacks in Europe is documented repeatedly in paintings of the seventeenth and eighteenth centuries. What has been invisible in textual history becomes visible in images, including the illustrated books on Haiti at the time, and in the iconography of freemasonry that extends from Haitian voudou symbolism to the watermarks on Hegel's writing paper!

LM: Surely this conjuncture (Hegel and Haiti) is something that emerges out of a European intellectual engagement with the problem of colonial slavery? Eurocentricism? I'm often not quite sure what it means exactly. Britain, for example, was an Imperial country that also had a tradition of Leftism, even liberalism, which has often been forced into existence by Imperial politics about liberation struggles, questions of colonialism ...

SBM: Yes, but the story of colonial liberation still keeps Europe in the centre, whereas work by, for instance, Linebaugh and Rediker – *The Many-Headed Hydra* – tells a very different story. 'Hegel and Haiti' put me in contact with scholars from multiple disciplines who are doing what I would call a genealogy, or a critical archaeology of globalization. In other words, it is global history, but not in the triumphalist mode that leads to an affirmation of the present global arrangements of power. Rather, the project charts the kinds of resistance that existed historically in the margins, in a space that was not nationally defined. If you look at Haitian history as a national story, it's a disaster, a classic case of failed development and political dictatorship under the influence of foreign capital and the US Government. But if you look at the impact of Haiti's slave revolution on Latin America, or how it frightened the slave-owners in the United States, or how the Polish viewed the events there, as well as other Europeans, not only Hegel, the impact is enormous. So it is not just another struggle for colonial liberation. It's a global story, one of radical cosmopolitanism, in which Enlightenment thought is already in protest against European hegemony. It has a different valence than thinking in terms of colonies against the mother country.

LM: Historians here in the UK have recently been pointing out that there is a history that starts in the colonies, and then impacts on the mother country. It cuts both ways. In many cases there would have been radical reform movements that would have also necessarily been, if not anti-Imperialist as such, certainly forced to consider British power inside the country as part and parcel of its Imperial status. Thinking about maps, one of the things about Empire is that there is a physical map, a graphic map, and I think it's very interesting the way you pointed out that Napoleon censors what should actually be used and what would be of great interest to France.

SBM: You are right, of course. The Putney Debates are an excellent example of what you are saying, and they figure centrally in Linebaugh and Rediker's book. But if you look at, say, Robin Blackburn's book, *The Overthrow of Colonial Slavery* [1988], it ends up being a story about how the support, let's say, inside Britain or the United States for the Haitians played into the Abolition Movement. But that's still a European story. C.L.R. James' classic work, *Black Jacobins* [1963], is still a book about how Haiti was having a *French* revolution. The title of the book tells you that. In moving away from Europe, I was brought into contact with the work of people like Linebaugh and Rediker – and Walter Mignolo, author of *The Darker Side of the Renaissance* (1997), and also Joan Dayan, whose book *Haiti, History and the Gods* (1998[1995]) examines voodoo as a *modern* philosophy. Sibylle Fischer has just finished an extraordinary manuscript, '*Modernity Disavowed*', that insists on the centrality of Haiti for the modern history of liberation. A decade ago, Paul Gilroy's *Black Atlantic* (1995[1993]) initiated this decentring of the historical discussion. He was one of the first to replot the territory of the globe and tell its history in a way that does not privilege nation-states, or national liberation movements. All of these books can be said to be examples of an archaeology of knowledge. They are genealogies of the *urforms* of global resistance.

MS: To pick up on the issue of maps, and the geography of East and West in particular, we have a cultural geography or topography-type question. Picking up on discussions in *Dreamworld and Catastrophe* again, we're interested to know if changes in the global landscape, both literal and metaphorical, make continuing to think about East and West redundant? How valuable is it to still be able to think about East and West as locatable, as mappable, as articulatable through the directions of visual mapping?

SBM: I don't believe that geography lines up with politics, not today, and probably never. There is no space today where the Left has a home, not even Cuba or China, where lack of democracy corrupts the socialist goals. A real problem for the Left is the fact that there is no geographical base outside of global capital – although Cuba is courageously attempting to enter the global economy on altered terms. The Soviet Union played an important role because even when the Left was strongly anti-Soviet, the very existence of the 'East' was evidence that capitalism was not some sort of natural phenomenon that emerged necessarily out of industrial civilization. This bifurcation of Modernity, East versus West, also made possible progressive politics on a global level – Left-international support for the Republic in the Spanish Civil War, to name just one example.

MS: I think about the changing colours of maps. And watching the geographical transformation over the last 12 years or so, they've been quite profound as a visual experience. To understand where boundaries lie, is to recognize how the world begins to redefine itself from, say, East and West to North and South. For example, the US looks south towards Mexico, not east towards the former Soviet Union. The formulation of the East and the West as a geographical metaphorics seems very much of the Cold War, very European even. The East–West doesn't exist in the same kind of way, doesn't signify as demandingly or as singularly as it once did. So, really, it's a question of trying to imagine what a map looks like when it starts changing. There are some great maps, of Australian origin for instance, that have Australia centre-stage, and the other way up. And that's exactly the way the world is from an Australian's point of view! Maps generally seem to reflect, affirm our Eurocentrism. But as the centres of power, interest, and significant activity shift, it's imperative that we learn how the world works through an alternative set of coordinates that were always already in place, and were already mappable, but somehow simply not registered by the majority of us.

SBM: Seeing the globe from the perspective of Haiti is liberating in that it makes the familiar appear strange. Haiti is particular, but not unique in the way that it opens up new perspectives. It is not just re-mapping *per se*, not just that East–West maps are being replaced by North–South coordinates, but rather that there is a real effort to visualize the globe without a centre. It is very exciting, but it is also problematic from a political point of view. Hardt and Negri's book *Empire* [2001 (2000)] makes the important point that contemporary globalization means immanence: there is no place outside of 'Empire's' political and economic reach. But it also means that resistance cannot remain local, or even national, much less nationalist. Even anti-globalization movements have to work on a global level today. That is the challenge for the Left in the twenty-first century.

Politics, History, Utopia

MS: Let's return to the question of time that we touched upon earlier. In *Dreamworld and Catastrophe*, particularly Section II, entitled 'Dreamworlds of History', you discuss the crisis of history, the question of how 'history has failed us'. We're hoping you could say a little bit more about this failure of history as it shows itself to be a question about the perception of time. Rather than being interested in how history has failed as such, we'd like to know how you conceptualize the problem of reading back against history. (And not just in a Benjaminian sense.) In light of this, and your way of looking back across the concept of progress, do you, perhaps, believe there will be a moment when the Left is going to have to think in terms of a past rather than a future? In addition, different configurations of time emerge across *Dreamworld and Catastrophe*. You talk about revolutionary time, and debates around the end of history – from Alexandre Kojève to Francis Fukuyama's *The End of History and the Last Man* [1992], and so on. And then of course you talk about global time. How do these three modalities of time interact with one another?

LM: It seems to me that you are also drawing attention to the idea of a perceived crisis in history – the conjunction of the success of neo-liberalism with the collapse of the former Soviet Union is produced by the success of a Right-wing political and economic agenda. So that if we accept that 'history' has been divided across these crises, isn't it perhaps the case that intellectuals, however much these crises might exist, must find ways of knitting the lost continuities of the Left back across them?

SBM: If the utopian dreamworlds of the twentieth century are shattered, if cynicism now dominates political thinking, then we on the Left need to work for a kind of restitution. If fragmentation has occurred, then the question is: how do we actually knit, or in some way heal, a broken tradition of politics that was based on the hope that our technological and scientific knowledge can actually make the world better – and not just for the wealthy few?

LM: If one accepts that this tradition is completely broken, then there are pieces of rubble – as you suggested earlier discussing questions of methodology – that we can pull out, look at again, and think again across this supposed unbridgeable gap. So, what interests me is that, as well as the juxtapositions of montage, this is also addressing the question: to what extent does one accept the fact that the Right can announce the end of History? Or, for instance, that, with the decline of the Soviet Union, the kinds of utopian aspirations that you speak of having seen still active there in 1991, actually can't be sustained, or at least it's very hard for them to be sustained, when the dominant thinking is that this is now relegated to the past. So that's the kind of utopian thinking, an engagement with a tradition of Socialism, and the Left, 'the radical aspiration', as Annette Michelson has called it.

SBM: Yes, but, of course, precisely because the Soviet experiment is in ruins, we can think of returning to re-appropriate aspects of it. Otherwise, we would be bound by its use of state terror to continue to protest against it. The defusing of the dangers posed by the Soviet Union was signaled by the artists of the pre-*glasnost'* period, who began to recycle the Soviet symbols as irony and parody – but also, it must be said, as nostalgia, for a dreamworld of socialism that was *supposed* to be.

LM: Whereas, I suppose you could argue that the art works of Komar and Melamid, and the other Satirists of the Soviet Union are, in their satire, making an engagement which is both a montage and *also* has something to do with a restitution that you would think is appropriate?

SBM: What I want to insist upon with this notion of montage is that if the Left returns to the past, it is not to redeem some sort of original ideal world from which we have been banished. Not at all. So the nostalgia is really for *the possibility of something else today*, not for what in fact existed in the past. The shattering of time is key, describing 'history' – the dreamworld of historical 'progress' – as shattered, and consequently a destruction of the conception of time-as-progress on both sides, East and West. The Right calls this the 'end of history' and celebrates it. But what about the Left, which looks to the pieces of a shattered past? How can we reassemble them in ways that free us from the triumphalism of the present?

LM: What's so gripping about this section of *Dreamworld and Catastrophe* is that it discusses historical method, the juxtaposition of these past practices, the juxtaposition of these past fragments with our present concerns which, as you say, might have the power to challenge the complacency of our times. As a political task I thought this was so striking.

SBM: Striking, maybe, but at the moment I'm not terribly optimistic. There is a political question here, and it is part of the pathos of our present historical moment. Benjamin was working on a project about the nineteenth century, while the world was being destroyed around him. There was not time for his 'big book' about the Paris arcades; a decade of working on it didn't help to defuse the political emergency of Nazism and World War II. The same holds true today. From a Leftist perspective, going through the rubble of past history is a dubious enterprise given the urgency of the present global situation. I would be hard-pressed to justify it as an effective political weapon at this moment.

LM: Surely challenging our present's complacency by any political means available to us is a necessity. One way does seem to be through this sense of looking for the materialities of history as a way of seeing into the future. That people can't read your most recent book without saying you're a Stalinist, that people can't think about September 11 without seeing it as a 'things will never be the same' afterwards – which is one of the most objectionable pieces of rhetoric, that sense of always trying to make a crisis after which nothing will be the same – when it seems to me that one of the things that the Left has to do now is, instead of building towards the future, it has to build towards the future by trying to rescue the past from these cataclysms.

SBM: I have actually used that objectionable phrase, that things will never be the same after September 11, because of the authoritarian US response. I have used that phrase because I wanted to say to Left intellectuals, 'stop writing as if only academic politics were at stake! We need to get back to the material, political world'.

LM: Yes I absolutely agree. But I think you're going back to the material world in the sense of a kind of political, historical, material sense which implies that one shouldn't necessarily accept mythologies in which time is figured in these moments, gaps ...

SBM: I'm thinking of an image, a photograph of *Trümmerfrauen* in Berlin after World War II – women who set about cleaning up the ruins after the military devastation, dusting off the bricks from shattered buildings, piling them up to be recycled as material for rebuilding. Sometimes I feel I am doing the same ...

MS: Two things. One, you're in a Department of Government in a top US university, and that puts you in a much stronger position to be able to respond more directly via whatever media and other forms are available. And two, one doesn't have to write about particular topics, politics let's say, to have their impact, the impact of politics, infuse one's writing.

SBM: Let's not be utopian. I'm in a Political Philosophy subfield of a Government Department, and some of my colleagues wish that I wouldn't write about Soviet Studies, which is not my field, but, rather, teach and write intellectual biographies of the Frankfurt School. That is, I shouldn't *use* critical theory, I should teach it. The fact that I do use it may be a strength of my work, but it is also its academic vulnerability.

MS: In old-fashioned terms that means you're functioning as an intellectual and not an academic.

SBM: I would like to think so. As far as it is possible. But the way neo-liberalism has affected university culture, at least in the United States, is to discourage one from being an intellectual who contributes to public debate, and to train 'professional' academics instead. There's a world of difference between the two. Neo-liberalism's idea of intellectual life is that in the great marketplace of ideas, everyone expresses her or his 'opinion', no matter how ignorant it is, while academics are useful only as human data-banks.

MS: I like the idea of academic vulnerability. It seems to have something to do with leaving yourself open, which can bring on two very different potential responses: the first is that it might instigate dialogue, which is nice, while the second is the inevitable attack and subsequent mauling of the one making themselves vulnerable, defenceless. But the idea is the right one.

SBM: Well, let's look at that possibility. Assuming that there is a political advantage in developing a methodology that avoids a certain kind of academic culture, what, then – getting back to the question of the Left, and of its disappearance, or its impotence – can a method that looks backward do? Can it have an effect on the present situation?

LM: I would say that this is very much what it has to do. It has to reverse its presumption. That is, it has to reverse the presumption that out of a utopian expectation you look towards the future. To a certain extent now, I think your implication is that if the utopian aspiration can no longer be a driving intellectual force, then to a certain extent it's progressive to look backwards. And that gets you away from nostalgia and so on. Although nostalgia itself always has a bad press, it might just mean a more sentimental side of the desire to try and recuperate moments of hope from the past.

Media, the Global Public Sphere, Community

MS: What impact do you think new communication technologies, from email to hand-held video cameras, are having on our sense of experiencing the contemporary world as a specifically global environment?

SBM: If we take the example of September 11, we can certainly speak of a global media, as opposed to a transnational media. The difference is that the space of global media is immanent, which means that you cannot separate or segregate national publics. In World War II, governments pretty much had control over the means of production of propaganda for their own people, and they generated propaganda specifically to demoralize the other side. Today there is no longer a geographical dividing line between 'sides'; these media spaces are integrated, overlapping, and multiple. As a weapon of resistance, the medium of the internet can operate at low altitudes, connecting people under the radar screen of Government censors, while satellite TV flies in above the censors. The very existence of al-Jazeera, the Arab version of CNN, has had a tremendous impact in shaping what we can call a global public sphere. Not only are 35 million people in the Middle East watching it, but increasing numbers of people through satellite connections *inside* the United States (and elsewhere) as well. Even if the language is Arabic, the images are accessible to a global public, and the US Government can't do anything to destroy its impact. This is new since the Gulf War, when the US monopolized global representations of international politics far more successfully. I don't know of any political occasion prior to the present when we've experienced such a superimposition of media spaces, such a lack of a controlling centre.

LM: About access to information in the United States, on the one hand there's a shutdown on the part of the Government which prevents information from flowing freely, and there seems to be quite a lot of support for the Government's rhetoric – the 'either you're with us or against us' position – but on the other hand there are people watching al-Jazeera because they want the information. Of course, these may well just be different groupings of people!

SBM: Or the same people, increasingly schizophrenic! If you get your news from alternative sources on the net, you would think you were in a different world from the one presented to the US by commercial media. I receive emails from Egyptian feminist organizations and from RAWA, the revolutionary feminists of Afghanistan, with information that cuts through the PR nonsense of the Bush administration posing as the liberator of Muslim women. We don't know how widely these messages are being disseminated. It takes a local demonstration to bring all the net-radicals out of the closet, but when that happens it gives a glimmer of the enormous potential. There is considerable Left-organizing power via the web that is only now being tested. The Chiappas revolt used internet communication successfully to create global solidarity. With September 11, the stakes are higher, while communication is more difficult, given the appalling ignorance in the US regarding Islamism and the Arab world. And the dangers are greater, given the extreme potential for violence. Of course, internet publics can be monitored, but with millions involved, how realistic is that? There is so much information on the web, and no one to read it all. I find the excess comforting. It's a political safety feature.

MS: Do you believe that we can think about this whole area of exchange, of email writing, messaging, as a modern public sphere? Is it a new form of the public sphere? What, also, about this question of the global public intellectual. Is it possible for something like this to exist? And what does it mean for you as an intellectual, as someone who tries to be a practising public intellectual, and works on globalization, to be involved in a global public sphere?

SBM: We need to work with this concept – a global public sphere – as a place for politics. Since September 11, it seems vital to question the 'think global, act local' slogan of Left politics in the 1990s. We have to act globally as well. But this is an extremely difficult matter, as there is no agreement regarding the discursive terrain. There is no already-existing global space that one might enter in order to engage in violence-free communication, to use Habermas's phrase. We need to build that space, and one way is, performatively, to address it. What does the 'Left' look like in a global public sphere? Can we even use this term?

To speak of the global is to speak about media. And, of course, a mediated community is not a community in the traditional sense of living together, working together. The collective spirit produced by media is fairly superficial. Empathic identifications are instantaneous, but they can just as instantaneously disappear. Without language in common, the global public sphere will have to rely heavily on images. It will be a visual culture – or musical, perhaps, but not a dominantly print one.

If we are talking about a global Left today, the 1960s is surely the precursor. The music, for example – John Lennon's song 'Imagine' was censored from the airwaves in the US after September 11! The V for victory sign was appropriated as a peace sign in the '60s; the raised fist signified growing radicalization. You saw these visual markers in demonstrations (in photographs of demonstrations) in Mexico City, Athens, Tokyo, Berkeley, Berlin. And you had the sense that with the mimetic spread of even this very small gesture, global solidarity was being built around a set of issues: anti-Imperialism, anti-racism, pro-national liberation. It might be argued that if the demonstrators had actually been in the same room together, they might not have understood each others' concrete concerns – although I'm not so sure. The imagined community of the 1960s was indeed a global social movement. Political solidarity transcended national boundaries. When the African-American medal winners at the 1968 Olympics in Mexico City raised their fists on the winners' podium, this image, in this context, was montaged with images of demonstrating students shot by government troops on the streets of Mexico City the week before – that was a very powerful media intervention. I am not aware of research in visual culture that has dealt with this prehistory of today's global public sphere. Such a study would be valuable. Again, this is history-writing with a political function ...

Such a history would show that global and local politics are not necessarily in contradiction. Today's media magnify the potential for synergy. Ithaca, where Cornell is located, is a Left-political, small town, where community newspapers, distributed for free, combine articles downloaded from the web with political commentary by local writers – and reprints from the past (Marx's '11 Theses on Feuerbach' appeared, with the suggestion that readers clip it for their refrigerator doors!) After September 11, faculty and students organized a Cornell Forum for Justice and Peace with a website and listserv. We are a documentation and information collective that serves as an interface connecting global and local action. This kind of politics is being established all over the world, producing a counterculture that might support a global Left with strong roots in local communities. We don't know at the moment how successful such a movement might be, whether it can resist the global hegemony that has such a dominant position within commercial media. This is the first great political test of the new media, and I am optimistic ... but cautiously.

Notes

1 Excerpts from an interview with Laura Mulvey and Marquard Smith in *Journal of Visual Culture*, London, October 28, 2001. The full interview was published in vol. 1, no. 3, December 2002: 325-40. On 27 October 2001, Susan Buck-Morss was in London presenting a paper entitled 'A Global Public Sphere?' at *Radical Philosophy*'s annual conference, entitled 'Look No Hands.'

References

Benjamin, W. (1999) *The Arcades Project* (Howard Eiland and Kevin McLaughlin, *trans.*). Cambridge, MA: Belknap Press (Harvard University Press).

Blackburn, R. (1988) *The Overthrow of Colonial Slavery 1776–1848*. London: Verso.

Buck-Morss, S. (1977) *The Origin of Negative Dialectics*. New York: The Free Press.

Buck-Morss, S. (1989) *The Dialectics of Seeing*. Cambridge, MA: MIT Press.

Buck-Morss, S. (2000) *Dreamworld and Catastrophe: The Passing of Mass Utopia in East and West*. Cambridge, MA: MIT Press.

Buck-Morss, S. (2000) 'Hegel and Haiti', *Critical Inquiry* 26(4), Summer: 821–65.

Dayan, J. (1998[1995]) *Haiti, History and the Gods*. Berkeley: University of California Press.

Fukuyama, F. (1992) *The End of History and the Last Man*. New York: Free Press.

Gilroy, P. (1995[1993]) *Black Atlantic: Modernity and Double Consciousness*. Cambridge, MA: Harvard University Press.

Hardt, M. and Negri, A. (2001[2000]) *Empire*. Cambridge, MA: Harvard University Press.

James, C.L.R. (1963) *Black Jacobins: Toussaint L'Ouverture and the San Domingo Revolution*. London: Allison & Busby.

Linebaugh, P. and Rediker, M. (2001) *The Many-Headed Hydra: Sailors, Slaves, Commoners, and the Hidden History of the Revolutionary Atlantic*. New York: Beacon Press.

Mignolo, W. (1997) *The Darker Side of the Renaissance*. Ann Arbor: University of Michigan Press.

4

ON THE STATE OF CULTURAL STUDIES[1]

Interview with Paul Gilroy

Introduction

A deep concern for the politics and ethics of diaspora and difference in music, media, and the art runs through the writings of Paul Gilroy. Attention to these pressing matters has been visible since at least the publication of his crucial co-authored *The Empire Strikes Back: Race and Racism in 70s Britain* (1982), and in early affiliations with the Centre for Contemporary Cultural Studies at the University of Birmingham. Gilroy is a cultural practitioner, a DJ, and, having returned in 2005 from Yale University where he was Charlotte Marian Saden Professor of Sociology and African American Studies, now holds the Anthony Giddens Professorship in Social Theory at the London School of Economics. Along with numerous key articles on Black British, European, and American visual, acoustic, and cultural studies, he is the author of *After Empire: Multiculture or Postcolonial Melancholia* (2004); *Against Race: Imaging Political Culture Beyond the Color Line* (2000); *Small Acts: Thoughts on the Politics of Black Cultures* (1994); *The Black Atlantic: Modernity and Double Consciousness* (1993); and *There Ain't No Black in the Union Jack: The Cultural Politics of Race and Nation* (1987).

In this interview Gilroy engages with the questions raised by the current state of Cultural Studies. To this end this interview circles around a commitment to the future of Cultural Studies, an interest that cannot help but tread the precarious path between an optimism born of the practices which mark sites of possibility and the fear of a relentless threat of the disciplinary habitus which beckons us towards the most suffocating and futile of environments. With the delicate balance of this situation in mind, this interview locates some of the reasons behind the polemical impulse lying at the heart of the history of Cultural Studies. Likewise, it questions why this impulse has, it seems, largely lost favour, been directed elsewhere, or been denied. Why, the interview asks, has such a liquidation occurred? The kernel of this interview turns against the current stagnation within the often reified and academicized shelters of cultural practice: the spaces of the institution, of the publishing house, and of thought.

While against neither the history of Cultural Studies *per se* nor against those attempting to animate the contemporary, it is against the production and consumption of simply more Cultural Studies for its own sake. As such, in taking the significance of this history and these current practices into account, this conversation is an effort to negotiate new ways of dealing with practices of cultural production and cultural analysis in an attempt to draw out and innervate the faltering and often over-determined political and ethical heart of Cultural Studies. Resuscitation? A transplant? Switch off the confounded machine and jack the whole thing in?

Knowing full well that any effort to write the history of the present is impossible, our task here demands that we can do nothing but write in, against, and for that present.

Marquard Smith (MS): In light of the framework laid out for the following discussion, in the first instance, I would be pleased if you would be happy to make a few general comments about how you see the current and future shape of the discipline of Cultural Studies as a space for both optimism and despair, how an earlier polemical criticality has largely given way to an often complicit mediocrity, how perhaps the over-sophistication of Cultural Studies, its very success even, has made it impossible to maintain a certain kind of ideological blindness necessary for the direct historical and speculative criticisms of previous moments. Or, to put it another way, part of the impetus behind the polemical nature of Cultural Studies was always its effort to open things out, its will to speak critically, its desire to identify questions for consideration. Now it seems that while there is no subject or object that is not proper to the discipline, this very need or ability to question has disappeared. Born of a necessary unease, Cultural Studies has become supremely confident. Is it possible that the successes of Cultural Studies, its expansion and dissemination as an interventionist and dislocating strategy, has dulled the precision of the competing tendencies that once acted as part of a productive crisis in the Humanities? Can Cultural Studies as a structure of meaning and feeling premised on contestation no longer afford to risk itself?

Paul Gilroy (PG): I take a much cruder view actually. I think that the change of tone you speak of has much more to do with the decline of the Left, and much more to do with the decline of a certain kind of confidence around what a Left critique should entail. That problem is compounded at a point when many people are finding it very difficult to be anti-capitalist. People find it very difficult to find political ethics which can bear that weight. Along with the debates that you are getting at, I see this as much more of an issue. I think that the Alan Sokal affair – in which the journal *Social Text* was hoaxed – is a very useful way of tuning into this (Sokal, 1996). Although that situation comes out of an American setting, there are analogous conflicts all around us in this country. It's important to remember that the people who were responsible for setting up the whole Sokal affair, the people who produced the phenomena of Sokal as a critic of 'p-c leftism' concerned only with culture at the expense of the real class politics that we should be engaged with, were the people on the Left! These were people who felt themselves to be guardians of an authentic radicalism that was being betrayed and undermined by all this chatter about culture.

I'm not saying that there aren't equivalent forces around on the Right that are much more gleefully wanting to celebrate and expose the follies of Cultural Studies. But if you think of the Sokal situation as a polemical intervention in a certain sort of spirit, in a traditional spirit if you like, it's really important to understand its source, and to see the pattern of realignment that this sort of intervention instigates, especially since that kind of hostility to the excesses of taking culture seriously is not usually something that has been claimed very much from the Left. I'm quite interested in that realignment, it's really more of a reconfiguration. That novel set of political relations is really a very important thing. I think that the corporate language of modernization and managerialism which is destroying the Left from the other side in this country has blocked the ability to respond because nobody wants to be seen as an anachronism, a fossil. I'm sure that this abiding antipathy is not only towards Cultural Studies but also towards the critical study of media and representation as anything other than a preparation of students for some sort of professional life in the cultural industries. I think that our Sokal moment is currently pending. As a result, Cultural Studies is very much in a defensive posture right now. It would be interesting to explore that.

Marquard Smith (MS): It's interesting and not a little surprising to me that you see Cultural Studies as being on its back foot at the moment. Apart from its difficulties in finding a secure or more appropriate place from which to be assessed in forthcoming Research Assessment Exercises (RAE) or Teaching Quality Assessment (TQA) appraisals, it seems to me to be supremely overconfident.[2] Perhaps the discrepancy between our differing impressions is overly conditioned by those who we have been talking to recently, and by the kind of Cultural Studies we might have in mind. It strikes me that of all the emergent disciplines in the Humanities, if you can call it a discipline – after a longish desire to refuse this categorization, I'm now reasonably comfortable with having to accept such organizations – it seems to be standing taller and prouder, perhaps even less flexible, than a lot of the others. And it was this inflexibility that I was hoping to pick up on, an inability to bend which sounds similar to the problems that you were just suggesting were a component of the Left at the minute. Perhaps the two are related. Having had no option but to seriously take on board the lessons of Cultural Studies over the last twenty years or so, and often having done so to great effect, other disciplines in the Humanities have also been developing independent lines of thought which only rarely seem to disturb the calm of Cultural Studies itself. That is, the supremely confident in Cultural

Studies are happy to farm themselves out as the definers and arbiters of inter-disciplinarity whilst simultaneously digging their heels in by consolidating their position as that site of inter-disciplinarity. Comfortable to determine how these aporetic events will take place, their resistance to infection, or at least the illusion of this resistance, seems unimpeachable, to them at least.

PG: I suppose that the real difference is not so much that we have different notions of Cultural Studies, but that you were able to go so rapidly to the site of the Humanities. Because of where I work, and how I work, and the conditions under which I work, I think I'm still probably a little bit circumscribed by somebody else's notion of what the Social Sciences entails. Under that sign, the situation is actually rather different. I don't think, for example, that the sorts of patterns I associate most with the way that Anthropology has managed the history of its encounters and conflicts with Cultural Studies critique over a long period of time have been really matched in thinking around, for instance, Sociology. In the field of Sociology, as is in many other places, there is a very strong current of resentment which suggests that all of these arguments around culture and its complexities were things that were already known and practised by Sociologists. The fact is, I think that's bullshit but it's very interesting that this position represents itself as common sense. Other people have been exploring this problem. What is more of an immediate issue for me is the kind of culturalization, a novel sensitivity to the workings of culture that has been evident in the implosion and collapse of Sociology as a discipline. This disciplinary predicament has produced a political battle around culture and its workings. It is very different from the way that you are talking about the interface between those who prefer working under the banner of Cultural Studies and the sorts of things that are going on in the transformation of writing cultural history, or in the new geography, or in the attempts to try to stretch and amend traditions of philosophical reflection so that they engage in a different kind of dialogue with the agenda that Cultural Studies has set over the last twenty odd years. And yes, there are some grounds for optimism. But I think that the contested versions of cultural analysis which have circulated where the integrity of Social Sciences has been challenged tell a rather different story. That's a funny situation, really, given that the people who have done most to define the discipline of Sociology in this country have tended very much to be people whose intellectual concerns have been closely tied to those sorts of areas associated with Cultural Studies. Even if they haven't always been sympathetic to the project, they've certainly been in that space or close to it. People like Zygmunt Bauman for instance and many others. Someone like Gillian Rose, whose work is informed by an implicit conflict with the concerns of Cultural Studies as a betrayal or trivialization of the critique of culture, but who still inhabits those same spaces. We should be talking more about the problems of Sociology and the collapse of Sociology as a particular kind of disciplinary context.

It's not indiscrete to admit that when my Department was trying to appoint people, there was an immediate conflict articulated: 'These people are Cultural Studies people, we don't want them!'[3] I'm sure that some version of that argument is going on in every institution, in every department. It is fascinating to consider what this says about the proper name Cultural Studies as a form of abuse. It makes you want to be one of those abject people! It's funny for me because, much of the time I find myself trying to dissociate myself from what I think of as the excesses of Cultural Studies, the point where it can become nothing much more than an uncritical affirmation of some of the worst tendencies in consumer culture, or whatever. But when I see the sort of bile that comes out, where certain sorts of work are identified and associated with Cultural Studies, it makes me want to become an advocate of Cultural Studies in a way that I don't usually feel myself to be.

MS: This matter of affiliation is an interesting one. Have you also noticed how many of those responsible for instigating the concerns of Cultural Studies, extending the duration of these critiques, and concretizing the future of this criticality through institutional legitimation, are returning to their initial disciplines? My concern here is that students educated through Cultural Studies will be left to wander around and fall through the gaps and fissures opened up between disciplines, leaving them essentially stranded, unemployable.

PG: Yes, I think that the context for that return is their sense of the impending assault on the University, their sense that the new managerialism and the new corporationism makes them vulnerable, and threatens to evacuate the space that they've been in. They think that they can defend themselves better when swathed in those moth-eaten old disciplinary cloaks. What's interesting for me is not so much their retreat into their disciplines, but their inability to articulate a defence of open-ended scholarly enquiry and their refusal to engage with the marketization and pseudo-professionalization of research degrees. The idea that people have been trained. Where is the principled opposition to the bureaucratization of marketization and all of that? No one is able or willing to do it. The only people that come close to making these objections are the old-style Tories, the ones who believe that education is a good in itself. It's curious to find yourself in some sort of sympathy with a position that has always been rather complacent and indifferent. It's a curious position to find yourself agreeing with Roger Scruton and George Walden about anything. But their commitment to the ideal of education as a good in itself is exemplary. Bizarre. Another morbid symptom for the new millennium.

MS: What worries me is the extreme menace with which the management of education directives tie us closer to the ever more rigid dictates of the RAE and the ever newer categorizations of the TQA. What damaging efforts do you think these regimes of supervision will have on the future of unique research and innovative teaching? (How have we found ourselves hostages to fortune?)

PG: I too believe that the bureaucratization of British academia is a cause for worry, and is having negative effects on both research and teaching. But let me be really clear about this. I'm not against a measure of accountability for people who are in many respects, not financially of course, but in many respects extremely privileged, privileged in the way that we can all organize our own time, privileged in the way we are able to have a degree of intellectual autonomy, which is *sui generis*. We're sort of like police officers in that we have this permissive 'original authority' under the law which entitles us to specify the content of our own work. I personally find that an incredibly valuable thing. I know that it has been abused, and I know that there are a lot of people whose idea of a life of semi-tenured scholarship is a life down the pub. So, I'm not overlooking that as a problem. But it seems to me that the bureaucratization and marketization of the sector is not necessarily addressing the question of accountability in the way that it needs to be addressed. For me, all of this began with the idea of credit accumulation transfer, attempts to specify general standards of value across courses and institutions that aren't amenable to that sort of evaluation. Things of that kind have consumed an extraordinary amount of resources that could have been deployed in other places. And, of course, I think that it is a really wonderful thing that so many more people get the chance to move into higher education. Although the research over who those people actually are, and the basis on which they are there, doesn't seem to suggest that there has been the kind of class cultural revolution that some people like to imagine has taken place. I look forward to that day but it hasn't actually happened yet. In fact charging people fees has driven away the older students in large numbers. They can't afford it. No mystery there. It's odd to suggest that Cultural Studies is any sort of therapeutic presence in the midst all of this. But I like to think that our concerns and the intellectual agenda that we've struggled to articulate corresponds very well with the positive questions that have come out of the transformation of that sector and its widening, curriculum change and development. The effects of Cultural Studies in schools and in FE [further education] as well as in universities, have fostered a different sense of where education might itself fit into the logic of personal development, and inter-subjective relations. This may even have been proved by the relative success of these initiatives in the marketplace. We probably wouldn't want to defend Cultural Studies on that ground, but the fact that it has been buoyant seems to me to suggest that it is a significant thing in changing the terms and boundaries of educational experience. As I say, I don't want to defend it on those grounds. But it seems this is something that the marketeers and corporate-type managers haven't really been able to reckon with. Certainly, the too rapid retreat into the certainty of a fortified discipline rather misses out that possibility.

What would also be interesting to know is what is going on in those disciplines which isn't appealing to students, what it is that they are being offered in, for instance, the field of Sociology or the fields of History or Literature which has been fortified against these exciting encroachments. That is a harder thing to specify for me. Of course the managerial culture is closely connected to a decline in the standards and depth of the educational experience. The customer mentality is associated with the mistaken idea that learning can be boiled down to a small pile of photocopied papers and skillful use of the overhead projector.

MS: That brings me to a question that I want to ask you about the academic, or the intellectual, and the kinds of possible interventions that they can make. From Gramsci and Williams to Foucault and Said, Barthes to Kristeva, Cornel West to Spivak, Cultural Studies has been offered many versions of the intellectual. More than experts in legitimation, the organic, specific, critical, amateur, dissident intellectual has been obliged to fight for the study of culture with an unprecedented degree of passion, with a commitment premised on a refusal of what Deleuze, citing Foucault, has famously dubbed the indignity of speaking for others. With this multifarious genealogy of responsibility in mind, what does it mean for you to be engaged? With the demands of an increased professionalism in the field of Cultural Studies, and with the simultaneously urgent obligation to insist on an attitude of intervention – and I am thinking here of your work for the GLC [Greater London Council] in the 1980s and your moving, recent piece on Stephen Lawrence (1997).[4] What is your role as an intellectual, as a black intellectual, in the public sphere? And do you think that there are distinctively different and specifically useful roles that you as an intellectual, as a black intellectual, can make into the fields of cultural production or cultural practice?

PG: I think that's all a bit grand. I think that trying to defend an intervention within the field of your educational institution, and trying to sustain a much more complex sense of national culture, a much more complex sense of how that culture is translated and rearticulated in the context of the Humanities and Social Sciences is one thing. I think that that battle is a very interesting one in this country, through the Cold War phase and beyond. In a way I don't think that that story has been told terribly well yet. There are elements of it around that will emerge in biographical writings. A little bit of it begins to come out in something like Fred Inglis's (1998) recent biography of Raymond Williams, although it's not necessarily told in the spirit, or in the style, or in the detail that is required. I think that story is worth telling. But then to move on from that discussion to a different kind of argument about what it has meant to be a public intellectual, or what it will mean to intervene in a wider field, or what it means to feel that you can enter the info-tainment telesector and win battles there, I think those are different problems. It is really interesting to see how much people have retreated from them, except where, of course, they are addressing people like themselves. To work not as a public intellectual but as a popular intellectual in that info-tainment telesector, where it becomes difficult to say anything at all, is something I think that people, rightly, have retreated from. I know that there are all these jokes about soundbite celebrity academics, but I can't see anybody functioning terribly effectively in that sphere. Even from the Right. Even they are undone by the pressures of the instant pay-off that is required. So, I don't see that bit. It's not even as though the feminist intellectuals who, of course, have had a very elaborate if dissonant relationship with the project of Cultural Studies from the very beginning, but have also been absolutely intrinsic to its successes as an intervention over a long period of time, leave their mark. It's very interesting to me that even they haven't been able to consolidate that breach. At the end of the twentieth century, the primary voice of feminist political critique in the world of the info-tainment telesector belongs to Germaine Greer. That is a disappointment and, whatever one thinks of her insights – and sometimes she is blessed with great insight and vision – it is a very telling indictment of several other successive generations.

MS: But as an academic, better Greer than Elaine Showalter speaking as head of last year's Modern Language Association on the reasons why young, overqualified, would-be academics in the States should give up their hopes of becoming valuable members of educational institutions and instead move into the culture industries. In terms of journalism, I know exactly what you mean. There is some interesting work to be done on the reasons behind why a newer, and highly educated, generation of female journalists writing for the 'quality' newspapers can offer such explicitly and politically motivated feminism in such an apolitical and ineffectual way. Apart from the despondency that comes with being told how to experience my cultural condition by a twenty-year-old – and male journalists are of course just as uninspired and lazy in their efforts – I'm concerned by how these obviously well-educated writers can be so insipid. Giving them postgraduate training in Cultural Studies seems to be a licence to ...

PG: That's what I'm trying to say. They've filleted Cultural Studies. In the same way that a lot of people in the corporate space have filleted it, have gutted it for what they want, and adapted it to the rhythms of their own complicity with consumerism. And I don't think that that should be a surprise. What's interesting is how disloyal those people are to what formed them a lot of the time.

The Nick Hornbies and the Bridget Joneses, that layer of British people interest me a lot as a recent phenomenon in our national life. The fictionalization of their journeys is pivotal. The relationship that those novels, if you can call them novels, bear to the sorts of critique that we have been talking about is profound. It's quite interesting just where those reflexive notes come from in, say, the figuration of that sort of masculinity that is on the edge of Laddism, but is something different. I don't know myself how much that 'something different' is involved in making those voices attractive that's what I'm unable to answer. In a sense Nick Hornby is a real successor to Dick Hebdige. I wonder about it, I wonder about how much real critique is there. It may not count for very much, but still. I remember coming back to this country from the States in 1995, going on a bus in London, and every young man I could see was reading a book by Nick Hornby. Everywhere I looked, they were reading *High Fidelity*! I couldn't believe it, I couldn't understand what had produced that outcome. I was happy, of course, that they still wanted to read.

When one thinks, also, about the impact of these forms of training and sensitivities around culture on the conduct of the political process itself, that too yields some interesting and uncomfortable insights. The sort of line that prominent spin doctors have worked out about the significance of football, say, is something that is deeply guided by cultural insights drawn from the Cultural Studies project. Actually seeing that mentality in Government, and seeing the influence of Demos and their strategies, (Demos is of course only a little window on that process) is very disturbing. There are lots of informal elements to it as well as its more formal signatures. So, a little bit of ruthless self-scrutiny when it comes to this unfortunate complicity is overdue. It really is overdue. The anti-Semitism of British political culture produces a figure like Peter Mandelson as the butt of all of this, but I think that there are some interesting questions to be asked about the quality of confidence with which these awful people imagine, with their totalitarian confidence, that they can make anything mean anything else. They can make anything mean what governments want it to mean, that there is an infinite pliability about the world of representation. All of this has a folk theory, it may be a folk theory but it is a folk theory in which Cultural Studies has been deeply implicated. Of course, that acknowledgement will never be made. And of course, pressing for it would be wrong. While I don't know what they teach on MBAs in detail, I expect that in addition to the history of, for instance, what Edward Bernays was doing in 1920, I'm sure that there is a very strong and refined understanding of a critical semiotics and so on. It's odd that nobody in the world of Cultural Studies has been prepared to reckon either with the political moment or that of its commercial moment.

My neighbours, of whom I am extremely fond, have an interesting company called 'Semiotic Solutions'. I don't know much about it, but I think it's a sophisticated kind of market research thing. In the work that they have done they have pioneered advising the corporate world on how to communicate, to make new meanings. There is a real politics there, particularly around gender and representation. And I'm sure that there is a version of that story that is replicated in a thousand places, and I know because I have to write references for my own students who have tried to move into those corporate worlds. And I think that we need to have something to say about that. And it has to be an ethical thing as well as a post-politics.

MS: To backtrack briefly by reiterating my earlier question around the role of the public intellectual, I would like to now inflect it in a different register. My first remark concerns the limited spaces available within which black commentators are able to speak. Here, I am gesturing towards the dilemma not just of tokenism *per se* but of what it means for some – and I am thinking, for instance, of Darcus Howe – to be representative of many, to speak for many. And here, I'm obviously picking up on exchanges in postcolonial thought on marginality articulated by many including Kobena Mercer and Isaac Julian, bell hooks and, of course, Gayatri Spivak. Second, I would like to draw on the painfully moving words you have written on the Stephen Lawrence case in the past, and the further twists that have been added to the complexity of the issues raised by this tragic matter since we last discussed it. I'm thinking here about the black production company that proposed to the Lawrence family that they appear on Channel 4 to give the 'alternative' Christmas speech, and the wranglings or misunderstandings around this. And this is to say nothing of the more recent developments.

PG: The person who directed it was not white. And anyway, the message for this moment is that I'm all for equal opportunity of access to the media-scape, for Channel 4 and its commissioning process. But, personally, I'm not going to get in a stew because I don't see any guarantees in having non-white directors doing those tokenistic things. You can't criticize somebody like Darcus Howe for what he represents one minute, and then complain about the fact that these opportunities aren't given to black production companies the next. Darcus' career is the proof that we get no guarantee that we'll get the outcomes we want by simply employing a black presenter. These arguments contradict one another. If you want fronting, if you want tokenism, have tokenism. But then don't complain about the fact that people don't sing the song you want them to sing. It's that degree of complexity that we have to applaud. I think that whatever Darcus represents, it's not him that is the question. It's the people that think that they can manage the problem of 'race' in Britain by holding him in a position of authority. That's the question. It's the Michael Jacksons and those powerful shadowy people who think that they can manage the disruptive potential of race politics in the moment of the Stephen Lawrence tragedy, in the moment of that anger, and the respectable nature of that anger, that they manage the problem by employing Darcus more. That's the issue and, in a sense, inter-generational relations do come into it. A lot of younger black people in the media world want to be Quentin Tarantino and John Woo! That's what they want. And I'm absolutely happy for them to want that, but I don't think that in wanting that, in being that, in becoming that, that they are going to be representing either Stephen Lawrence or me, or any of the possible networks of meaning that might be used to connect that family's tragedy to the wider life of British society as a whole. Having a bit of melanin in your body doesn't actually render you immune to conservatism and consumerism and now-ism and me-ism. I wish that the world was simple enough to be able to say that. There isn't even a unified organization of black media workers! Something like twenty years after such a body was first proposed, its still doesn't exist. There is no forum in which the people who seek to intervene in that world can address one another as equals, responsively, to advance their professional and political interests. So I think we have to ask ourselves why those fundamental structures are so pitifully underdeveloped. Just before Christmas 1998, I went to speak at a conference that the British Film Institute had organized at the National Film Theatre about black British film production. And it was an interesting day precisely because it became apparent very quickly that so many people wanted to be Quentin Tarantino. And that surprised me. I thought that there was still a residual conscience around, and I think that there is. But it belongs to a different generation. It belongs to the Linda Bellos generation, or it belongs to the Menelik Shabazz generation, or it belongs to the Darcus Howe generation. I think that there are some questions which need to be asked about how bad people have been at reinventing their own political traditions in ways that are attractive.

It was a curious thing. When the British version of the Nation of Islam, much split and caught up in sectarian conflicts, had their rally of ten thousand men, supposedly, in Trafalgar Square in 1998. I remember going down there and having a look. And the fact that there were less than ten thousand there, is in a sense, secondary. What is interesting is who was there, and what they were doing, and how they were behaving. It was very curious to me that the first person I heard speak from that platform was a young Sikh man who was fêted and respected as a young warrior by the assembled crew of the Nation of Islam. The second person was the French leader of the Nation of Islam who came, and spoke, and prayed in French, and wore his uniform and all the rest of it. All very, very interesting. Even those absolute theocratic differences were being mediated. Then the third thing that happened was that they started playing Bob Marley records on their big sound system! The political and cultural vacuum that agenda suggests to me is interesting. And, without wanting to be drawn into making too glib statements about the nature of the post-modern, I think that it is very interesting to me that people don't know, or have perhaps somehow temporarily forgotten, how to speak in a certain sort of political language. In a way, and without any disrespect to the Lawrence family, and their tragedy, and their suffering, the iconization of that moment fills that space with a kind of narrative of terrible loss and suffering that people are comfortable with precisely because it means that they don't have to think or say anything other than to introduce that icon of victimage.

Of course it's disturbing that for the Cultural Studies movement we were discussing earlier on, one of its sharpest interventions is around the whole question of race, and representation, and policing, and so on. And it's very interesting to see that from the police's side, there is a much greater degree of sophistication and command of what it means to intervene and to manage, and to represent, and to spin and so on. The front page of *The Guardian* today has an item, rather jokingly written up by Nick Hopkins (1999), about the Metropolitan Police Force commissioning a sort of rap video to organize their recruitment of black officers. Conflict in that world should be very apparent too. I've known for a long time that one of the few places that it was actually an asset to have a Sociology degree was in the police force. I begin to wonder now whether a Cultural Studies qualification is becoming a similar kind of commodity for entering that space. It's only a matter of time ...

MS: Do you think that this might have anything to do with the reasonably recent emergence of 'White Studies'?

PG: I would say that the kind of anxiousness, the kind of lack of certainty about the constitution of racial identity amongst black people is not something unique to them. It is not dissimilar from other symptoms in a wider crisis about the limits and anxieties over the boundaries of ethnicity. Facing that, some academics have opted to try to represent whiteness as a kind of ethnic substance, but I think that is a rather defeatist and trivializing response to this crisis. How can I put it? When you watch those five young men bowling along in their Kentish London style, and when you appreciate that their hatred and their hostility is part of a longer history of racial attacks in that area, and when you also appreciate that it is in a sense non-specific – that racism is one important and vicious individual element of it, but that it includes a whole complex of other fields and responses – whilst the Stephen Lawrence tragedy actually gives us a chance to see just how deeply beliefs, and attitudes, and responses cut into the life of national institutions, I think you don't want to contain them there. You also want to see how those questions articulate with localism, and regionalism, and nativism, and nationalism, and no-nothingism, and a generalized non-specific hatred and hostility towards anything different which is only experienced in terms of anxiety and loss. So, I think that there is a cue here for a very different kind of way that we might begin to understand the constitution of a multicultural Britain. And I think that Cultural Studies, with its resources for thinking the elaboration and history of conflicts in and through culture, conflicts which articulate national identity in a number of quite different and contrasting ways, has actually got rather a lot to contribute to that process.

Again, I wonder where a lot of that energy is going? And, I rather suspect that a lot of the people who are in a better position to guide it are people who are not academics, but people who have come through our kind of academic relationship with Cultural Studies but have moved beyond it into the world of art, or the world of media, or into other areas of cultural production equipped with some of those tools, the toolkit, the sandbox, that Cultural Studies offered them. I'm thinking here of someone like Chris Ofili, and the sorts of games that his work plays which are informed by an exposure to questions of identity, and culture and power, and nationhood, and so on. In a way, he is the *reductio ad absurdum* of all of that. And it is interesting to see the forms of celebrity and prestige that might be attached to it in its ironic constitution.

MS: Political in its apoliticism.

PG: Exactly. It's very interesting not only that he won the Turner Prize in 1998, but to walk around The Tate seeing people experiencing that work. It may seem harsh to blame it on Stuart Hall, but in a way you have to see those links ...

MS: They can't blame Tarantino for Ofili as well! His brand of 1970s kinky-porn-retro is no Jackie Brown, and it's definitely no Jack Hill.

PG: A lot of American critics read Tarantino's films as celebrations of hybridity, and exactly within the currency of anti-absolutist notions of ethnicity. That's the line that someone like Stanley Crouch, the Right wing critic, takes. His is the loudest voice cheering on Quentin Tarantino precisely on that basis, because it's showing that race isn't a fixed code in the body ...

MS: But presumably he's arguing against the likes of a Spike Lee or a bell hooks, and others who, I imagine, would be very anti-Tarantino ...

PG: In the case of Spike Lee there is a rather greater degree of ambivalence. If you think, for example, of the opening sequence of *Girl 6*, it features Quentin Tarantino acting himself in a way which acts out precisely the kind of critique that you would anticipate someone like Spike Lee levelling at him. He is bullying and harassing the young black actress who is trying to get into the movies. I think that bell hooks has a rather different line. What's significant for me is that the most interesting movie that's trying to manage and play with these figures and intervene at precisely the point that we are speaking about has not been made by Tarantino or Spike Lee but by Warren Beatty. In a way, *Bulworth* (1998) is depressing to the extent that it is so obviously bound to precisely that sort of Leftist, 1968, Cold War Marxism. It's very interesting to think the relationship between something like *Reds* (1981) and *Bulworth*. It's an attempt to deconstruct the dangerous pieties of a whole set of arguments about the nature of racial identity. And it's a very, very powerfully and interestingly figured film precisely for that reason. I think that it is clearly informed by a very scrupulous reading of the literature around whiteness and white studies.

MS: *Bulworth* looks to me like a combination of *CB4* (1993) and *Wag the Dog* (1997).

PG: Yes, it's certainly pitching for those markets. But I think it is a wee bit more savvy than either of those films. And, presumably, precisely for that quality it is failing comprehensively in the American market. I don't know, but that's my guess. It seemed to disappear very quickly there. But I think that I would want to defend it very, very strongly as an imaginative intervention.

MS: To shift gear, would you tell me a little about your current research.

PG: I've just finished a book for Penguin, *Between Camps* (2000) which is about the ethics of multi-culture. It is an attempt to restore an ethical dimension to thinking about race and politics, because I think that this has been absent. It has partly been flushed away because of the sorts of professional interests involved in the construction of the world of race-relations research as a professional community. I think that as the political context created by the memory of the industrial killing of Jews and others in Europe has begun to fade, we can't take for granted any kind of ethical position in the work we want to do on race and on politics. And I think that we have to return in a very deliberate, and rigorous, and principled way to the problem of how we want to bring ethics back into that work. In a way, that's one strand of the book. There's a second strand which connects up to that because it's also about trying to reckon with the enduring force of elements of the Fascist cultural revolution in the world that we inhabit. In particular, in its primal staging of post-modernism in a relationship between self and soma, in what Zygmunt Bauman calls the 'custodial' relationship to one's own body that's so much a signature of it. In particular, I've tried to address notions of fraternity, and fraternal solidarity, mutual belonging, constituted around the world of sport as a form of mass spectatorship. Reckoning with that history, and reckoning with its relationship to racialization over a long period of time, thinking about that in relation to debates about the nature of a generic fascist culture, and a fascist aesthetic, things of that kind. That's the sort of ground that I have tried to enter. At the same time, I've tried to look at the impact of those histories on a changed relationship to the representation of blackness. I've tried to focus on the point where blackness ceases to be abjection primarily, and becomes a signifier of bodily prestige in a different sort of global economy of info-tainment centred primarily on the world of sport and on the supra-human figures that dwell there, the Michael Jordans, the Mike Tysons ('Tyson Caged Again' said the front page of *The Sun* the other day), and the John Fashanus, Lennox Lewises, and Derek Redmonds ... to try and open that up, and to open it up in the context of an argument which suggests that the industrialization of killing in Europe has a significant relationship to things that were going on in colonial history. It's time to revisit that problem. I haven't done it adequately of course, but I want to air that again, and to do something to reactivate an old line of argument which has not felt shy of making the connection, not been intimidated out of seeing that connection, to find those sorts of threads in Primo Levi, or Jean Améry, in aspects of the Holocaust survivor's literature reconfigured to a Cold War world where the issue of national liberation struggles, and so on, was being articulated. But also to see how many of the black intellectuals of that Cold War period were people who had also distinguished themselves in combat against the Nazis. A lot of us read Fanon as though his line on violence was not something that has been informed by the fact that he had been in the French army shooting at Nazis, and had got medals for fighting in that war. So in a way it misses the point to read his argument about violence and evil, and the role of violence in the desegregation of white supremacy, outside of that unacknowledged history. And I think that there are many other versions of that story. In my book, I talk a little about Léopold Sédar Senghor in the prison camp, being in the Resistance, and so on. And there are other people.

MS: Last time we met, we were briefly talking about the importance of the war experience as the impetus behind much of the impulse in the work of the early cultural study of Raymond Williams and E.P. Thompson.

PG: Of course. Raymond and Thompson both on their tanks. Yes, so, in a way I'm not sure that we have made the best of those formative experiences. I've always believed that you don't understand their nationalism unless you understand that moment. Edward Thompson used to talk a lot about the kind of patriotism you could feel for the idea of Europe. Never mind his little Englandism, there is something about those experiences that was very formative. And I think I wanted to revisit some of those experiences in the lives of black intellectuals precisely because I think that they are a resource for the future of a different sense of what Europe is, and I didn't want us to be shut out from that history.

There are other aspects to it. I have tried, I suppose polemically, to bring back into line the question of the figuration of The Negro soldiers in the emancipation of the Camps. When I was working at Yale, I spent a lot of time in the Fortunoff Video Archive of Holocaust Testimony that Geoffrey Hartman and Shoshana Felman and others have sustained over the years, although financially I know that they are under a lot of pressure. Now that there are so many other organizations with bigger profiles trying to do similar work. There, I looked at a lot of the video testimony of people who had been liberated by black soldiers. I was very interested to see what they said about that. You do get the figure of the negro in Tadeusz Borwoski very ambivalently, or you do get it in Elie Wiesel, of course, who was liberated by black soldiers. I'm interested in those encounters, and not just from the point of view of what the inmates said, but also in what the Afro-American and Japanese-American soldiers had to say about those experiences.

I got very interested in the history of a film that was made by an African-American filmmaker, Bill Miles, and a Jewish-American filmmaker, Nina Rosenblum, called *Liberators* (1992) which was about the experience of these men and their presence at the opening of Dachau, and Buchenwald to the eyes of the world, and there is of course a great deal of photographic evidence to substantiate this. I got very interested in the political responses to this film, and just how many problems it caused in the context of New York politics, for a contemporary anti-racist initiative to be articulated around this history of bearing witness. The image of a Hasidic man embracing Jesse Jackson at the Apollo Theatre Gala opening of the film was very, very powerful. It freaked a lot of people out, and I think that the film was very, very rapidly discredited. The idea was that it was invented, that they had overdone it as a result of their politically correct zeal. The black soldiers had been at Mauthausen, and Gunskirchen as 'liberators', but they couldn't have been at Buchenwald even though there was a photograph to show that they had been there. There was a sense in which the film was rapidly enveloped in a controversy about veracity. The makers were accused of revisionism, the idea that you are projecting blacks into this story where they don't belong means that you end up in the Faurisson camp, and all of this kind of thing. This was a very, very interesting episode. In a way, what it pointed to for me was a different periodization for the history of blacks in Europe. It took me back to the First World War and to the impact of black soldiery, African-American soldiers, soldiers of the West India Regiment, in the life of Europe at that point. The African-Americans weren't even allowed to be in the American army, they joined the French army! And the history of their relationship to the French army is also extraordinary. Their marching bands were a means through which African-American culture was first conducted into the cultural life of Europe. Very interesting, very powerful. And of course, it is at that very moment that Adorno comes along and says that jazz is fascistic because of its military character.

I've tried to rewrite something of that story, and to do it in ways that, hopefully, instantiate a slightly different cosmopolitan historiography. I hope. That's what I've tried to do. I don't know whether it works, but I've just tried to write history on a slightly different scale which is alive to, first of all, the power of raciology in distorting modernity and, second, alive to a different rhythm in the way in which we think of the relationship between Europe and its unfolding, and the presence of black cultures in that space. So someone like Josephine Baker, say, and her romance with France, takes on a slightly different aspect. Or the stories of Afro-Germans who are swept up in the implementation of the Holocaust, but who live through it because they are film extras, or circus people going around with animals. There are those stories of how the German propaganda movies needed real live black actors. So the stories that can be told about that are interesting, they tell us something about the nature of raciology. We need to know what that is, but of course it isn't always something that fits in with our proscription. The idea that black infra-humanity might work in our favour because you become patronized in a way that people take care of their pets or livestock. I've tried to explore that problem. And then, on the other side, to explore the contemporary figurations of black supra-humanity. So, we have the infra-human and we have the supra-human black – the Michael Jordan-type figure. But then, there's the question of what falls between. Where you just get to be ordinary. Ordinary. To deal with it in the spaces of the everyday. To be other, not exotic. The material on sports is likewise interesting. I began to get very, very concerned with the figures of Jesse Owens and Joe Louis, and the historical meaning of the Louis–Schmelling fights, and seeing what Louis and Schmelling themselves had written about them. There was a politicization of race and power at that moment in the 1930s. Until I was researching this book, I had not read *Mein Kampf*. And I thought that it was incredible that a liberal education does not include that encounter. And it was shocking to read it. The sections on sport in there are a revelation. Of course, a lot of it is very familiar because it reads like *Scouting for Boys*, or something. And that's exactly the point. Elements of it do touch that colonial history in ways that are really shocking.

MS: *Scouting for Boys*, sounds like a training manual for paedophiles ...

PG: Well I haven't tried to explore that problem, the libidinal economy of that fascist revolution is something that people still find very difficult to know what to say about. Klaus Theweleit's two-volume *Male Fantasies* (1987) is really all that there is. While I haven't discussed his work, I obviously really respect that intervention, it's an extraordinary body of work. But I'm not sure about the detail of it at all. It's a beacon of possibilities, there is so much there to explore. I don't know about the detail of it, I just don't know. I think that there is something about the ways that we periodize all of this knowledge, how we understand colonial war in relation to the 1914–18 war, how we understand the history of killing technologies in these fields. Around the Theweleit intervention there is a lot of discussion around the occupation of the Rhineland, the use of black troops, the whole way in which we can reconstruct the raciology of that history through, for instance, the secrecy that surrounds the sterilization of the Rhineland Bastards. I don't think that that has really been done in a comprehensive way. For example, if you take the figure of Eugen Fischer, Germany's dean of racial science, the first person to study the application of the principles of Mendelian genetics to a human population in South West Africa amongst the Reheboth Bastards, very much there in the aftermath of Lutwein and Von Trotha's assault on the Herero people. It is Fischer who writes the standard textbook on racial science with two other writers – Hitler read it in Landsberg – Fischer then becomes the rector of a University in Berlin at the same time as Heidegger becomes the rector of Freiberg. Great friend of Heidegger, because he's from Freiberg himself. They converse. In fact, there is an interview with Fischer's daughter which says, 'well of course, Heidegger visited my father till the end of his life, and they talked much about the experience of the white man in Africa'. I think the friendship between the two of them opens up a whole other line on Heidegger's relationship between Volkism and metaphysical racism and anti-black racism. Unfortunately, the archives are closed. But it's very suggestive. The figures of Heidegger and Leni Riefenstahl are an interesting cast of characters. Just to provoke a little bit, I've tried to engage with these key figures because I think that the undignified postures people assume in trying to protect their genius are deeply, deeply problematic. For me, a wholesale condemnation is not at all problematic. I take the Adorno line on Heidegger and I take the Susan Sontag line on Leni Riefenstahl, so I don't think that there is anything to be redeemed at all. I think it's all Nazi from end to end.

Between Camps (2000) deals with different things, which isn't to say that it is difficult. It's just an attempt to say, let's take raciology seriously as something that constitutes other relations in modernity is hard. So it's been a struggle. I like to think that the book is clearer than the things that I've written in the past because I've tried to write a different kind of a book. I've tried to write a book that wasn't just an ordinary academic book, and I don't think it reads like an academic book. I think that if you come to it as an academic you will be disappointed because it's not a big theory book. It just says, let's have a think about this stuff to do with the history of fascism and what it adds up to, and let's use a different kind of a meditation on it, or a history of fascism written on a slightly different scale, as a resource for thinking about the future of European culture. Richard Wright comes along after the war, and he says that everything that happens around black culture in Europe after 1945 is a response to the aftershock of fascism. And this is somebody whose writing is going to be translated by the Maquis, whose stories of privation and struggle as an African-America seem to resonate precisely in that context. So, we need a better history of that. And we need to bring it into the Cold War. For myself, I wanted to bring myself into it. I was born in 1956, my father was a conscientious objector in World War II, he wouldn't fight the Nazis, didn't want to be made to kill anybody by a government. And yet my whole formation as a London child was in the shadow of the war, and I wanted to explore that ambiguity partly, I suppose, because I began to realize that that history had been very important for me in shaping my antipathies to nationalism. When you have one migrant parent and one pacifist parent, it's an interesting lesson in the powers of nationalism. So, I wanted to understand a little bit about that in my own formation. I started writing it before I realized that those were the things that were acting through me, so it's been a nice experience of self-discovery too. I don't feel any more benign about nationalism, but at least it's good to know a little bit more about the sources of those things, to be able to tell yourself a better story about them.

Notes

1 This interview originally appeared as Marquard Smith, 'On the State of Cultural Studies: An Interview with Paul Gilroy', *Third Text*, 49, Winter 1999–2000, 15–6.
2 The Higher Education Funding Council for England (HEFCE) has distributed public funds through the RAE since 1992 in order to, in their own words, promote and fund 'high quality, cost-effective teaching and research in universities and colleges in England' in an effort to ensure 'accountability' and promote 'good practice'. The TQA is conducted by the Quality Assurance Agency on behalf of HEFCE in an effort to 'promote and support quality and standards of [teaching] provision'.
3 Editor's note: At the time of the interview, Gilroy was based in the Department of Sociology at Goldsmiths College, University of London.
4 See Paul Gilroy (1997). The black teenager Stephen Lawrence was murdered on 22 April, 1993. The five prime suspects were acquitted in 1996. In the 1998 public inquiry they suffered from a bout of collective amnesia, a condition rectified for the ITV interview with Martin Bashir on 8 April, 1999. The Stephen Lawrence Inquiry, launched in 1993 by Macpherson, appeared in February 1999 and included accusations of institutional racism against the Metropolitan Police Force for their dealings with the case.

References

Gilroy, Paul (1987) *There Ain't No Black in the Union Jack*. London: Routledge.
Gilroy, Paul (1993) *The Black Atlantic: Modernity and Double-Consciousness*. Cambridge, MA Harvard University Press.
Gilroy, Paul (1994) *Small Acts: Thoughts on the Politics of Black Cultures*. London: Serpent's Tale.
Gilroy, Paul (1997), 'Scales and Eyes: 'Race' Making Difference', in Sue Golding (ed.), *The Eight Technologies of Otherness*. London: Routledge. pp. 190–96.
Gilroy, Paul (2000) *Between Camps*. London: Allan Lane.
Gilroy, Paul (2000) *Against Race: Imagining Political Culture Beyond the Color Line*. Cambridge: Harvard University Press.
Gilroy, Paul (2004) *After Empire: Multiculture or Postcolonial Melancholia*. Routledge: London.
Gilroy, Paul, *et al* (1982) *The Empire Strikes Back: Race and Racism in 70s Britain*. New York: Routledge.
Hopkins, Nick (1999) 'Met police ready to take the rap', *The Guardian*, Thursday June 10.
Hornby, Nick (1995) *High Fidelity*. London Gallancz.
Inglis, Fred (1998) *Raymond Williams*. London: Routledge.
Sokal, Alan (1996) 'Transgressing the Boundaries: Towards a Transformative Hermeneutics of Quantum Gravity', *Social Text, 46/47*, (Spring/Summer): 217–252.
Theweleit, Klaus (1987) *Male Fantasies*, vols I & II. Minneapolis: University of Minnesota Press.

5

DISABILITY STUDIES, THE HUMANITIES, AND THE LIMITS OF THE VISIBLE

Interview with Lennard J. Davis

Introduction

Lennard J. Davis is Professor in the English Department in the School of Arts and Sciences at the University of Illinois at Chicago. In addition, he is Professor of Disability and Human Development in the School of Applied Health Sciences, and Professor of Medical Education in the Medical School. Amongst his many books, he is author of *Enforcing Normalcy* (1995), *My Sense of Silence* (2000), *Bending Over Backwards* (2002) and editor of *The Disability Studies Reader* (1997 [2007]), and has a book forthcoming on the cultural history of obsession (2008). Here Davis begins by speaking about the role of the public intellectual in discussions of class, disability studies, and activism in the public sphere. He then concentrates more fully on Disability Studies as a valuable area of knowledge and of academic study, and one that also needs to question some of the very dogmas of disability culture itself. In this way, and breaking away from the identity politics of the 1980s and 1990s, Davis is able to introduce a more nuanced discussion of hybrid identities, the normal and the abnormal body, and the extent to which disability is crucial to any account of human embodiment. Disability Studies, then, shows itself to be not just a minoritarian discourse but in fact always already embedded in paradigms of the Humanities, the Social Sciences, the arts, and studies of visual culture. In addition to contributing to the emerging conversation between Disability Studies and Visual Culture Studies, and to generating a dialogue on the points of convergence between disability and visuality, Davis also seeks to explore the ways in which 'disability' and 'visuality' are so often constitutive of one another.

Activism: History, Theory, Practice

Marquard Smith (MS): Lenny, following Antonio Gramsci's nomenclature (1971 [1941]), you have called yourself an organic intellectual, 'being taught not necessarily in the schools, but on the streets, articulating the issues of [your] class' (Davis, 2002). I'd say you are also a public intellectual, perhaps in part because of this. And Disability is an avowedly political movement. Alongside your academic activities, you publish essays in *The Nation*, the *Chronicle of Higher Education*, and elsewhere. You have been interviewed numerous times on National Public Radio, and you give lectures around the US, Europe, and beyond. Often taking advantage of the stuff of high and low culture, of books and cinema as a starting point, you're interested in generating widespread debate around topics such as disability rights, civil rights, equality, citizenship, integration, identity politics, legislation, physically-assisted suicide, and the future of genetics (Davis, 2005a–j, 2006a). In a word: justice. Would you let us know something about how your background has led to this commitment to activism in the public sphere.

Lennard J. Davis (LD): I slightly blush at some of the things you say. I would begin with the fact that I grew up in a family where my parents were both deaf and working-class. And immigrants too, to the United States. As a child, that immediately gave me a sense of otherness, and also outrage at the way I would see my parents be treated. My parents were not outraged themselves. Very rarely were my parents ever outraged. They were more 'get along' members of the working-class. Their sense of themselves was very much to be good workers, to not make any waves, to just get along. From my point of view, the example I use from when I was a kid is this: I would ride on the subways in New York with my parents and my parents would talk to each other in sign language and every single person on the subway would stare at them. I would start at one end of the subway car and stare back. I started doing this when I was five, six, seven maybe. I would stare back at every single person until they averted their eyes. I would work my way down the entire subway car and by the end of that the first people would start staring again and I would have to start all over again. There was certainly an obsessive compulsive aspect to it. I would wonder: 'why are you staring at my parents, they're just talking to each other, don't you understand this?' I had a very strong sense of the way society treated them.

The funny thing about this defensive position I held vis à vis my parents and the world is that I abandoned it for much of my life. I went to university, and the last thing in the world I ever had on my mind was disability issues, deafness. For me, the whole point of my education was to get away from this working-class background and disability – what I saw as limitations on me. Even though my parents had some interesting strengths and complications, for me, like every kid, I just wanted to get away from it – but even more so from the issues of class and disability. I remember at university that when my graduate professor, Steven Marcus – who like me was born in the Bronx, so we'd talk about it, and he knew my parents were deaf – suggested that I wrote a dissertation on gesture and Dickens. He was a Dickensian. I said 'No!' I was horrified. It was the last thing in the world I wanted to do – yoke myself back to my origins.

I made my name as someone who wrote on the history of the early novel and fiction novel theory. It wasn't until my mid-career that I became involved in Disability Studies. It was a major awakening in my life. A university education, back in the 1960s, had made me much more aware of my working-class background than my disability background. I was comfortably a Marxist, but disability had nothing to do with my Marxism. So, it wasn't until about the early 1990s that I became interested in Disability Studies. It all started because of my wife. She was always telling me that I should write about the interesting experiences I had as a kid, and I always said 'yeah, yeah, maybe ...' But I never did. Suddenly, I changed my mind. I had already started doing journalism of various kinds, and I was writing for *The Nation*. Then I got a letter with information about a conference on the topic of children of people who were deaf. And I thought: 'this is a weird conference!' I was *sort of* interested. I found out that it was in Austin, Texas. I actually got in touch with the *New York Times* and asked if they wanted a really crazy *Sunday Times* story on these wacky people who were all children of deaf people meeting at this conference? They said no! [laughs] I decided it might make an interesting story anyway, so I bought myself a ticket and I just went! The only way I could actually even get myself to go was to think of it as a journalistic experience. I went there, and I had one of those classic life-changing experiences. I realized that deafness was a very important part of my life and I hadn't really left it behind, that I was, in some ways, bi-cultural, and I had just abandoned this whole crucial part of my childhood because I was able-ist, because I was audist.

So I went to this conference and I met all these people. The majority of people who go to that conference are, essentially, interpreters for the deaf. But one or two or three people were academics, and it had not occurred to me that my experience as a child was something that you could study from an academic perspective. As soon as I came back, I decided to see what information on 'deafness' there was in the archive, and there wasn't that much.

Edward Said had been my dissertation director, and I suddenly put it together for myself that he had articulated the contradictions and issues of the Palestinians, that he could do this because he was a public intellectual and that here was a group of people who *weren't* Palestinians and they *weren't* Vietnamese, but they *were* deaf and they were my parents' generation and beyond that why couldn't I articulate the issues that were involved.

So I just started researching 'deafness' and then I began to see that I couldn't research deafness without researching disability, so I started looking into all the material that was there and I felt that what was missing, at the time, was that there was so much theorizing about gender, there was theorizing about queerness, and about every major subject in cultural studies, but there was no theorizing about disability so, that's what I could do.

So I started writing *Enforcing Normalcy*. I originally called the book *Theorizing Disability*. I literally don't remember writing a book, it literally wrote itself. I was just so ready to write that book and it was so 'of the moment'.

So, that's how I got into Disability Studies. In terms of the whole 'public intellectual' thing, I'm not sure exactly what that means. I write things for the newspapers, and I do radio commentaries. You were asking me about activism. Well, there are a lot of people who do disability activism. That's great, and I support it to a great degree. I don't agree with everything in the party line. I'm for assistance in dying for people who have six months or less to live, and many disability activists in the US don't. But I came to a realization for myself: I grew up in the 1960s, I was part of the strike at Columbia, I was arrested, I went to Washington, I was part of demonstrations, I cut my teeth on the Civil Rights movement. I was 11 or 12 years old, standing on the corner of Bleeker Street and Sixth Avenue in Greenwich Village, collecting money for CORE, the Congress on Relational Equality. So, activism was always part of my life. But at some point I realized that I wasn't that effective standing with a placard in a large group of people yelling. That's not how I can be the most effective. I can be the most effective teaching classes, writing articles, articulating a point of view. In some ways, people might not consider me an activist, I consider myself an activist but it's one of those things: are you really an activist or just an intellectual? I've always felt that the role of the intellectual is crucial. (Said of course had written about that [Said, 1996]). I say all this with a certain amount of guilt and regret, but demonstrations are not the place for me to reach people. I do reach a lot of people through journalism, lectures, radio commentaries, op-ed pieces, and the like. I think that's the kind of activism that's important to me, although not everybody does. And I recognize that.

MS: I want to pick up on this relationship of disability to your personal experience. In your memoir *My Sense of Silence: Memoirs of a Childhood with Deafness* (2000) you write about growing up as a hearing child of deaf parents.[1] It really is such a moving book. You say that because of your parents' deafness you became hypervigilant. And you still are. As a child, you knew that they couldn't hear you calling them, they couldn't hear your screams, they wouldn't come to your aid, you couldn't rely on them to conform you ...

LD: That's true, that's true.

MS: *You*, on the other hand, had to guard *them*. You had to be their ears and listen on their behalf: who would hear the burglar? The ceiling collapsing? Who would warn them? In *My Sense of Silence* you also write that your first 'word' was 'spoken' in sign language. Sign language is of course a most visual language.

LD: It is ...

MS: And, in fact, throughout the book you do a lovely job of conjuring up the ways in which a CODA (Child of Deaf Adults) can show how our normative understandings of the dynamics between the aural, the oral, and the visual break down. Please tell us some more about these dynamics ...

LD: There's a professor named Ben Bahan who teaches Deaf Studies at Gallaudet University and says that deaf people are 'people of the eye' – that they are 'visu-centric'. Deafness is all about a certain kind of visuality. And that's absolutely true. When deaf people talk about being deaf, one of the things they talk about is this frontal, physical one-on-one-ness that has to do with looking. Actually there's a word in sign language that I'll try to explain to you. It's the sign for the word 'Concentrate'. You take your two flat hands, and you put them on the sides of your forehead, and you pull them forward like blinders on a horse. When a deaf person talks to another deaf person – I will imitate this for you – you are just focused on each other. The classic hearing people converse by looking in away from each other and occasionally glance at one another. That's considered polite! [laughs] The only times people stare at each other is out of aggression or sexual interest. Apparently, the only other people that have fixed eye contact with one another are nursing mothers and their children. Deaf people experience each other in a very physically visual way. Because of this, they often feel that hearing people are stand-off-ish.

Growing up as a child of deaf adults, one of the things you have to do is negotiate these two different worlds. It's literally two different worlds of visuality. If you don't do it right, you're misperceived. Hearing people will say there's something wrong with you, you're too in their face, literally. This actually happened today with my cousin who is British. I got up this morning, and I was very frontal and energized with her. And I was talking about how my daughter doesn't like me doing that with her in the morning. And my cousin said that she completely understands that! [laughs] She said it's too much. Yes, there is a kind of intense visuality. There's another thing too. It's a cliché, but still ... it's the idea that if you lose one sense the others become more powerful. Well, the senses are all about gathering information. I was actually thinking about this as I was coming over to talk with you. Here we are, sitting across a table from one another. We may be smelling each other right now, but hopefully we're not too aware of that. But we're certainly looking at each other. I'm looking at you and you're looking at me and we're reading each other's body language. I'm looking at the rings on your fingers, your shirt, I think 'Would I buy that shirt?' [laughs] ... I look at your shaven head, your semi-shaved face. I can see that your smile's a little tense because I'm looking at you ... There's a whole complicated dynamic going on there. I'm just gathering information. Now sound is another form of information that you gather.

If you don't have that, sound, then you really have to put a lot of eggs in the visual basket. Hearing people do that anyway. Analysis of body language has been conducted which suggests that what people are saying in conversation is only thirty per cent of what people are getting (Birdwhistell, 1970). What they're *getting* is all the physical stuff they're *seeing*. If you're blind, you're not getting the input in this way. People rarely think about blindness as an information-gathering problem. They think of it as a tragedy or an absence. But you have other ways of gathering information. When you talk to blind people, they're gathering information all the time. The point is this: if you're deaf you're more attuned to a certain kind of visual stimuli. It's commonplace to say that, but it's true. And then it manifests itself in human interchange.

The other thing is that sign language is a kind of concrete language. The way that sign language works requires that the face *shows* degrees of things – whereas when we speak we let our voices show those degrees. For emphasis, I have to *show* you that on my face. I don't know if you've noticed whether my face is particularly expressive or not. But I know that it's *nowhere near* as expressive as it would be if I were talking to you in sign language. I have learnt to put a pall over my facial features when I'm talking to people who are hearing. My father was always accused of being angry or irrational or whatever, and when he was you'd see it because it would be painted on his face! Like a Turner painting as opposed to a Mondrian painting – you'd see the waves and the wind!

So to be what I am is actually a schizophrenic existence. And the other thing is this: because I occupy a liminal position – as someone who's not deaf and someone who is not hearing (in this sense that I'm not fully culturally hearing – though I can hear – while I was brought up to be culturally Deaf – though I'm not deaf) – I'm always negotiating between these two worlds.[2] My job would be to present the hearing world to my parents and to present my parents to the hearing world. But I wasn't a simple conduit. I was a membrane. I allowed certain things to pass through the membrane, and I did not allow other things to pass. For instance, my father could be outrageous, and I would not let the hearing world see this because I knew that the hearing world would think that he was doing this, that, or the other *because* he was deaf. My father would say: 'Tell them I'm really furious about this or that ...' And I would say: 'My father says that he believes that you shouldn't do that ...' Then, on the other side, I'd hear the hearing world say something like: 'Look, there's that stupid deaf person'. And I'd say to my father: 'He says that you have a nice jacket on'. There is a kind of disingenuousness about all of this: creating a safer space for both worlds. But it's also been a general interpretive problem, and that's how I put it in terms of my academic work. How do you present one world to another world? And, how do you present one world to another world in a strategic way? For example, in terms of Disability Studies, I think that *Enforcing Normalcy* is a book that attempts to portray the world of disability in a very positive light to people who don't understand it, and to show that it's a valuable area of knowledge, and of academic study. Lately, though, what I've been doing, since *Enforcing*

Normalcy, is questioning some of the fixed beliefs or dogmas of disability culture and that's not made me, necessarily, the friend of some people, although of others, perhaps. So, the whole thing is I'm always occupying this liminal position and with the dangers attendant to it.

MS: I was just wanting to ask you something about the consequences of the success of *Enforcing Normalcy*. It's a weird situation to be 'representing' Disability Studies, to speak 'on behalf of' Disability Studies, and that this isn't necessarily something you want to do. (You're well aware of the difficulty of what Gilles Deleuze, in conversation with Michel Foucault, calls 'the indignity of speaking for others' [Deleuze and Foucault, 1977: 209]).

LD: There are a lot of people in Disability Studies who are disabled. Although many are not – and that's an important point to make. Over the years, at various points I've said something like 'Well, I think I've completed my work in Disability Studies' or 'I shouldn't be really doing this ...' Early on I said this and David Mitchell said to me: 'No, your voice is important. We don't want to ghettoize Disability Studies'. I've always appreciated that. But, the fact is, that I'm not a person with disabilities. I am a bi-cultural person who is part-Deaf, but that's about it. As we move into the other side of identity politics, I think it's very important that we're beginning to question, that we're rushing to question the whole idea of identity. Mixed identity becomes really important, and hybrid identities, and a sort of post-post-modernist questioning of the absolute categories of identity is really important. We have to try to understand what is liberating about identity but also what is not. The formation of rigid identities can be very oppressive. So I think my position is a useful one, although of course it's not the only one. But, as I say, I still occupy that liminal position between people with disabilities and people who do not have disabilities – yet.

MS: I'd like to follow on from and reaffirm what you've just been saying by returning to *Enforcing Normalcy*. The question of 'disability' emerges as a discussion around the categorization of words, of language, of how words come to function as categories within language, and only ever in relation to other categories such as the 'normal', the 'normative', 'able-bodiness', and so on. This historicization and deconstruction of 'normalcy' and its dialectics has been terribly important for everyone concerned, and that includes the able-bodied community: the question of disability is not just a question for Disability Studies. Would you outline a schematic diagram of *Enforcing Normalcy* as a project?

LD: I started the research for *Enforcing Normalcy* by simply asking the question: When do we start using the word 'normal'? I did what every academic does, I want to the *Oxford English Dictionary*, and the *OED* surprised me in saying that the word was relatively recent. I had assumed that this had to be a word that was around a long time. But, in fact, you don't find it until the middle of the nineteenth century. It's used earlier, but in somewhat different context. I'll tell you a funny story about this ... Around that time, I went to see the movie *The Madness of King George,* written by Alan Bennett. In the movie, they keep using the word 'normal' in the middle of the eighteenth century! Because I had done my research, I knew that they didn't use the word in that way. So I wrote to Alan Bennett. I just sent him a little annoying, academic letter. He was very lovely, he wrote me back a little postcard with a picture of the town that he was saying in 'I wish I had known that because it would have been a very interesting challenge to write this without using the word "normal"'. The point is that we all assume – and here we get into the question of historicity – the way we're living now is the way everybody always lived. We know they didn't have computers, and so on, but we do *assume* that there are certain universal touchstones: like we know what love is, like we know what it means to be crazy, and so on. Certain obvious things that we know! Yet it turns out, when you start researching these kinds of things, that it isn't universal at all, that you're living in a very particular moment, a cultural moment. One of the early influences on me, on others like me in my generation, was Michel Foucault. I went to his lectures at the College de France in 1972–73 when he was lecturing on what would become *Discipline and Punish* (1975). Foucault teaches us that cultural paradigms emerge, and that it's important to be sensitive to them. I think that my entire life's work has been, in some sense, about studying those cultural paradigms, about how something happens in a culture that arises and changes our way of thinking and seeing; and how this is a discontinuous arising.

So, the insight that the idea of 'normal' was only a moment in history, that for a hundred thousand years there'd been no 'normal' and, suddenly, relatively recently, there was 'normal' made me understand that many things spin off of that idea. From the point of view of visual culture, for instance, our ideas of what the body is. If you say to somebody 'What's a human body?', they say 'Well, its obvious what a human body is'. But, in fact, I think that our sense of shape, form, of the normal body, the abnormal body, the ideal body, are heavily shaped by our cultural developments. My argument in *Enforcing Normalcy* is that before about 1830 culture had a sense more or less of an 'ideal' body, and that that 'ideal' was something unattainable. But, once you develop the idea of statistics and the norm, then the 'normal' body is actually well within reach – although it's of course all caught up with our creation of a desire for the norm. Let's face it, another terms for the 'norm' is just the 'mediocre'. It's the 'ordinary'. It's the 'middle' of the bell curve. We shouldn't desire to be mediocre! So there are certain kinds of strategies that people have used to transform the 'norm' into what I call the 'ideal norm'. You see that everyday on TV, at the gym: people working out to try to attain the 'ideal norm' body.

Our very sense of what we see, in a picture, how we understand a representational painting, the history of the nude, the history of the sculptural nude, is an ongoing development and articulation of *first* the idea of the 'ideal' and *second* the idea of what the body should be and must be. Very few of us actually see – until the Internet really – a huge number of bodies nude. So we have to rely on artists to give us a sense of what the human body looks like! Which is a completely bizarre idea. If artists are telling you what bodies are, then you're instantly in a world of ideology and fantasy. In a weird way, you have to say that our *real* sense of what a body is, is based on that profoundly and deeply ideological fantasy of the body. What, then, if you think about our body, our bodies, in terms of experience: how do you experience your own body? You experience it as a sort of random, complicated set of sensory information, and occasional mirror images that don't' fit together that well – the Lacanian sense of a body as a series of moments or fragments (Lacan, 1977). We need to pull that together into some kind of seamless whole that we can call a body. Ultimately, that is not about the body, but it's about culture, and about the development of cultural ideas, ideals, and norms.

MS: Which takes me seamlessly to my question about identity politics, and this is a question that's also about the politics of representation. We've already touched on some of these things ... I have a little quote from *Enforcing Normalcy*:

> [t]here is a strange and really unaccountable silence when the issue of disability is raised (or, more to the point, never raised); the silence is stranger, too, since so much of left criticism has devoted itself to the issue of the body, of the social construction of sexuality and gender. (Davis, 1995: 5)

This sentiment is also referred to by Michael Bérubé who provides the 'Forward' to your more recent book *Bending Over Backwards: Disability, Dismodernism & Other Difficult Positions* (2002). And he goes on to write:

> ... disability studies did not start to become an important area of study exclusively because of the recent work of Lennard Davis or David Mitchell or Sharon Snyder or Tobin Siebers or Rosamarie Garland Thomson or G. Thomas Couser or Brenda Jo Brueggemann, valuable though all of their work has been; rather, disability studies has started to become an important area of study because the long (and largely unheralded) work of disability activists in the past three decades has finally begun to change American law and culture, making disability more visible and thinkable in the midways of American life, and because disability itself is so important to all our lives, so crucial to any account of human embodiment. (Bérubé, 2002: ix–x)

To Bérubé's list, I'd also add the work of Helen Deutsch and Felicity Nussbaum (2000), Georgina Kleege (1999), David Hevey (1992), David T. Mitchell and Sharon L. Snyder (1997, 2000), Nicholas Mirzoeff (1995), Katherine Ott, David Serlin and Stephen Mihn (2002), David Serlin (2004), and Henri-Jacques Striker (1997). But name-checking isn't the point. The point is to follow up on this final statement from Bérubé: that disability is crucial to any account of human embodiment. I very much agree. In fact, along with these other activists and authors, your work on 'disability' as an unstable historical, political, and cultural 'category' has done much to shift the discussion on disability. And it's not simply that it's been shifted from a marginal discourse to something more mainstream, or that interrogating this category has done much to destabilize more familiar, conventional figurations of the body – although both these things are true. What I'm getting at is more acute: I'm suggesting that the question of 'disability' in Disability Studies has become a way of rethinking the dilemmas of/in the Humanities and Social Sciences. Actually, to expand on Bérubé's statement, I'd make an even bigger claim: that this most recent generation of disability activists and scholars have orchestrated a shift from Disability Studies as a minoritarian discourse *per se*, to a state of affairs in which these discourses of disability are understood to always and already be embedded in paradigms of the Humanities, the Social Sciences, the arts, and studies of visual culture ...

LD: There's a lot in that question! [laughs] OK, so, it's a question about contexts and trajectories. Disability Studies has been around for 20 or 30 years. Long before I started writing about it. I didn't' know about it because it was firmly entrenched in the Social Sciences, and had a very positivistic social science side to it. Therefore it wasn't interesting to me. There I was in the early 1990s, interested in what you might call a Leftist version of post-Marxist postmodernism. So we felt that we were re-inventing Disability Studies *in* and *for* the Humanities. That was the thing that mattered to us. There was a group of us that founded an important committee at the Modern Language Association that looked into Disability Studies. The Committee was made up of David Mitchell, Sharon Snyder, Rosemarie Thomson, Brenda Brueggemann, and Georgina Kleege, and many other people. (Michael Bérubé also eventually came onto the Committee.) The whole idea was to bring the Humanities to Disability Studies, or bring Disability Studies to the Humanities, in order to think about it in a different way. It was about how crucial Disability Studies was to the very nature of the humanistic adventure. In a way, it's like the argument that was made about how gays and lesbians were crucial to understanding what 'gender' was all about. Or, how crucial African-Americans or black people or slavery was to the formation of the United States or American consciousness or our sense of eugenics and race, and so on. It wasn't out of line with thinking at that time, that the 'marginalized' person wasn't marginalized for no reason! They were marginalized specifically to create the sense of the majoritarian position. It's very much like Giorgio Agamben's notion of *homo sacer* (1998). That you need to create a special category of being in order to form the state. A particular Germany forms itself by killing Jews. A particular sense of German nationalism comes from destroying the other. It isn't that that person is 'marginalized' in any sense, it's that that person is *crucial*! In terms of disability, it isn't about nationalism *per se*. It does have elements of nationalism, but it's really about the formation of the modern human subject. The formation of the modern human subject comes from many things, and one of these things is defining a sense of normalcy and defining a sense of abnormality, and putting those definitions into discourse. And this is something you see played out again and again in the history of art and the history of cinema. It's a great way to win an Academy Award. Think Dustin Hoffman in *Rainman* (1988) or Daniel Day Lewis playing Christy Brown in *My Left Foot* (1989) or Gena Rowlands as the grandmother of a disabled child in *The Mighty* (1998) and you can go on. It's a great way of making your career!

Can I say one more thing? It's a point I made in *Enforcing Normalcy*. Disability is largely perceived visually. My definition in the book is that disability is a disturbance in the visual field. That's been controversial. When they criticize the book, that's one thing they criticize. They say: 'What about blind people? What about blind people perceiving the world?' I don't swear by that definition but I think that it's still relatively true in the sense that our visual gathering of information is very important. The point is that when it comes to our visual sensorium, disability is more often than not *perceived* (if not always *experienced*) visually. Hence the disturbance. What's 'wrong' is a limp, what's 'wrong' is seeing people signing, what's 'wrong' is 'blind' eyes, what's 'wrong' is erratic behaviour.

Sensoria: Disability, Biocultures, and the Limits of the Visual

MS: OK, so, to break into the second half of the conversation, and to sum up, what can disability activism, differently-abled practitioners, and Disability Studies teach Visual Culture Studies, and its studies of visual culture? What are the salient lessons that we can draw out from the things you've been saying ...

LD: We always need to keep in the forefront of our brains the idea that – and I've made this point before – when we talk about the body, when we talk about the classical image of nude, the physicality of the image of the human body, we can't do that in a universal or abstract way. We always have to touch base with the historical and cultural basis of representations of 'normality'. And to be aware of that. To be unaware of normality is like being unaware of racism! People are happy to say: 'Racism is bad'. But no one ever calls 'normality' bad! That's our Achilles' heel. 'We' *like* normality. 'We' *like* racism! How do we consume normality? I mean, in other words, we live in a culture of consumption. We consume normality. And by consuming normality, we're consuming the very hegemonic dogma that creates disability. Every time you buy hair gel, or you buy cosmetics, or you go to the gym, or buy low-carb food, and so on, you're contributing, by way of consumption, to an enforcing of normalcy. It's the same, whenever you're dealing with a product in a consumer society that has to do with creating the normal body ... you are essentially creating the disabled body. Every time you look admiringly at a beautiful painting that depicts the human body, you're doing the same thing. Every time you buy that idea, whether you buy it in museums or whether you're buying it in a pharmacy or in the movie theatre, you're voting for investing in putting reinforcing girders around a concept of normality that's oppressive. So, that's the challenge, to try to understand the social formation that creates normality, and therefore creates abnormality, and therefore creates the social conditions that will discriminate against people who are abnormal.

MS: I think it's terribly important to expose this dualism. This idea of 'disability' being always and already embedded in wider discussions of the body, subjectivity, and identity, is something you and I tried to develop in our recent themed issue of *Journal of Visual Culture* entitled 'Disability-Visuality' (Davis, 2006b). The themed issue isn't there as a token gesture, a gesture of goodwill to 'special interest' groups, an acknowledgement that the journal is willing to take on 'minoritarian' discourse. Rather, it's a way of forcing Visual Culture Studies to draw its attention to the fact that 'disability' is a structuring, founding principle within one's thinking about visuality. If we're working within, say, a privileging of the occularcenticism of Western metaphysics, then the matter of blindness is never far away. The very tenets of Visual Culture Studies are all too often implicated in the dualistic thinking you've been outlining.

LD: When conceiving of this themed issue, the fact that we started from this perspective is really crucial. Someone else could have easily made a more minoritarian gesture. In Disability Studies we always talk about people 'getting it'. It's actually a wonderful experience when you teach a course on Disability Studies and you have a group of undergraduates or grad students, and there's always this two-week period when nobody 'gets it'. And then, suddenly, somebody gets it, and then somebody else gets it, somebody else gets, and so on. By the end of the semester, everybody gets it. It's interesting. I'm not religious, but it does have a religious 'awakening' quality to it. Students begin to see that to be alive is to reckon with the concept of disability. Some start out saying, 'I'm not disabled' and then by the end of the semester you learn that they have a sibling or a parent or a grandparent with a disability. It's almost as if the entire class comes out as disabled – at least in the sense of being connected to disability.

In the last 10 or 15 years, within every academic discipline that I know of, Disability Studies has arisen within it as a kind of dawning insight. So yes, Disability Studies would obviously be crucial to any serious notion of what visuality is. But the fact that it hasn't been discussed that widely is testament to the fact that it's part of our political unconsciousness.

MS: I think we did well with that issue of *Journal of Visual Culture*. Of course Disability Studies has long been involved in a critique of visual culture, or rather, a critique of both (1) Western culture's privileging of the ocular *per se*, its occularcenticism, and (2) the ways in which scholarship in the social sciences, humanities, and arts has similarly privileged the field of vision. Here I'm thinking of important writings by the likes of Rosemary Garland-Thomson (1996a, 1996b), David T. Mitchell and Sharon L. Snyder (1997, 2000), Susan Crutchfield and Marcy Epstein (2000), Petra Kuppers (2003), Ann Pointon and Chris Davies (1997), Carrie Sandahl and Philip Auslander (2005), and of course your own writings, in particular *Enforcing Normalcy* (1995), *The Disability Studies Reader* (1997), *My Sense of Silence* (2000), and *Bending over Backwards* (2002). For the themed issue, I think we were trying to do something quite unique, three things simultaneously: to test the temperature of Disability Studies and Visual Culture Studies; to propose that something interesting comes from bringing these areas of study (and their principle interest, 'disability' and 'visuality') into contact with one another; and to show how this productive dialogue might bring about a paradigm shift of sorts.

The issue was a fantastic meeting place, for contributors coming from a diverse range of disciplines and fields of study such as Art History, Communication Studies, Comparative Literature, Disability Studies, Fine Art Practice, Museum Studies, Philosophy, Psychoanalysis, Urban Studies, and Women's Studies. All the contributors did a great job of attending to both the mundane and the extraordinary realities of embodied lives lived on the edge between 'disability' and 'visuality'. And how such experiences and activism are the starting point for a questioning of 'disability' and 'visuality' as it takes place in a multitude of encounters in various settings, such as the museum, the classroom, or the public domain. The contributions also provide us with ways of understanding how we experience and behave when we encounter objects and practices within these spaces, such as films, documentaries, the visual and applied arts, journalism, memorials, and comedy. The articles in that issue of the journal engaged with and questioned numerous points of convergence between visual, tactile, auditory, and material cultures, and in doing so they revealed points where these collisions begin to break down in messy and productive ways.

Most importantly, in addition to beginning a conversation between Disability Studies and Visual Culture Studies, and to generating a dialogue on the points of convergence between disability and visuality, the issue also sought to explore the ways in which 'disability' and 'visuality' so often constitute one another. By this we were referring to the extent to which visuality is both determined by and determining of our understanding of disability. And how disability can bend our existing conceptions of visuality out of shape, thereby gifting us all kinds of new ways of thinking the problems of the visual.

This issue of *Journal of Visual Culture* brings me to your interest in bio-cultures, the inter-disciplinary study of biocultures, or biocultural studies: a concern with the historical, cultural, social, and scientific aspects of the body as they emerge by way of discourses and disciplines of public health, medical education, bioethics, medical sociology, and the history of medicine ... [3]

LD: I worked on Disability Studies since the early 1990s, so it's been about 15 or 16 years. As I already told you, I went from researching deafness to researching disability – to me this seemed a logical outcome. (Although in the United States at any rate, there was tremendous resistance to a shift such as this on the part of Deaf people, to thinking of themselves as disabled. But I think it's changing, and in part because some key people working within Deaf Studies understood that Disability Studies was important.) So for me, the next step was biocultures because I found that although I remain interested in Disability Studies, it felt to me that Disability Studies was part of something else. If you look around, what you see in Women's Studies, in criminal justice, in History, in African-American Studies, Latino Studies, Gay and Lesbian or Queer Studies, Cultural Studies, and so on, is that one of *the* organizing principles is some idea about the body, biology, technology, health some idea about the environment, some idea about the relationship between knowledge and the biosphere.

I thought I'd invented the term, but it turns out that it had already been used by David Morris is his book *Illness and Culture in the Postmodern Age* (2000). (David Morris and I are actually editing a themed issue of *New Literary History* on bioculture (forthcoming 2008). This will be an important literary foray because as an introduction we've written a Biocultures Manifesto – a call to arms, as it were. It is a term whose time has come. It's a way of speaking about the issues that Disability Studies raises, the issues that are raised by a whole range of cultural studies of visual and other cultures, and that those working in the Humanities need to know more about the Sciences. And that people working in the Sciences are having to come to terms with the fact that their theories are incomplete. Some are quite receptive. There's a willingness to explore. The example that I often use to talk about this is the issue of race. There's a lot of biomedical studies of race, there's a lot of material coming out of human genomics about race, but weirdly the scientific work don't really rely on the treasure trove of research that's been done on race in the last 30 years in academia in the Humanities and Social Sciences. One of the great accomplishments of academia in the last 30 years – and maybe there aren't that many – has been the amassing of a *huge* amount of knowledge about race. And, it's as if that knowledge doesn't exist to a scientist.

If, for instance, you look at the work that's been done in geonomics ... they ask people 'What's your race?' Self-reporting is the criteria! And people say 'I'm this' or 'I'm that', and they just enter it as data! We know that the issue of race is a really highly complex cultural and political issue. We know that race doesn't *exist* apart from its social construction. Given this, what kind of science are you doing? In an experiment you have to be careful to avoid feeding bad information into the process. If you're putting in garbage you get out garbage. That's essentially the nature of the research on race. So, we need to talk to each other, we need *a biocultural understanding of knowledge* that will combine the work that we've done in the Humanities on the body and identity, with the very valid work that science can do.

MS: Is the prospect of biocultures going to give us a utopian note on which to end this conversation?

LD: For me, the utopian view is probably openly an academic utopia that can lead to a civic utopia. So, in the first part of the academic utopia there's no longer a Department of English and there's no longer a Department of Neurology. There's a Department of Englo-Neurology, and there's a Department of Bio-Art History, and so on. On a first hearing it sounds funny, but on a second hearing it sounds totally what you want! I think one of the great tragedies of our culture is that in the 18th and 19th centuries the Humanities and the Sciences split. We decided that there were two branches of knowledge. That did us some real harm. The Humanities got the values, morals, and ethics. The Sciences got the facts. The former is supposedly 'soft' while the latter is 'hard'. One doesn't need to parse that metaphor very far before you see that it's based on gendered stereotypes. Men do science, feminized men and women do literature and the arts. We forgot that if you divide truth you get half truths or two truths. I don't think there's anything magical about it. I think that knowledge is a complicated thing and I think that ultimately – and I'm going to give you one of those big statements that are kind of meaningless – Science lacks humility. Not scientists, but Science. There's a sense that there's absolute knowledge, and after the postmodern interrogation of history and knowledge that's taken place during the last few decades, we should all know that things are more complicated than that. It doesn't mean that there's a kind of truth, and it doesn't mean that there aren't things you can stand for, and fight for. But it means that we have to understand the limitations of what it means to be human, and what knowledge is fundamentally about, which isn't creating monuments out of granite but making flesh-like pictures in the air, which is one way of thinking of sign language.

MS: That's lovely, a very nice way to end. Thank you.

Notes

1 Davis (1999) has also edited his parents' correspondence and wrote about their lives in *Shall I Say a Kiss?: Courtship Letters of a Deaf Couple*. Gallaudet University Press.

2 I'm using the convention of 'Deaf' to mean being part of a cultural/linguistic group while 'deaf' means the simple biological fact of hearing loss. So Marlee Maitlan is Deaf but

your grandmother who wears a hearing aid and who became hearing impaired at 65 is 'deaf'.

3 Lennard Davis is the founder of Project Biocultures. See http://www.biocultures.org/index2.php.

References

Agamben, Giorgio (1998) *Homo Sacer: Sovereign Power and Bare Life* (Daniel Heller Roazen, *trans.*). Stanford, CA: Stanford University Press.

Bérubé, Michael (2002) 'Forward: Side Shows and Back Bends' in Lennard J. Davis, *Bending Over Backwards: Disability, Dismodernism & Other Difficult Positions*. New York: New York University Press.

Birdwhistell, R. (1970) *Kinesics in Context*. Philadelphia: University of Pennsylvania Press.

Crutchfield, Susan, and Epstein, Marcy Joy (eds.) (2000) *Points of Contact: Disability, Art and Culture*. Ann Arbor: University of Michigan Press.

Davis, Lennard J. (1995) *Enforcing Normalcy: Disability, Deafness and the Body*. London: Verso.

Davis, Lennard J. (1997) *The Disabilities Studies Reader*. New York: Routledge.

Davis, Lennard J. (1999) *Shall I Say a Kiss?: Courtship Letters of a Deaf Couple*. Gallaudet: University Press.

Davis, Lennard J. (2000) *My Sense of Silence: Memoirs of a Childhood with Deafness*. Urbana: University of Illinois Press.

Davis, Lennard J. (2002) *Bending Over Backwards: Disability, Dismodernism & Other Difficult Positions*. New York: New York University Press.

Davis, Lennard J. (2005a) 'Why "Million Dollar Baby" infuriates the disabled', *Chicago Tribune*, February 2.

Davis, Lennard J. (2005b) Commentary, 'What Defines Disabled?' 'All Things Considered', National Public Radio, http://www.npr.org/templates/story/story.php?storyId=4581539

Davis, Lennard J (2005c) Radio Interview, 'Morning Edition', National Public Radio, February 18, http://www.npr.org/templates/story/story.php?storyId=4504009

Davis, Lennard J. (2005d) 'Why Disability Studies Matters?' *Inside Higher Education* February 21, http://www.insidehighered.com/views/why_disability_studies_matters

Davis, Lennard J. (2005e) 'Feints, Jabs, Low Blows, Roundhouses and the Gentle Art of Counterpunch: Art's Power Comes with Responsibility', *Chicago Tribune*, March 6.

Davis, Lennard J. (2005f) 'An end to it all; The issues raised by the Terri Schiavo case linger and are as complicated as life itself; Medical facts are cast aside', *Chicago Tribune*, March 27.

Davis, Lennard J. Writer/producer (2005g) 'Go Ask Your Father' episode of 'This American Life', May 13, http://www.this.life.org

Davis, Lennard J. (2005h) Commentary, 'Physician-Assisted Suicide: All Things Considered', National Public Radio, September 27, http://www.npr.org/templates/story/story.php?storyId=4866181

Davis, Lennard J. (2005i) 'Penguins: A Poor Case for Intelligent Design, Family Values', *Chicago Tribune*, November 6.

Davis, Lennard J. (2005j) 'The Right to Die and Disability Rights: An Interview with Lennard Davis' in *The Ragged Edge*. www.raggededgemagazine.com

Davis, Lennard J. (2006a) 'Life, Death and Biocultural Literacy', *Chronicle of Higher Education*, January 6.
Davis, Lennard J. and Smith, Marquard (eds.) (2006b) 'Disability-Visuality', *Journal of Visual Culture*, 5 (2): complete issue.
Davis, Lennard J. (2007) 'Deafness and the Riddle of Identity', *Chronicle of Higher Education*, January 7.
Davis, Lennard J. (n.d.) Project Biocultures, http://www.biocultures.org/index2.php
Deutsch, Helen, and Nussbaum, Felicity (eds.) (2000) *'Defects': Engendering the Modern Body*. Ann Arbor: The University of Michigan Press.
Deleuze, Gilles and Foucault, Michel (1977) 'Intellectuals and Power', in Donald Bouchard (ed.) (Donald Bouchard and Sherry Simon, *trans.*), *Language, Counter-Memory, Practice*. Ithaca: Cornell University Press, pp. 205–17.
Foucault, Michel (1975) *Discipline and Punish: The Birth of the Prison*. New York: Random House.
Garland-Thomson, Rosemary (1996a) *Extraordinary Bodies: Figuring Physical Disability in American Culture and Literature*. New York: Columbia University Press.
Garland-Thomson, Rosemary (1996b) *Freakery: Cultural Spectacles of the Extraordinary Body*. New York: New York University Press.
Gramsci, Antonio (1971 [1941]) 'The Intellectuals', *Selections from the Prison Notebooks* (Q. Hoare and G.N. Smith, *trans.* and ed.). New York: International Publishers.
Hevey, David (1992) *The Creatures Time Forgot: Photography and Disability Imagery*. London: Routledge.
Kleege, Georgina (1999) *Sight Unseen*. New Haven, CT: Yale University Press.
Kuppers, Petra (2003) *Disability and Contemporary Performance: Bodies on Edge*. New York: Routledge.
Lacan, Jacques (1977) 'The mirror stage as formative of the function of the I as revealed in psychoanalytic experience', *Ecrits: A Selection*. New York: Norton.
Mirzoeff, Nicholas (1995) *Silent Poetry: Deafness, Sign, and Visual Culture in Modern France*. Princeton, NJ: Princeton University Press.
Mitchell, David T. and Snyder, Sharon L. (eds.) (1997) *The Body and Physical Difference: Discourses of Disability*. Ann Arbor: The University of Michigan Press.
Mitchell, David T. and Snyder Sharon L. (2000) *Narrative Prosthesis: Disability and the Dependences of Discourse*. Ann Arbor: The University of Michigan Press.
Morris, David (2000) *Illness and Culture in the Postmodern Age*. Berkeley, CA: University of California Press.
Ott, Katherine, David Serlin and Mihn Stephen (eds.) (2002) *Artificial Parts, Practical Lives: Modern Histories of Prosthetics*. New York: New York University Press.
Pointon, Ann and Davies, Chris (eds.) (1997) *Framed: Interrogating Disability in the Media*. London: British Film Institute.
Said, Edward (1996) *Representations of Intellectuals*. New York: Vintage.
Sandahl, Carrie and Auslander, Philip (eds.) (2005) *Bodies in Commotion: Disability* and *Performance*. Ann Arbor: University of Michigan Press.
Serlin, David (2004) *Replaceable You: Engineering the Body in Postwar America*. Chicago: Chicago University Press.
Striker, Henri-Jacques (1997) *A History of Disability*. (W Sayers, *trans.*). Ann Arbor: University of Michigan Press.

6

NAMING, NETWORKS, AND SCIENTIFIC REGIMES OF VISION

Interview with Lisa Cartwright

Introduction

Lisa Cartwright is Professor of Communication and Science Studies in the Department of Communication Studies at University of California, San Diego. She is author of *Screening the Body: Tracing Medicine's Visual Culture* (1995) the co-author of *Practices of Looking: An Introduction to Visual Culture* (2001), co-editor of *The Visible Woman* (1998), and author of two forthcoming single-authored books, *Moral Spectatorship* (2008) and *Images of Waiting Children: The Visual Culture of Transnational Adoption* (2008). In this interview Cartwright speaks about the links in the US academic context between Visual Studies, Film Studies, and Cultural Studies, and the challenges for emerging fields of inquiry and inter-disciplinary programmes of institutional legitimation in such environments. She also explores issues raised by her recent and ongoing research in the Medical Humanities and on media culture, considering the global network of mediated and re-mediated visual culture, and our need to be attentive in that context to the phenomenological experience of the body *as* body.

Ways of Looking, Naming, and Knowing

Marquard Smith (MS): You were an early member of the graduate programme in Visual and Cultural Studies at University of Rochester in upstate New York – and also for a while its Director. Tell me about the spirit in which this innovative programme came into being ...

Lisa Cartwright (LC): The PhD Programme in Visual and Cultural Studies at Rochester was founded as a programme in Comparative Studies in the late 1980s by an inter-disciplinary group of people: Kaja Silverman and Constance Penley, who were appointed in the Department of English; Craig Owens, Mieke Bal, Norman Bryson, and Michael Ann Holly in Art History; and Sharon Willis in

Comparative Literature. This constituency resulted in a balance between Film Studies and art history, with three or four founding members in each field. I joined the English faculty a year or two later, just after Norman left Rochester for another job and Craig died. My appointment was made primarily to serve the undergraduate Film Studies and English majors and to participate in both the comparative studies and English graduate programmes. A year after I joined the faculty, Constance and Kaja left Rochester for the University of California system, followed by Mieke, who left for Amsterdam but continued to be affiliated, returning on a regular basis to teach seminars and advise PhD students. Her and Norman's influence continued to be strong through the work of students like Lev Manovich who had studied with them before the changing of the guard and the official shift in nomenclature to visual studies.

Janet Wolff (who went on to become Dean at Columbia, and is now Professor of Performance, Screen, and Visual Cultures at The University of Manchester in England) and David Rodowick (who came to King's College, University of London to set up a programme in Film Studies before moving on to the Department of Visual and Environmental Studies at Harvard University) joined the Rochester faculty in the early 1990s, and with them came the official nomenclature shift to visual and cultural studies. With David, we recouped some of what we lost in the departures of Kaja and Constance. David had just published the *Difficulty of Difference* with Routledge, his analysis of feminist psychoanalytic film theory, and was beginning his work on Deleuze for Duke, a press that, under Ken Wissoker's direction, would go on to publish many of the faculty and former students of the programme (Rodowick, 1991, 1997). Rodowick's two books reflected approaches that would become major influences on the students in residence. Psychoanalytic feminism continued to be reworked by some of us including Sharon Willis (as reflected in *High Contrast* (1997), a psychoanalytic theory and criticism book on race and cinema), and myself in my new book with Duke, *Moral Spectatorship* (2008), which is a rethinking of turns not taken in late twentieth-century psychoanalytic theory. During David's time at Rochester, Laura Marks drew on Deleuze in her dissertation on third cinema and the skin of the film, which became an outstanding book with Duke that broke new ground in the not-yet-burgeoning subfield of Deleuzian film studies that David had helped to forge (Marks, 1999).

With Janet, we gained a crucial link to the Birmingham school of cultural studies, and to the social sciences. This was perhaps the most distinctive aspect of the programme in comparing it to graduate programmes offering visual culture emphases during this period (Cornell, for example). Many of the original and new members of the Rochester core faculty group had expertize in Cultural Studies, but none before Janet had direct training and experience with Stuart Hall and in the British model, and none of us had trained, as Janet had, in sociology. These two aspects of her training made for some crucial shifts in the programme. For one, we included in our core group of faculty members from education (Warren Crichlow) and anthropology (Robert Foster) who were working within cultural studies frameworks. This made it possible for graduate students to pursue a kind of supervised fieldwork that would not have been as knowledgably guided by those of us trained in humanities research approaches. For example, Brian Goldfarb's fieldwork in classrooms and museums which grounded the dissertation that became his book with Duke, *Visual Pedagogy*, was strongly shaped by the methodologies and theories that Janet and Warren introduced (Goldfarb, 2002).

MS: This leads me nicely to the whole question of naming: to the discipline or sub-discipline or field of inquiry or movement variously known as Visual Culture Studies or Visual Studies or Visual Culture. (For me, it's Visual Culture Studies for reasons I've outlined elsewhere.) The question of naming has been and still continues to be so pressing as part of the process of intellectual and institutional legitimation, in light of the knock-on effects it has on the kinds of research we do, and so on. On this matter, let me quote from an article you published in the first issue of *Journal of Visual Culture* back in 2002. There you write:

> The stakes in naming [a discipline or field of inquiry] are high when the objects, methods, or orientations of one's work may not be accommodated within the boundaries of the departmental home's title. Disciplinary naming gives shape to research agendas, canons, and how we enter into intellectual politics, determining our potential to carry on research in certain methodologies and not others, and with certain objects of study and not others. (2002: 10)

Do you still feel that the stakes in naming are as high, and play themselves out in the same ways, or do you believe that things have changed in the last few years, and if so how?

LC: The stakes in naming remain high, especially around the use of the term culture or cultural. My comment that you recall above sounds critical of what gets excluded in naming. I want to emphasize here instead that what got included in naming the Rochester Program Visual and Cultural Studies made possible the continuation, or at least the continued designation, of some research agendas that came under fire and were eliminated at other institutions in the years since I wrote that comment. I am thinking of the dissolution of the Birmingham cultural studies programme in particular, and the general disparagement of cultural studies in the United States by the late 1990s.

A little background is in order. When Janet joined the Rochester faculty and became director of the comparative studies programme in the early 1990s, it was decided that it was time for a change in name. The programme name Comparative Studies wrongly suggested students were engaged in comparing texts or comparing media forms and the respective approaches to analysis attached to them across the disciplines. That is when the programme officially became Visual and Cultural Studies. Whether and how to include the terms culture and cultural was a central discussion point among the core faculty. This was before the big controversies about the terms and the cultural studies field. The decision was to go not only with 'cultural' but also to insert the word 'and' between the two terms, rather than describing the programme as 'Visual Culture Studies'. This left things open for types of cultural studies work not explicitly or primarily about the visual, while also leaving room for work in visual studies but not cultural studies. This decision was a practical one that would become more meaningful over time, for example with the backlash against cultural studies in the US and Britain that came well after this decision, and with the formation of the Visual Studies PhD Programme at Irvine, which never included the term cultural in its title. Personally I felt somewhat proud to have the term cultural in my academic title with these later developments. Regarding the backlash against cultural studies, well, although my own work was never grounded most centrally in American cultural studies paradigms (for instance, I don't work on the popular or the mainstream media), I remain strongly committed to that field. Marita Sturken and I give it extended coverage in our *Practices of Looking: An Introduction to Visual Culture* (2001). Throughout the late 1990s and early 2000s I was repeatedly surprised and bemused by colleagues around the country who affiliated with the field by publishing in its journals and adopting its approaches, but then bailed on cultural studies as soon as the field became the object of criticism.

MS: What effect do you think the subsequent institutionalization of Visual Culture Studies has had on the kinds of initiatives, scholarly projects, and research practices that take place under its auspices, and that are carried out in its name ... the kind of projects to which you have been referring?

LC: Visual culture studies has had different lives in different field contexts. Art history was a foundational home and remains a strong base for it. Many of the graduates of the Rochester PhD Program found (and continue to find) jobs in art history. Others went (and go) to film studies, where visual studies is also recognized as an area of expertize. The University of Toronto started a Centre for Visual and Media Culture under the direction of photo historian Louis Kaplan. This is a fabulous, well-organized centre that supports undergraduate degree programmes in Visual Culture and Communication, Art and Art history, and Fine Art History, served by an outstanding faculty and a new facility at the suburban Mississauga campus. Art history remains the most active supporter of visual studies, I think, with film and media studies and communication departments also playing a role in explicit support of the field. In 2002 I joined the faculty of the Department of Communication at the University of California at San Diego. Although we have a high percentage of humanities-trained faculty, we are a social science department. I work closely with social scientist colleagues and students on a regular basis. At the same time, UCSD's Visual Art Department has a strong profile in visual studies, having hired both Lev Manovich and Grant Kester out of Rochester in the late 1990s. Both are now senior faculty members with high profiles in art history and beyond. Also in art history, Nick Mirzoeff tried very hard to get a visual studies programme off the ground at the State University of New York at Stony Brook and then joined the art faculty at New York University's Steinhardt School of Education, where Marita Sturken is also appointed – in Communication. The picture that unfolds in both of these cases, UC and SUNY, is that founding people in Visual Culture Studies exist in art history and communication departments but the institutions don't have what it took at Rochester and Irvine to make an inter-disciplinary programme get off the ground, at least not yet. The key elements at both Rochester and Irvine were a relatively small-scale, informal inter-disciplinary research networks, and departmental placement within the same school and under the same dean. At San Diego, visual art and communication are in different schools and under different deans, in addition to being physically far apart.

But I think the main innovation in the field comes in programmes that offer media practice as a component of visual culture study.

MS: These questions of naming, of institutionalization, of legitimation, of visibility, are of course issues that crops up again and again in/for the associations and societies 'representing' research and scholarship in and across the Arts, Humanities, and Social Sciences. Without doubt, Visual Culture Studies and scholars of visual culture have made inroads into these associations. The College Art Association (CAA), for instance, has a Visual Culture caucus. There are always half a dozen sessions with 'visual culture' in the title at the annual conference of the Modern Language Association (MLA), as there is at the biennial conference of the Association for Cultural Studies (ACS). Likewise, there's usually one or two presentations at the annual conference of the Association of Art Historians (AAH) with titles such as the 'The visual culture of violence in medieval manuscripts' or 'The queering of London's visual culture in the 1950s'.

Overall, though, it's my impression that Visual Culture Studies is perhaps most welcomed, most visible, and sits most comfortably – as do scholars of visual culture (although not numerically necessarily) – at the Society for Cinema and Media Studies (SCMS). You have spent many years contributing to the SCMS in various capacities, do you also get the sense that this is the case, and if so why?

LC: I think that art history continues to provide the most visible base for visual studies, and it probably remains a comfortable base for those who got their degrees and taught in that field (Mirzoeff, Holly, for example). The field's basic commitment to visual art and artifact makes it a natural for the study of anything visual, obviously. But the Society for Cinema and Media Studies continues to support the kind of visual studies theories and methods that constitute the field for scholars like myself whose focus is not fine arts primarily. SCMS has been great about recognizing the theory and method-specific aspects of visual studies. To be clear, for me visual studies is not simply a term we should use every time we write about a picture or acts of looking. What constitutes a field, crucially, is theory and method, not object of study. SCMS, like the College Art Association, includes a diverse range of professionals who work in a diverse range of methods and theories. SCMS remains explicitly committed to the kinds of non-empirical critical methods and theories that are fundamental to visual studies. For this reason, I see it as a more specialized professional association than CAA or MLA, which have far larger constituencies. Empirical work in film and media is more broadly supported by other associations including the International Communication Association (ICA), where you nonetheless find panels devoted to visual culture.

I have divided my time among the Society for Cinema and Media Studies, where Lev Manovich and I were on the plenary that introduced the 'and media studies' to the official title and the Society for the Social Studies of Science and a couple of other science studies associations. In the end, I feel most at home in SCMS and will probably invest more of my energy there in coming years. This is because I find myself continuing to be aligned with its philosophy and mission with regard to studying visuality and visual culture as their views and mine change over time.

MS: Following on from these thoughts about the SCMS, it's well worth pointing out early-ish in this conversation that your research and writing interests are decidedly *not* art historical. You're a scholar who comes to Visual Culture Studies, who comes at studies of visual culture, from a position that's decidedly 'not' that of an art historian. Perhaps this just has to do with the subjects and objects that interest you, with your education, your time at Rochester, and any number of other factors. Whatever the explanation, I mention this for two reasons specifically. The first is, as you've just been saying, that so many of the scholars responsible for shaping the emergence of Visual Culture Studies are art historians or scholars who have worked with, through, and against Art History – and here I'm thinking of for instance Sveltana Alpers, Michael Baxendall, Norman Bryson, Douglas Crimp, Hal Foster, Michael Ann Holly, Nick Mirzoeff, Keith Moxey, and Griselda Pollock. Or they are scholars of lit crit or critical studies that have long-term intellectual and institutional connections with the concerns of Art History such as Mieke Bal and Tom Mitchell. Art History is a customary stepping-stone – often also a whipping boy – to Visual Culture Studies. The second reason I mention this is because your important and influential book *Practices of Looking: An Introduction to Visual Culture* (co-authored with Marita Sturken [2001]) is so decidedly 'not' a book of Art History, even of Art History in an expanded field.

After that long preamble, I'm not really wanting to ask you a question about your relationship to the discipline of Art History or to visual arts practice. I want to know what it means for you to be contributing to, highlighting, alternative genealogies of Visual Culture Studies' emergence that come directly out of, say, Sociology, Communication Studies, and Cultural Studies ...

LC: Increasingly, I find myself more at home talking to producers of art and media. My background was in art and film production (I attended the Whitney Program and NYU film school for my undergrad education) and I have never lost my sense of seeing the world through frameworks offered by modern and contemporary artists. For example, increasingly in teaching undergraduates in a social sciences communication programme I find myself turning to projects like Komar and Melamid's 'World's Most (and least) Famous Paintings' series to explain phenomena such as globalization, or Catherine Opie's photography to teach gender. But I have no desire to work within art historical paradigms. Rather, I prefer to emphasize the ways in which these works are produced in dialogs with contexts outside the art world, through organizing concepts such as domestic taste or self-fashioning, and body image. I think this approach is fairly typical among those of us trained in cultural studies.

My place in a science studies programme and my work in that field allows me to engage with people interested in the place of visual culture there. Jackie Stacey's new book in production with Duke on genetics and cinema entitled *The Cinematic Life of the Gene* (forthcoming) is an example of this conversation as it has extended from art history (from work by the likes of Barbara Maria Stafford [1991; 1996]) into the film studies realm where feminist theory continues to thrive. Particularly interesting right now is the work of the German media theorist Marie-Luise Angerer on affect theory and cinema and Vivian Sobchack's new work in *Carnal Thoughts* (2004) on embodiment. Both scholars work through film to media theory, introducing new ideas about embodiment and experience, but moving away from the older emphasis on the body as an entity captured in representation and towards theories that account for experience and sensation without stripping away culture and ideology as entities of concern.

Convergences, the Medical Humanities, and Our Global Media Culture

MS: Your own research and writing projects cut across and between Visual Culture Studies, Film Studies, Communication Studies, and the history of science, technology, and medicine, as well as Feminist and Critical Gender Studies. In so doing, you're often captivated by the convergences between the objects, subjects, media, and environments of these fields of inquiry – and the realization that these things are always already and inevitably caught up in one another's concerns. Will you tell me more about the significance of 'convergences' for Visual Culture Studies, and of how Visual Culture Studies is ideally placed (if you consider this to be so) to deal with such 'convergences'.

LC: I think this question brings me back to the thought that visual culture as a field allows us to shift away from the focus on the object, the object made to be seen, and on the classes of things made to be seen. Instead we can consider the sensory and cultural experiences of looking in its contexts of other sensory experiences, other cultural practices. It may seem that we have taken our focus on the visual too far, with all our books and essays and curricula organized around media, the arts, visual things. But in fact I think we have not gone far enough with what it means to see in the context of cultural practices of looking. For example, we have barely begun to consider the implications of sensory ability in the increasingly visual contexts like internet communication, and news media. How do people who are visually impaired access, for instance, the increasingly visually complex pages of the web? What happens when the images on these pages are captioned – how does that translation constitute a kind of interpretive change? Explaining the relationship between image and caption as one of simple description fails to capture the interesting question of how visual knowledge and experience change when 'translated' into other representational and sensory forms. There is much work to be done on looking relative to the senses and ability. I wonder if this is a thought that you and Joanne Morra had in producing *The Prosthetic Impulse* (Smith and Morra, 2006). Here a 'visual' theorist like Vivian Sobchack goes directly to the point in discussing her prosthetic leg in a way that immediately brings the visual into a convergence with touch and feel.

MS: Thanks, yes, that's very much the kind of thing we were trying to do in that book. And I think in your contribution to that collection you were similarly attentive to the phenomenological *experience* of the body *as* body in your contribution to that collection. Which takes me nicely to your first book *Screening the Body: Tracing Medicine's Visual Culture* (1995) which is a perfect instance of this. Here you engage with film archives, obscure film objects (early scientific medical films), the conditions of their production and circulation, and scientific and medical techniques and technologies of vision. You write about the X-ray, radiography, ultrasound, recording instruments, virtual endoscopy, microscopic anatomy, and a series of ways of looking, seeing, and knowing that come out of these techniques and technologies: the medical gaze, physiological viewing, the microscopic gaze, and the gynaecological gaze. How the body is figured and refigured through and by way of technologies. (And this is something you return to in your co-edited collection on the Visible Human Project (Cartwright, 1997; Cartwright *et al.*, 1997).) Why give such importance to these ways of seeing, as well as (as you've done in some of your more recent writing) to the kinds of research that contemporary computer scientists and programmers are conducting into developing new modalities of perception and cognition?

LC: These ways of seeing become increasingly important as these modalities of representing the body become more pervasive in everyday medical practice. The issue that concerns me most is objectivity. There continues to be a drive towards objective representation in medical practice. In relationship to the visual, this concerns me because representational objectivity is a kind of holy grail. An example of this: the drive to image brain structures and processes in hopes of finding hard evidence of the location of pathology, certain modes of cognition, and so forth. There is a sense that if we can see difference, we can know the location or source of a condition, or a state of being. I am very wary of this trajectory of thought. It isn't a matter of mistrusting representation. Rather, it is a matter of believing that to see is to know, and that apparent, empirical differences in structure are always meaningful.

MS: So, in a sense, your concerns are with visuality, opticality, and virtuality, in how scientific and medical techniques and technologies of looking, seeing, perceiving, and cognition come to define, delineate, and circumscribe the conditions of possibility for our understanding of things such as the body, our reproductive systems, our invisible materialities, our carnality even? From the surface of our skin as the most visible contested topography of 'the human' to our DNA as the most invisible battleground on which to wage a campaign for the future of the human ...

LC: Yes.

MS: As an aside, in re-reading your work in preparation for this interview, I spotted that across your oeuvre – from discussions of the cinematic and televisual apparatus, to the disciplining of the body in the grip of the scientific and medical gaze, to the matter of the 'morality' of spectatorship – you return again and again to the problem of space: whether it's the space of the cinema, or the lab, or the waiting room. You're acutely attentive to the space or location or stage where historical, social, and experiential encounters take place. I know that Spatial Culture Studies doesn't exactly roll off the tongue, but ...

LC: Anne Friedberg's book on the gaze has been for a long time now a central work of visual culture theory that addresses questions of space (Friedberg, 1994). The recent work on spacial culture that I find most compelling is about mobility and access (Friedberg, 2006). How do people with motor or sensory differences negotiate the built environment? David Serlin (2006), one among a number of scholars who work across visual culture and disability studies, is beginning to address questions like this, in his case with reference to architecture and/for the blind. I was delighted by a piece in Rosemarie Garland Thomson's *Freakery* anthology by David Yuan (1996). This piece touches on walking and falling down, the negotiation of space relative to the coordination of motor and sight which we take for granted. For a year or so I stumbled and fell quite a bit, and then my ability to turn my head was limited for about a year after that due to a surgery from which I am now rehabilitated. Walking required concerted attention to looking. My field of vision was limited to what my body squarely faced. As my perception of and access to the spaces I inhabited changed on the basis of this new point of view, so my sense of the relationship between sight and spacial negotiation changed as well. Because of this I am very interested in the connection between visual perception and space, though there is little work on it in visual studies.

MS: Going back to this topic of invisibility and immateriality – although maybe in a funny kind of way it's also a matter of space – I have a question about the virtual and the global. I'm interested to hear how you conceive of our visual and material (and immaterial) global media culture? That's to say, in attuning ourselves to and engaging with the past, present, and future of our global media culture – from our networked economy to political activism to new-fangled sense of ourselves – how are we to come to grips with it?

LC: In *Images of Waiting Children*, one of my two books coming out with Duke [University Press] this year, I am concerned with global visual culture in the circulation of children through transnational adoption networks. It is one thing to talk about circulation of goods and people, quite another to talk about circulation of children in a sanctioned marketplace. Children constitute a unique example. The market in children makes us confront the liberal humanitarian impulse to work on behalf of others in crisis while throwing into relief the problem of the creation of markets set up to transfer the management and control of children not only from family to family but across nations, across language groups, across cultures. The psychic trauma this produces in the rapid change the child experiences is a limit case for understanding globalization for adult subjects as well.

MS: That's an interesting response, and far more important than the more frivolous things I had in mind, such as the kinds of debates going on around Web 2:0 communities: what are we to make of participatory environments such as YouTube and MySpace, as well as blogs, wikis, podcasting, and so on? Have we entered a brave new democratic world, or are we simply being bombarded by a series of new marketing buzzwords and business opportunities? With this user-generated content, what happens to debates of policing and surveillance? Quality control? To the future of activism itself, and online or electronic activism in particular? (I must admit, I do check out clips on YouTube and MySpace regularly. One of my favourite pastimes at the moment is watching footage of Silent Discos – it's fascinating and hilarious to watch the sights and listen to the sounds of hundreds of people with headphones on dancing in open air venues or clubs in Riga or Lisbon, and there's even footage of a flash mob silent disco in the forecourt of Liverpool Street station in London during rush hour!) My question, then, is whether Visual Culture Studies is well placed to take on the challenge of delineating, making sense of, critiquing even, this global network of mediated and re-mediated visual culture? As it engages with cultural practices, can it, for instance, effectively harness the expertize of or think by way of Media Studies, Information Technology, Computer Studies, and so on?

LC: It makes sense to talk across fields. Some criticize visual studies for losing sight of the specificity of media forms and practices and what is produced in each. I think it is crucial to recognize the convergence of media forms and the ideological formations, to use an old term, that cut across forms and structure the way each media form is variously used.

MS: Of course, there's always going to be a utopian and a dystopian 'take' on this ...

LC: My take is pretty much on the side of utopia in the sense that I think we have moved beyond cultural critique to recognize the transformative nature of critical practice towards new modes of media production and use including everyday technologies like cell phone cameras but also medical imaging modalities like ultrasound, MR imaging, and PET scans. If there is going to be one thing that visual culture study can do that will transform the use of academic work, that is in the convergence of criticism and media practice. I took to heart the training provided in the Whitney Program of the 1980s where artists were taught semiotics, Marxism, and psychoanalysis as a means of informing their practices. Ron Clark and Yvonne Rainer were dead on right in that approach. Their pedagogical philosophy of spanning the theory/practice divide in artworks that made critical commentary set the stage perfectly for the convergence of criticism and media practice in the work of digital artists from different generations of critically informed producers such as Ian Bogost, Lev Manovich, and Natalie Jeremijenko.

References

Cartwright, Lisa (1995) *Screening the Body: Tracing Medicine's Visual Culture*, New York: Routledge.

Cartwright, Lisa (1997) 'The Visible Man: the male criminal subject as biomedical norm', in Jennifer Terry and Melodie Calvert (eds.) *Gender and Technology in Everyday Life*, London: Routledge, pp. 123–37.

Cartwright, Lisa (2002) 'Film and the digital in visual studies: film studies in the era of convergence', *Journal of Visual Culture,* 1/1(7-23): 10.

Cartwright, Lisa (2008) *Moral Spectatorship: Technologies of Voice and Affect in Postwar Representations of the Child.* Durham, NC: Duke University Press.

Cartwright, Lisa (2008) *Images of Waiting Children: The Visual Culture of Transitional Adoption.* Durham: Duke University Press.

Cartwright, Lisa and Sturken, Marita (2001) *Practices of Looking: An Introduction to Visual Culture,* Oxford: Oxford University Press.

Cartwright, Lisa, Penley, Constance, and Treichler, Paula A. (eds.) (1998) *The Visible Woman: Imaging Technologies, Gender and Science,* New York: New York University Press.

Friedberg, Anne (1994) *Window Shopping: Cinema and the Postmodern,* Berkeley: University of California Press.

Friedberg, Anne (2006) *The Virtual Window: From Alberti to Microsoft,* Cambridge: The MIT Press.

Goldfarb, Brian (2002) *Visual Pedagogy: Media Cultures in and Beyond the Classroom.* Durham, NC: Duke University Press.

Marks, Laura (1999) *The Skin of the Film: Intercultural Cinema, Embodiment, and the Senses.* Durham, NC: Duke University Press.

Rodowick, David N. (1991) *The Difficulty of Difference: Psychoanalysis, Sexual Difference and Film Theory.* New York: Routledge.

Rodowick, David N. (1997) *Deleuze's Time Machine.* Durham, NC: Duke University Press.

Serlin, David (2006) '*Disabling the* Flâneur', *Journal of Visual Culture,* 5(2): 131–46.

Smith, Marquard and Morra, Joanne (2006) *The Prosthetic Impulse: From a Posthuman Present to a Biocultural Future.* Cambridge, MA: The MIT Press.

Stacey, Jackie (forthcoming) *The Cinematic Life of the Gene.* Durham, NC: Duke University Press.

Stafford, Barbara Maria (1991) *Body Criticism: Imaging the Unseen in Enlightenment Art and Science.* Cambridge: The MIT Press.

Stafford, Barbara Maria (1996) *Artful Science: Entertainment and the Eclipse of Visual Education.* Cambridge, MA: The MIT Press.

Sobchack, Vivian (2004) *Carnal Thoughts: Embodiment and Moving Image Culture.* Berkeley, CA: The University of California Press.

Willis, Sharon (1997) *High Contrast: Race and Gender in Contemporary Hollywood Films.* Durham, NC: Duke University Press.

Yuan, David D. (1996) 'The Celebrity Freak: Michael Jackson's "Grotesque Glory"', in Rosemarie Garland-Thomson (ed.) *Freakery: Cultural Spectacles of the Extraordinary Body,* New York: New York University Press, pp. 368–84.

7

PHENOMENOLOGY, MASS MEDIA, AND BEING-IN-THE-WORLD

Interview with Vivian Sobchack

Introduction

Vivian Sobchack is Professor Emeritus of Critical Studies in the Department of Film and Television at University of California, Los Angeles. She was the first woman elected President of the Society for Cinema and Media Studies, and is on the Board of Directors of the American Film Institute. Her books include *Screening Space: The American Science Fiction Film* (1980 [1997]), *The Address of the Eye: A Phenomenology of Film Experience* (1992), and *Carnal Thoughts: Embodiment and Moving Image Culture* (2004). She has also edited two anthologies, *Meta-Morphing: Visual Transformation and the Culture of Quick-Change* (1999), and *The Persistence of History: Cinema, Television, and the Modern Event* (1996), and her essays have appeared in journals such as *Quarterly Review of Film and Video*, *Artforum International*, *Camera Obscura*, *Film Quarterly*, and *Representations*. Here Sobchack speaks about doing inter-disciplinary work between Media Studies, Film Studies, and Cultural Studies, her interest in being part of mass and popular culture, and the ways in which subjective, phenomenological, embodied, lived experience drives our encounters and engagements with visual (rather than just simply visible) culture.

Inter-disciplinary Thinking, Mass Media, and Popular Culture

Marquard Smith (MS): For the record, thanks very much for agreeing to meet with me.

Vivian Sobchack (VS): For the record, you're welcome.

MS: So, to my first question ... Vivian, you think, work, write, feel your way between the disciplines of Media Studies, Film Studies, and Cultural Studies. How do you conceive of inter-disciplinary study, its necessity, its inevitability?

VS: I love that question. One, because you didn't put Film Studies first, which is where I started. Two, because I like your suggestion that it was 'necessary' and 'inevitable'. It actually never occurred to me to do anything but inter-disciplinary work even when I was doing disciplinary work. I had been an English lit major as an undergraduate and I wasn't particularly compelled at the time to go back to graduate school for various reasons. The idea of working very narrowly on some forgotten poet just didn't knock my socks off. This was in the 1960s. When, in the mid-1970s, I actually realized you could study film, other than go to school to make them, I decided to get an MA.

What appealed to me about film as an object of study was not only that I loved it in itself because it's such a sensuous and totally enthralling medium, but also because it seemed to be an anchor from which you could go anywhere. Just anywhere. You could become interested in painting, or architecture, or want to follow through on some philosophical or social issue. To me, film was a medium that inherently prompted interdisciplinarity – and this was long before the influence of Cultural Studies and globalism. So right from the beginning film provided me with this, a deep intellectual pleasure and the pleasure of having a legitimate reason to study anything I wanted.

MS: So film shapes the 'subjects' and 'objects' of your engagement? Your engagement with things comes *out of* film; it goes from to beyond the text itself, the cinematic text? The text acts as a fulcrum?

VS: Yes, that's absolutely right. Indeed, I started out as a formalist. I was dazzled by the problems and pleasures of the cinema sensually and formally. Nonetheless, I found close reading very boring! It wasn't boring to close read as you watched a film, but it was really, really, really boring to write a close reading. And, if you did, there was always the question: to what end? So, I have always been interested in close *seeing* but not necessarily in close reading, which was of course was a big thing, when I started writing about film in the late 1970s. Nonetheless, I've done one or two fairly close readings in early essays, these on *The Grapes of Wrath* and *A Clockwork Orange* (Sobchack, 1979; 1981). For the most part, when I do close read, I tend to focus on scenes or moments rather than whole films. I prefer to read fragments for a purpose, as provocations or responses to larger theoretical questions. I loved taking a short fragment and really working with it, interweaving description of it with theoretical or philosophical or cultural meditation about it. For me, it's never been just the formal reading of a film for its own sake.

MS: Working in and between Media Studies, Film Studies, and Cultural Studies means working with the popular. The popular has been central to – and is of course privileged in – the emergences of these fields of inquiry, these disciplines or sub-disciplines. What role does the popular and/or the vernacular play in all of this for you? I ask this question with three things in mind: first, that you deal with the experience of photographic, cinematic, televisual, electronic, and multi-media technologies of representation – all forms of mass production, consumption, and dissemination – as they all in their own unique ways constitute and mediate our sense of ourselves. Second, because you draw on objects and subjects of popular culture, from film, television, music videos, camcorders, and cell phones to computer games, on-line shopping, and PDAs. And third, because you utilize sources from popular culture such as film reviews, advertisements, and self-help manuals written for mass audiences ...

VS: Let me begin to answer this question of the popular by saying that as a child, I spent a lot of time wondering if other people perceived not only *what* I did but also *as* I did. This fascination was probably the result of an eye operation I had when I was four and spent a whole week with my eyes bandaged. So, questions about the experience of perception were always personal for me, right from the beginning although I'd like to think my interest was not merely narcissistic. I had – and still have – a very personal attachment to the large questions I ask. Even as a child, I asked very large philosophical questions, whether they were framed in childish ways or not. I've always found it strange to be alive and embodied in the world – to have two rather than three eyes or hands. I was always asking: what does this *mean*, what does this mean to *me*, not just personally but also as a human being, rather than, say, a cat or a goldfish or an alien. (This probably explains why, in the 1950s, I loved science fiction films.) Watching films tends to provoke these big questions – which is why I love film!

These perceptual questions about what it was to be a human being always were also social questions. That is, I was – and am – not just immersed in but also *part* of a mass and popular culture – different from but also the same as others with whom I share it. (Whether you're an auto mechanic or a professor, can you avoid having Paris Hilton enter your consciousness?) So, as a scholar and 'participant-observer', I believe my experience living in mass and popular culture is incredibly valuable precisely because it provides some common ground from which to write about more philosophical or theoretical questions. In sum, I do believe I'm part of a greater commonality – whether it's a common culture that we share or the fact that we're all embodied and have to deal with the consequences.

It's interesting that it's so difficult for my students to rely their own individual experience as a place to start intellectual inquiry. I don't know if this has to do with their feelings of uniqueness or humility – or their ideas of what it means to be 'professional'. But I point out to them that it's more arrogant than humble to think that their experience is so unique that no one else can possibly share or interpret it. 'Are you that special?' I ask. They're shocked at that! Wanting to be scholars, they turn up thinking that the personal is 'too subjective'. What does *too* subjective mean? Real objectivity *includes* subjectivity – personal experience is a place to begin a more general exploration of perception and expression, not its purpose or its end point.

Now, I couldn't have articulated this when I first started writing about film – in the 1970s, which was just about when public university film programmes were getting started in the United States and before the proliferation of 'high theory'. Nonetheless, my own personal experiences of mass and popular culture have always been the engine that, from then to now, has driven me to ask certain questions and *discipline be damned*! One can't think, 'Oh, cinema is my area of expertize, so I'd better not talk about photography and certainly not about digital culture'. Instead, I say, 'Plunge ahead girl!' It is only by thinking about the possible variations in one's modes of perception and expression across moving image media – looking at both similarities and differences – that you can say something meaningful and specific about any particular medium.

MS: You might have pre-empted my next six questions!

I think you've just suggested that the personal is popular. Actually I've just realized that your previous response – your personal response on the purpose of the personal – ties in very nicely with a question I wanted to ask about the anecdotal. Why do you regularly use the anecdotal form in your writings?

VS: One the one hand, my affection for the anecdote comes out of my phenomenological approach, which emphasizes starting with what is given in experience. On the other hand, it emerges from my interest in new historicism, where the anecdote is often used as an oddity meant to trouble grand narratives, or, alternatively, as somehow generative of larger historiographic speculations precisely because it's a fragment of something *not* given. Besides telling a good story of some kind, the anecdote always remains open, suggesting a larger context. It's like a pebble thrown into a pond – it causes ever-widening ripples.

The personal anecdote or story fragment is a very powerful place to start phenomenologically unpacking the possible structures of experience. A lot of people misinterpret phenomenology, believing it's just about subjectivity. This is absolutely *not* the case. Rather, phenomenological method begins with a description of what appears – or is first 'given' – to consciousness. Then the task is to start recognizing that certain scientific, cultural, psychological, and historical presuppositions and predispositions have constructed the shape, and dimensions, and particular limits of what is less 'given' than 'taken up' by us and 'naturalized' as 'the way things are'. This recognition – achieved through what are called the phenomenological reductions – allows one to broaden one's perception, to undo habituated hierarchies of what something 'is' in any fixed sense. It opens both the 'thing' you're looking at and consciousness to different forms and ways of seeing. In this regard, because of their small size, the anecdote and story fragment allow me/one to turn and test them in a series of variations that expand their possible phenomenological interpretation and meanings. Over the last few years, I've gotten a lot of attention (so much so that sometimes I feel as if I should be dead!) from people who tell me that they love the way I write using personal anecdotes. They're bemused by the fact that normally they dislike the personal voice, and find it narcissistic or confessional. They think the reason they like my work is because I write well, which is certainly very flattering. But it also pisses me off because my use of the personal voice is really a methodological manoeuvre. It starts with the personal and anecdotal and then unpacks its specificity to reveal its more general structures – ones whose possibilities resonate sufficiently to be imaginatively 'inhabited' by others. Let me give you an example, I was asked to write a short piece for *Film Comment* on two contemporary horror films – and I hate to watch most horror films! (Sobchack, 2006) I agreed to do it – but I wrote in the essay that I wasn't sure I was the right person to comment on these films because I tend to watch them by looking at my lap instead of the screen and catching the films out of the corners of my eyes! But, from a phenomenological perspective, this way of watching a movie, I realized, was itself interesting. So I started to unpack the structure of the experience of seeing films in this way, to think about *not* seeing rather than seeing: waiting for sound cues that tell you when you can look up, but still mostly looking away. This is an oblique form of vision – it's off to the side; it occasionally sneaks a peek. This kind of vision also notices the space of the theatre. Not only the darkness but a sense of my body really sitting there, in its materiality, anticipating peril and assault. And this structure was narratively and formally reflected in the horror films themselves – not only in the characters' reactions but also in the films' use of visual occlusion to conceal and reveal. (The piece was called 'Peek-A-Boo'.) Unpacking this experiential structure revealed that even though I was cinephobic about horror films, the kind of visceral and bodily present-tenseness I felt, the 'now-ness', the awful extension of the present, was the same general structure the horror cinephile enjoyed – although differently valued. I would never have explored this kind of perceptual experience if I had discounted it, if I'd said 'Oh I don't do horror films', or if I'd pretended that I watched the films in the way you're supposed to – eyes wide open. There are valuable things that emerge if you can allow yourself, at least in the beginning, to trust your own particular experience. It can lead to the fleshing out of more general structures. Then you don't end up with the merely personal.

The other side of my interest in the anecdote comes from new historiography. I teach a seminar in philosophy of history and one of the books I use is the wonderful *Practicing New Historicism* by Catherine Gallagher and Steven Greenblatt (2001). The first two chapters are particularly useful and focus on the anecdote and its functions in writing history. One is on Ernest Auerbach and the way that, in *Mimesis*, he used the anecdote – a small fragment – to stand as a microcosm of the much larger literary work of which it was a part. Here the whole world is found in a grain of sand. The other chapter, however, is on the anecdote as a spoiler that ruptures the coherence of a larger whole. It's the oddity that doesn't fit into the official historical narrative and disrupts it.

I like the dialogism as well as the dialectic between these two models of the anecdote. And the anecdote can be liberating. Students often flounder about as to what they might write, or how to frame their dissertations (whether historically focused or not), but once you give them license to use the anecdote as a starting point it's amazing what emerges – whether they are using it as a microcosm or as a spoiler. It seems to allow them to move from 'oh dear, I have to be an academic, a philosopher, or whatever' to something very existentially present, and about which they are curious.

Phenomenology, Synaesthesia, and Embodied Vision

MS: All this talk of the personal/popular and the anecdotal in no way detracts from – it even affirms still further – the fact that you are a phenomenologist. You're interested in the lived-body being-in-the-world, as you once put it.[1] What does it mean for phenomenology to be your tool of choice, a research procedure, a methodology, a mode of engagement, when considering our acts of seeing, perceiving, viewing, encountering, understanding, mis-understanding even, visual culture? I think you've already touched on this, but if there were anything you'd like to add ...

VS: I've just finished teaching a class called 'Visual Perception'. I do it with a phenomenological emphasis. As a methodology, phenomenology is about performing perceptual variations and interrogating one's presuppositions – what seems given and hardly worth mentioning. It's cautionary about too quick a leap to theorizing or rushing to cite Foucault or Deleuze. It's also very open: when you begin, you don't know where you're going to end up. My irritation with feminist/psychoanalytical readings of mainstream Hollywood film came from their predictability. You knew what the input was and you knew what you were going to get coming out. Very soon, everyone could do a Lacanian and deconstructive analysis that would trash the patriarchal Hollywood film. Boring! While such readings were politically motivated and initially illuminating, the methodology itself determined the outcome and in a very narrow way.

What appeals to me about phenomenology is that it offers a set of critical commitments to a rigorous, but open way of looking. The very first film I show in 'Visual Perception' is Derek Jarman's *Blue* (1993). I ask students what they see. They're grad students so they're not so naïve as to say 'Nothing'. They usually respond that they see a field of blue. I ask them if that's it? Phenomenological description shows it to be much more: the field of 'blue' keeps changing colours, our focus changes; our sense of depth changes, we move our eyes; there are coloured after-images, there are artefacts from the scratches on the film; our vision widens, so that the exit signs in the theatre are part of the visual field. There are all sorts of experiences going on that are dramas of vision and intimately tied to the narrator's discussion of blindness, let along blueness!

This is a very simple gloss of a very complex phenomenological analysis. But the general tendency at first is for students to say: 'Okay, it's blue. Let's get on with it and talk about the film in the context of Jarman's biography or in relation to the social history AIDS'. I'm not against discussing any of these things. But they need to be – quite literally – fleshed out. Phenomenology does not supplant social analysis, or ideological analysis, or poetic analysis. It *embodies* and *thickens* them. So, for me, phenomenology is a methodological commitment to not rush to presume that when you say 'I see blue' that that's the end of it. Or, when I ask 'What do you see?' there are students who want to quote Foucault, which is not what they see! Phenomenology insists you dwell in the moments of perception before moving on to more abstract or theoretical concerns. It insists you experience your own sight before you (dare I pun?) cite others.

MS: Continuing this discussion of phenomenology, in a chapter from *Carnal Thoughts* entitled 'Is Any Body Home? Embodied Imagination and Visible Evictions' you speak about the inverse ratio 'between *seeing* our bodies and *feeling* them: the more aware we are of ourselves as the cultural artefacts, symbolic fragments, and made things that we see in – and as – images, the less we seem to sense the intentional complexity and richness of the corporeal existence that substantiates them'.[2] You go on: 'In a culture like ours, so preoccupied with images of bodies and bodies of images, we tend to forget that both our bodies and our vision have lived dimensions that are not reducible to the merely visible'.

You're fascinated by the lived body, what you call the 'embodied and radically material nature of human existence'.[3] You write that the actual focus of *Carnal Thoughts* is 'on what it is to *live* one's body, not merely *look* at bodies – although vision, visuality, and visibility are as central to the subjective dimensions of embodied existence as they are to its objective dimensions'.[4]

Why such a commitment, and such a long-term commitment, to questions of embodiment and embodied vision?

VS: First of all ... it's very strange ... or perhaps not ... most people assume that I became interested in the body when I had cancer and my leg was amputated. But if you really look at my work, I was dealing with embodied vision in one way or another early on. My amputation became merely a very intellectually (if not physically) fortunate – albeit very dramatic – laboratory to continue certain investigations of what it was to be that strange 'thing' we call a body: not only a set of capacities but also sensual and sentient matter. I grew up bookish. I was the eldest of two daughters in a family where, as the eldest, I was praised for being independent. I was given the right to make a lot of decisions and to be assertive about my opinions. Which was great until I hit puberty! Suddenly it was my sweet and adoring sister daddy approved of, not the independent and argumentative male-identified adolescent I'd become. I realized that I was caught in a terrible double bind – not a good enough boy and not a good enough girl. And this dilemma made being embodied even stranger than it had been. I can remember standing in front of a mirror, pulling my long hair back, searching my features, and thinking: 'If I didn't have long hair, would anybody know I was a girl or a boy?' Those were more innocent days as far as sexual knowledge was concerned. Certainly I was aware of sexual difference, but it didn't seem to be that much of a difference because I wasn't yet all that sexualized. I was more aware, however, of how your body determined the way people made judgements about you or treated you. So from early on, I found being the body that I was somehow an arbitrary thing, the result of chance. (I thought a lot, too, about how I might have been born in China or Africa and wondered if I'd still be 'me'.) Anyway, I struggled with my body. I wasn't athletic – always the last picked for teams in gym class (which I hated). And I struggled with being a female body, when I was a bit older seeing my effect on men and enjoying the power I seemed to have, but also despising its superficiality and the fact that I enjoyed wielding it. So, for me, embodiment was a conscious problem – and a problem for consciousness.

Quite late in life (and I'd already had a child), things changed, I discovered phenomenology, particularly Merleau-Ponty's existential phenomenology. I was introduced to his thought first, not Husserl's. I love Merleau-Ponty's emphasis on embodiment. He keeps Husserl's phenomenological method but, by emphasizing the embodiment of consciousness, its materiality, he also introduces culture and history into the 'life-world' Husserl wanted to get to the heart of. Embodied, we can never get behind things to some 'pure essence' of phenomena – 'essence' is always qualified by existence, and always open to variation and further elaboration. If there are any universals to 'human being', they come with embodiment: we inhabit and co-constitute space and time and give it value of some kind, we have senses through which we make sense, and even if bodies are conceived differently, they have material sub-strate – what Merleau-Ponty came to call the element of 'flesh' – which we share with the world and all the animate and inanimate life within it.

I am a materialist. I don't believe in the transcendental – transcendent yes, but not the transcendental. So Merleau-Ponty for me, in emphasizing embodiment and the body as a set of capacities and not just a thing really spoke to me – as did his insistence on our engagement with a world that co-constituted its meanings, on the importance of the body and its intentional gestures as enabling intersubjectivity as well as understanding and mis-understanding. His work really spoke to me. It spurred me on. It provided license and a vocabulary that allowed me to articulate things I'd been sensing but couldn't say for a very long time.

MS: And yet, this embodied, materialist existence, this living 'in the flesh', is always already mediated? I've never read it put better than this: '... however direct it may seem, our experience is not only always mediated by the lived bodies that we are, but our lived bodies (and our experience of them) are always also mediated and qualified by our engagements with other bodies and things ... [and] by historical and cultural systems that constrain both the inner limits of our perception and the outer limits of our world'.[5]

VS: Yes, 'living in the flesh' is always mediated experience. Merleau-Ponty suggests we come into the world on a 'bias' – our bodily situation, from the first, is never 'neutral' and no experience is ever 'direct' or 'pure' because it always happens in – and is mediated, formed, and transformed by – culture and history and, of course, our engagements with others and things. Certainly, our bodies are the agents that realize our intentionality and consciousness in the world, but they are constituted as the particular bodies they are (and the bodies we perceive them to be) by others as well as ourselves. Culture shapes them and history shapes them – not only personal history but also epochal history. Phenomenology is sometimes criticized for thinking of the body as foundational – there's no experience without it – but confuse this with the misconception that this means the body is 'natural' and that what phenomenology calls 'direct experience' means it is unmediated. What 'direct' actually means is 'transparent' and 'habituated'. So, our experience of our bodies is never 'raw' – it's cooked from the first breath we take in the world. Obviously, there are different forms of mediation – including technological mediation – that transform our bodily situation and thus the way we see ourselves or perceive the boundaries and limits of our world. So, in terms of imaging technology, with the advent of painting, then photography, then cinema, now digital technologies, we keep (as they say of cosmetic surgery) 'having our eyes done'.

MS: Despite or perhaps because of this mediation, you speak, for instance, of the cinesthetic subject, our carnal responses to film, of vision's relation to touch, of how our capacity to touch, smell, or taste come to the cinema with us ...

Let me frame that a little: in the end, for you phenomenology is a way for us to engage with *visual* culture as an object of study – rather than a 'visible culture' that, as you write, is simply a reductive culture in which 'vision dominates our sensory access to the world and in which a discrete and reductive emphasis on visibility and body images greatly overdetermines our more expansive possibilities for seeing and making sense of our enworldedness'[6] Of this visible culture, you go on to say that 'the sensual thickness of lived experience has been thinned to the superficiality of two dimensions, and we have lost touch with what really matters about ourselves and others'. Yet you conclude by sounding an upbeat note of optimism: 'What we need ... is not to rid ourselves of images but to flesh them out'.

VS: For the most part, I think that what goes by the name of 'visual culture' is really 'visible culture'. That what gets talked about is not 'visuality' but 'visibility'. Similarly, instead of talking about embodiment – what it is to *live* a body, what it is to *live* acts of seeing not merely with one's eyes (as if that were possible) – most scholars talk about 'the body' – positing it as merely a thing, or as a visible object belonging to someone else. This seems to me a continuation of the objectivist project – despite the fact that people writing about 'visuality' and 'the body' are critiquing that project. I find a certain poignancy in all the recent stuff on the body; you can feel a straining towards something more, but also a pulling back – from what? From a complementary discussion of the subjective dimensions of vision and its full entailment with our other senses: touch, hearing, smell, taste. It's important not to forget that our bodies are not things as other things are. We're not 'in' our bodies like a car is 'in' a garage. Certainly, our bodies provide us material premises that allow us to have a world but they're also a dynamic ensemble of senses and capacities that make meaning together.

I think the distinctions between visible culture and visual culture are terribly important ones. Although it's changing, the tendency still is to only talk about the side of vision that is about the visible, not about the visual. But you need both sides to achieve vision. Thinking about visuality links vision to the body and our other senses which are not, to use a phrase, 'asleep on the job', but active in giving the things we see a visible thickness and dimension. If, in fact you don't acknowledge vision as embodied and richly informed by our other capacities for sense-making, where does that leave you? It certainly doesn't leave you with a good time at the movies! This conception of a cinematic vision that is somehow abstracted from an actively lived body is nonsense. Christian Metz's characterization of film spectators still ticks me off twenty or thirty years after I first read it: 'Spectator-fish, taking in everything with their eyes, nothing with their bodies' (Metz, 1982). What the hell does that mean? What contempt does that display? Where the hell is he at the cinema?

MS: So the synaesthetic ...

VS: All our senses are involved and intercommunicate when we see films. That's how we make meaning of the world and things we see on the screen. Objectively, we are given only sight and sound but we experience these in ways other than visual and acoustic. It's hardly news that we have kinetic responses to films, which shouldn't happen if only our vision and hearing are engaged at the movies. As I've argued (and I hope demonstrated) in an essay called 'What My Fingers Knew', we also *feel* films: we touch and are touched by them, and this is tactility not merely in a metaphorical sense.[7] Look at how we blithely talk about texture in relation to vision and painting. Most of us don't go up and actually touch the painting on the wall. But we understand from what we see the depth of the paint on the canvas. On the screen we see the roughness of tree bark or the satiny smoothness of a gown – but this seeing 'roughness' and 'smoothness' would be impossible if vision were not intimately informed by our sense of touch. But it is not that you just sit there and cognitively remember, in some very quick way, what something feels like. Your body knows. There is a tingle in your fingers, around your skin. It is not that you are feeling the specificity of the satin up there or, for that matter, your own clothing. Rather, informing and apprehended through vision, the sense of touch gets generalized, and enhanced and intensified at the same time as it becomes diffused across a range of fabrics, if you will. We shouldn't be able to feel texture just by looking but we do. Our skin and the skin of the film merge in a cooperative production of meaning. To some (I'm thinking film scholars in love with the logic of analytic philosophy), it is absurd to talk about 'the skin of the film'? Laura Marks, of course, does this quite effectively in her work (Marks, 2000). All of our senses cooperate, each informing the others. We are synaesthetic by nature, even if most of us are not clinical synaesthetes. So any act of vision is constantly – and without a conscious thought – informed, to varying degrees, by our other senses. We would never get so involved with the worlds created by film if we used only our vision and our hearing to make sense. Each sense gives us a discreet mode of access to the world. But the others don't just turn off when one or two of them are dominant.

Space and Being-in-the-World

MS: When I began preparing for this interview, it hadn't occurred to me that I was going to be asking you a bunch of questions on space. But the more of your work I reread, the more I realized that 'space' comes up again and again, implicitly and explicitly, in so many different ways. From your first book *The Limits of Infinity: The American Science Fiction Film* (Sobchack, 1980) to your most recent book *Carnal Thoughts: Embodiment and Moving Image Culture* (Sobchack, 2004) you've been interested in space. (This is made all the more evident since *The Limits of Infinity* was enlarged and reprinted as *Screening Space: The American Science Fiction Film* in 1997.) This is by no means simply an interest in the outer space or inner space of Science Fiction cinema or television or literature; of space as the final frontier. To infinity, and beyond!

Concerns with space are evident throughout *Carnal Thoughts*: spatial perception, spatial schemas, spatial morphologies, lived space, lived geography, spatial processing, contracted space, Euclidean visual space, hyperbolic space, maps, points of orientation, topological space, imaginary geographies, electronic space, virtual and cyber space, modalities of spatial disorientation, spatial ungrounding, becoming lost in worldly space.

So I have a few questions to put to you about space ...

The first is this: In one essay in the book, 'The Passion of the Material', you say that '[c]entral to any understanding of the connection between ethics and aesthetics, [is] the question of "the limit between the body and the world"'. (This is, as you write, a question posed by both Maurice Merleau-Ponty in *The Visible and the Invisible* and Jean-Paul Sartre in his novel *Nausea*.)[8] Is it too dramatic to say that this question, this question of space – the space *between*, and the space *of*, the body and the world – is the question that underpins your oeuvre? (I realize you've already said bits and pieces about this during our conversation, but would you like to offer a more explicit response?)

VS: My first chapter in *Carnal Thoughts*, 'Breadcrumbs in the Forest', is about being lost in worldly and cinematic space – and also, I hope, some very funny and telling stuff about gender and space. In that essay I talk about having felt sure of my world as a child but then becoming unstable as I got older and became a girl. For the longest time, I had a certain terror – it wasn't a phobia but it was nonetheless a terror – of getting lost, in space. For many years, I had recurrent anxiety dreams about getting lost, not being able to find my way. So, when I was writing the chapter and thinking not only about my own dreams but also about films in which characters get lost, I first went to Freud's *Interpretation of Dreams* ... but although it discussed dreams about losing *things*, there was nothing about getting and being lost oneself. (It turns out Freud himself got lost in Italy (on a street of 'painted women') and writes about it in his essay on the uncanny!) Anyway, this issue of locating oneself in the world or being spatially disoriented was the essay's central concern, a good part of which was also a meditation on cinematic narratives in which characters get lost in worldly space. In this one, no science fiction was allowed!

Then, of course, the very first book I wrote (it was my Masters thesis), *The Limits of Infinity*, was about the science fiction film – which is all about the exploration of space. I had grown up in the 1950s watching SF films and they fired my imagination. I mean, for several years, I wanted to be a scientist – but I wasn't good at math. That scotched it, you know. I still am fascinated by science: contemporary neuroscience particularly, but other kinds as well. My interest in technology also stems from SF, even when it scares the shit out of me. I really am inept – I understand technology conceptually, I understand computers, but put me in front of one, and I have to do something and something goes wrong and I'm sure I've broken something. I guess, in many ways, those 1950s films were very formative. They were about limits and the promise of limitlessness, about liberation, about thinking in other and new ways, and about the 'fringes' of what could be thought and seen. And this was at a fairly conservative time. Those films really sparked my imagination – however dinky they are from today's perspective. And they were about space.

But there is the spatiality of the cinema itself that makes me a cinephile. Spatially, you can go anywhere without really getting lost. In my 'Breadcrumbs' essay, I talk about how, when I was very young, I thought north was always the way I was facing – and, of course, it wasn't. Well, at the movies, north is always ahead of you – on the screen. Anyway, that's comforting for someone who has always been spatially challenged. Living in New York; I'd always get out of the subway and turn right, even if it was the wrong direction. I have no idea why. So I really ... space has always been a kind of a conundrum and somehow perilous to me. It is only over the last ten years, in Los Angeles – maybe it is because I can usually see the Hollywood hills – that I can say 'that's north', and that I can get find my way if I do get a little lost.

But when I wrote the first version of the SF film book, I never tied it to my pre-occupation with space. I also didn't even know what phenomenology was then; I'm not even sure that I had ever heard the word. I was fascinated with 'being in the world' – on the one hand, its spatial possibilities and, on the other, the expression and containment of these by cinema. Later, in *The Address of the Eye* (1992), I ground being and seeing and cinema as, from the first, movement – action – in space, not, as Deleuze does, in time which I think is constituted as a reflexive reflection on that spatial movement. So, in a strange way, those very early spatial preoccupations come back in my interest in existential phenomenology – and the fact that I see movement in space as the ground of temporality. So, concerns with space have informed almost all my work.

In some ways this is not surprising. Modernism was all about time, and temporality: and one of the moves into the post-modern, although I hate when this is seen as causal, has been the turn to an emphasis on spatiality. Now, I think the tide is turning again – back to an emphasis on temporality. With the expansion of space and all the things in it, we increasingly have no time. So now the preoccupation is the reclamation of time. The last thing I wrote was actually on slow motion, on intense or hyperbolic slow motion.

MS: As an aside, I thought it was worth mentioning another kind of space: the space of interior design. While I was flicking through *The Limits of Infinity* – sometimes I flick through books as well as read them to get a different sense of them as visual and tactile objects – I realized that by way of the film stills in the book you'd offered a visual essay on screen space, the set designs, the interior decoration, the *mise-en-scène*, the material culture of science fiction cinema! I don't know whether this was intentional or not. The stills that are particularly apposite for me are from *Fantastic Voyage* (1966), *THX 1138* (1971), *2001: A Space Odyssey* (1968), and *A Clockwork Orange* (1971) – perhaps they just seem spot on because late 1960s and early 1970s Science Fiction cinema evidences *my* favourite speculative 'aesthetic' for how the future is going to look ...

VS: I never would have put it the way you have! I just love the idea of the stills being a visual essay on screen space and the material culture of SF. But I did have something vaguely similar in mind. I had a hard time getting those stills although it was easier with copyright issues than it is today, I had a hard time, because I wanted pictures that focused more on *mise-en-scène* and composition, on what the film space looked like, its iconographic qualities.

When I started that book, it was to raise the question of genre. Genre was a relatively new issue in Film Studies. Scholars were writing about these very codified genres in which there was a clear historical background and certain very identifiable, repeatable, iconographic figures – in the Western, the train, the horse, the stagecoach, all of these different kinds of guns that tell you about the characters and the like. So the Western and the Gangster film were the two main genres written about (by men), and I came along with the science fiction film to challenge some assumptions about genre. I was interested in it inherently, but also because its figurations and iconography were more plastic than in other genres. And so, it became very important to think more broadly about iconography, not so much about the constancy of objects and more about the look and sound and editorial juxtapositions and the composition of the *mise-en-scène*, of things like symmetry. Symmetry does not really happen in the world very often and so it is strange: in *A Clockwork Orange*, Kubrick constantly uses symmetry to defamiliarize the world. In *THX 1138*, George Lucas has characters wearing white against a featureless and white background; their bald heads punctuate the space in startling ways that again suggest some alternative and unfamiliar world. I was always very visually attuned to these things. So it was very hard getting stills because stills tend to be of characters rather than the *mise-en-scène*. And I was very happy to be able to get the things that I got. It is great that you noticed that.

MS: It is a fantastic example of material and visual culture. Also, I just love the idea of what the future looks like. I remember watching *Solaris* (1972) for the first time and just being amazed at the stage sets and how, pushing the obvious point, the future, or the way in which a historical period imagines the future, is always completely of its own imaginings. It's simultaneously a look of the future, it's of the now, and, because of this, it's somehow always already dated too.

VS: Yes, that's right. I remember going to Epcot Centre several years ago. I had been there many years before and had gone through the ride in a sphere called, I think, Spaceship Earth, which was sponsored by AT&T. Using animatronics, it was a dramatized history of telecommunications. Anyway, I was really looking forward to seeing this now old fashioned vision of the future, but, of course, they had completely updated it. I was so disappointed. But it's hard to keep up with the future – or envision it. A good friend of mine is the head of research and development at Disney Imagineering and – thoughtful about how the future gets so dated after it's visualized – their design team talked this through and decided to purposefully make the future 'retro'. In Disneyland and Disney World, so the rockets and such in Future World (or whatever it's called) are based on Jules Verne and H.G. Wells. It's looking *Back to the Future* rather than ahead ... This says something sad about the state of our imagination, don't you think – let alone the state of the world?

Notes

1 In *The Address of the Eye: A Phenomenology of Film Experience* (1992) (Princeton, NJ: Princeton University Press) you write: 'The lived-body being-in-the-world establishes the concrete ground (that is, the premises as well as the necessity) for all language', p. 41.
2 Vivian Sobchack, 'Is Any Body Home? Embodied Imagination and Visible Evictions', in *Carnal Thoughts*, pp. 179–204, p. 179.
3 Ibid., p. 1.
4 Ibid., p. 2.
5 Ibid., p. 4.
6 Ibid., p. 187.
7 Ibid., pp. 53–84.
8 Ibid., p. 286.

References

Metz, Christian (1982) 'Story/Discourse (A Note on Two Kinds of Voyeurism)', (Celia Britton and Amwyl Williams, in Christian Metz, *trans.*) *The Imaginary Signifier: Psychoanalysis and the Cinema*. Bloomington: Indiana University Press, p. 97.

Gallagher, Catherine and Greenblatt, Stephen (2001) *Practicing New Historicism*. Chicago: Chicago University Press.

Marks, Laura U. (2000) *The Skin of the Film, Intercultural Cinema, Embodiment, and the Senses*. Durham, NC: Duke University Press.

Sobchack, Vivian (1979) '*The Grapes of Wrath*: Thematic Emphasis through Visual Style', *American Quarterly*, 31 (Winter): 596–615.

Sobchack, Vivian Carol (1980) *The Limits of Infinity: The American Science Fiction Film*. Cranbury, NJ: A. S. Barnes and Co., Inc.

Sobchack, Vivian (1981) 'Decor as Theme: *A Clockwork Orange*', *Literature/Film Quarterly*, 9(2): 92–102.

Sobchack, Vivian (1992) *The Address of the Eye: A Phenomenology of film Experience.* Princeton, N.J: Princeton University Press.

Sobchack, Vivian (1996) *The Persistence of History: Cinema, Television, and the Morden Event.* AFI film readers. New York: Routledge.

Sobchack, Vivian (1997) *Screening Space: The American Science Fiction Film.* Chapel Hill, NC: Rutgers University Press.

Sobchack, Vivian (1999) *Meta-morphing: Visual Transformation and the Culture of Quick-change.* Minneapolis: University of Minnesota Press.

Sobchack, Vivian (2004) *Carnal Thoughts: Embodiment and Moving Image Culture.* Berkeley and Los Angeles, CA: California University Press.

Sobchack, Vivian (2006) 'Peek-a-BOO! Thoughts on seeing (most of) *The Descent* and *Isolation*', *Film Comment*, 42(4) (July–August): 38–41.

8

PERFORMANCE, LIVE CULTURE AND THINGS OF THE HEART[1]

Interview with Peggy Phelan

Introduction

Having worked in the Department of Performance Studies, Tisch School of the Arts, New York University, from 1985 to 2002, Peggy Phelan is now the Ann O'Day Maples Chair in the Arts at Stanford University. She is the author of *Unmarked: The Politics of Performance* (1993), *Mourning Sex: Performing Public Memories* (1997) *Twentieth Century Performance* (Routledge, 2008), and the forthcoming *Death Rehearsals: The Performances of Andy Warhol and Ronald Reagan*, as well as survey essays for the art catalogues *Art and Feminism* (2001) and *Pipilotti Rist* (2001). She is co-editor with the late Lynda Hart of *Acting Out: Feminist Performances* (1993) and with Jill Lane of *The Ends of Performance* (1998). Professor Phelan has also written plays and performances and has exhibited her visual art. She has made significant contributions across the Arts and Humanities, particularly at the points where live culture, feminism, psychoanalysis, deconstruction and critical theory meet. In this interview Professor Phelan speaks about some of the awkward grey areas between Performance Studies and Visual Cultural Studies, as well as the themes and topics at the heart of her writing and her practice. These include feminism, performance, psychoanalysis and aesthetics; for Phelan, most of these themes touch on mourning, death and love.

Marquard Smith (MS): The last few years have witnessed if not a wholesale shift than certainly a transition of sorts from the study of theatre in English Departments to Theatre Studies programmes and to the development of programmes in Performance Studies. Do you believe this is a purely academic exercise or that, with a bit of luck, it tells us something about a certain recognition of the transformation of the practice of performance?

Peggy Phelan (PP): I think this transition is based on a combination of factors. In the United States at least, there was an economic incentive for rethinking Theatre Studies. As Joe Roach points out, theatre departments in the US – and it's probably the same in the UK, although I'm not sure if it's to the same degree and at the exact same time – in the 1950s made extensive investments in the physical plants of their universities. Many universities have multi-million dollar theatre complexes and therefore, very few universities are interested in getting rid of Theatre Studies. Richard Schechner [1995] did propose that theatre departments go out of business and become performance studies departments in an essay in *TDR*. His proposal received a lot of attention, and provoked a certain kind of healthy anxiety I think. But I don't think programmes in Theatre Studies are disappearing. And having just joined a drama department, I hope it is also clear that I don't think theatre departments should close shop. I do think there will be more effort to fuse the best of theatre and performance studies in the future.

Performance has become a central lens for understanding events as disparate as the war in Iraq and Madonna's newest video. We have entered a realm of all-performance-all-the-time. This is not to say that 'the real' has disappeared, but it is to acknowledge that it is impossible to recognize 'the real' without a concept of performance in view. I think that the recognition of the centrality of performance to contemporary life and thought reflects some shifts in the academic scene, but these shifts are themselves responses to a more pervasive performance world-view.

MS: Your co-edited collection *The Ends of Performance* was in fact explicitly both a celebration and a critique of the institutionalization of Performance Studies. As a recently emergent field of study, what can Performance Studies tell Visual Studies – keeping in mind that, at least as far as I am concerned, there is an obvious distinction between Visual Studies or Visual Cultural Studies as an academic area of inquiry and the visual cultures that are made and made use of, that take place out there in the world, the visual cultures in which we've been engaging critically for years in numerous ways long before Visual Studies came along?

PP: It's an extraordinarily complex question! First you're asking me to speak analogically: how is Performance Studies like or distinct from Visual Studies? And then you're also asking me to talk about a larger question with which I think both Performance Studies and Visual Studies have to contend, and that's Cultural Studies. These are distinct questions. I want to begin by just reflecting upon the CAA meeting in Philadelphia in 2001. Laurie Beth Clark and Nick Mirzoeff organized a discussion on Visual Studies in relation to Art History. I was asked to speak about Performance Studies as a model for Visual Studies. And I found myself in the session being more cautious than I had anticipated. Everything seemed to be available for the newly emerging discipline. There has been an extensive critique of Performance Studies along these lines – 'if everything is performance ... how do you define what it is?' – and my response to this question is always: 'well, if everything is language, why do we have English Departments!' [laughs] Nonetheless, there has to be a way to talk about the border between what is performance and what is not. I am completely behind the discipline of Visual Studies and I think it can enliven and enrich Art History. But as one begins the complex game of institutionalizing a field, it is important to delimit your study or else the field can become too amorphous. I think the example of Cultural Studies is useful to bear in mind. Institutionally, it is now very vulnerable. As you know, the programme was disbanded in Birmingham, and it is under attack in the US as well. The main argument against Cultural Studies is that it lacks disciplinary specificity. Some see it as a little bit of this and a little bit of that; it has a sort of 'jack of all trades, master of none' problem.

I think Performance Studies had a healthy anxiety about that problem, and while perhaps the field was beginning to fetishize the question of liveness, the question nonetheless did help to consolidate the field and to give it some kind of border. And I think similar questions will be important for Visual Studies as well: what constitutes the border between the visible and the invisible? How does our blindness to the opacity of the not-seen frame our experience of the visual?

MS: Would you speak a bit more about your essay in *Unmarked*, 'The Ontology of Performance' [1993]? What do you think is at stake in your emphasis on performance as an art of disappearance?

PP: I was trying to make clear that the ephemeral, indeed the mortal, is absolutely fundamental to the experience of embodiment, to the *facticity* of human history itself. Although the essay has prompted a lot of criticism, I still stand by most of it. I was trying to move the field away from a constant preoccupation with the content of performance, a descriptive fixation on what performance enacted, and towards a consideration of performance as that which disappears. I thought this aspect of performance allowed us to answer some important philosophical and political questions about loss, history and death – questions that I thought performance art had done much to pose. I wanted the field to engage more directly with questions around historiography, psychoanalysis, trauma and, therefore, ethics. I think this interdisciplinary work has been very good for the field.

MS: Picking up on this matter of disappearing, in *Unmarked* you say that you are if not against then you are certainly suspicious of a politics of visibility – a politics which seeks empowerment through visibility and exposure. 'Visibility is a trap', you say, following Jacques Lacan's invocation in *Four Fundamental Concepts* [1973/1981]: 'In this matter of the visible, everything is a trap'. In effect, you say you're against economies of vision as surveillance, as voyeurism and as colonialism's fetishistic will to possession [Phelan, 1993: 6–7]. Instead you propose a possibility of being or becoming 'unmarked', an 'active vanishing' that 'refus[es] ... the payoff of visibility' (p. 6). In your book you attend to questions of the need to move from matters of visibility to invisibility, disappearance, de-materialization. You ask: what does it take to 'value the immaterial'? Could you speak a little more about the background to this critique of visibility and this critique's concomitant call for a need to attend to the process of disappearance?

PP: *Unmarked* was written in the very late 1980s and early 1990s. In that period in New York (and elsewhere) the Left was absolutely obsessed with identity politics and visibility politics. The idea was that if you could give the disenfranchised access to representation, these groups could secure political power. I was suspicious of this for the feminist Lacanian reasons that you mentioned before, and also because I knew that this was part of what capitalism does so well – acquire new audiences! If one could increase the range of representation's demographic addresses, capitalism could add more markets to its expanding stage.

Unmarked was read, quite correctly, as a psychoanalytic text. But it was also about the way in which capital works: I was interested in finding ways to resist the relentless acquisitive drive of capitalism. Much of the energy and inspiration of performance art in the 1970s derived from an attempt to dissolve the materiality of the art object, and to create, in the moment of performance, something of value that did not have an object. This might be described as a quest for an intersubjective experience. I wanted to return to that impulse because I thought it was a brilliant critique of commodity culture, and very radical. By the time I was writing, however, that impulse had been overtaken by the usual capitalist worldview in the United States, and especially in New York, where the galleries, and museum culture more generally, had become so dominant. In places like Eastern Europe or Brazil, of course, the history of performance art played out quite differently.

When I was writing *Unmarked*, however, I was trying to think about resistance to commodity culture. As the performance artists of the 1970s made clear, one mode of resistance is to think about things that don't consolidate into objects that can be sold. I was interested in the *immaterial* allure of performance as one possible way to imagine new economies of value. One of the reasons why capitalism is so damn successful is that it understands we have an implicit system of value, discernment and end-judgement. I was trying to propose an economy of intersubjectivity, if you will, or an economy – now this has become a problematic term, but at the time it wasn't so bad – an economy of cultural capital independent of object commodification. And this was what that stream of the argument was about. But it hasn't really been taken up. The response to *Unmarked* has been much more about the technology of the ideal performance archive and the nature of disappearance.

MS: In *Unmarked* you say that 'performance's only life is in the present' (p. 146). This is a statement about the problem of mediation (of film, video, photography) between liveness and the experience of performance, and the memory of that fact, against the ability of recordable medias to document and reproduce performance, a statement about the undocumentable event of performance, and thus its ontology. You say that recorded or documentary footage, photographs of performances, and so on are distinct from performances themselves and are in a sense transformed visual acts in and of themselves that don't even bear an indexical link to the performance proper. We might say that they are in fact their own discrete works of art. Could you say some more about this proposition, with which I wholly agree, and also if you think the internet and its 'real-time' relays offer an addendum to this argument.

PP: That's a really good question. A couple of things: I was not saying, although I've heard people say I *was* saying, that we must not have photographs, videos or sound documentation of performances. I'm quite happy to have those! I teach and I use them all the time. I'm not against technology. But I think when one is showing a video; one is not, as it were, having the performance be re-performed. Video is a different medium and it pursues a different aesthetic. So I do stand by that part of the argument.

If I can paraphrase myself reasonably successfully, 'performance betrays its ontology to the degree to which it participates in the economy of reproduction'. That's not exactly it, but it's close. This word 'betrays' has been a bit of a problem. I think I was read as a high priest saying 'we must not have betrayal!' I understand that we live with betrayals of all kinds. I was trying to point out what distinguishes performance, ontologically, from the photographic and recording arts. Performance's ephemeral nature, I was arguing, is absolutely powerful and can serve as a rejoinder to the 'preserve everything', 'purchase everything' mentality so central to the art world and to late capitalism more broadly.

Philip Auslander has written a book called *Liveness* [1999], in which he disagrees with most of my argument.[2] Fair enough. But he misreads my essay in significant ways. He likes to say he doesn't *believe* in the unconscious and I think he thinks this relieves him of the obligation to contend with the psychoanalytic dimension of my argument. I can accept that, although I am not sure it is a legitimate mode of argument. At one point he says that I don't seem to notice that Angelika Festa's performances are performances with technology in them. Of course I notice it, and I spent a long time talking about what's on those monitors because I was not in any way trying to say that live performance cannot have video, audio, or technology. I was trying to notice where performance's political power lies. It has to do with this critique of the commodity. So that was what that was all about, and I am not so stupid [laughs] as to think live performance eschews technology. Performance is a technology. Medieval theatre was a technology. It was not the new technology, not, say, electronic technology, but it was technology: a plank and two boards, the definition of theatre. That's a technology!

Now we have streaming video, web casts, all sorts of media capable of recording and circulating live events. They can give us something that closely resembles the live event but they nonetheless remain something other than live performance. But these are very useful and very interesting tools and I am not against their use at all.

But in terms of the ontological question, it's simply not the same thing. For me, live performance remains an interesting art form because it contains the possibility of both the actor and the spectator becoming transformed during the event's unfolding. Of course, people can have significant and meaningful experiences of spectatorship watching film or streaming video and so on. But these experiences are less interesting to me because the spectator's response cannot alter the pre-recorded or remotely transmitted performance, and in this fundamental sense, these representations are indifferent to the response of the other. In live performance, the potential for the event to be transformed by those participating in it makes it more exciting to me – this is precisely where the 'liveness' of live performance matters. Of course, a lot of live performance does not approach this potential at all, and of course many spectators and many actors are incapable of being open to it anyway. But this potential, this seductive promise of possibility of mutual transformation is extraordinarily important because this is the point where the aesthetic joins the ethical.

Embodiment, Trauma, Death, Mourning

MS: Towards the end of *Unmarked*, you write that 'performance art usually occurs in the suspension between the 'real' physical matter of 'the performing body' and the psychic experience of what it is to be em-bodied' (p. 167). Add to that Elin Diamond's compliment on the dust-jacket of *Unmarked* that your book is a 'moving study on the ethics of the visible', my question is this: Is the point between these two things – between the real physical matter of the performing body and the psychic experience of what it is to be em-bodied – the point where Performance Studies, or perhaps performance itself, finds an ethics of the *visible*?

PP: Oh, that's nice! I wouldn't have thought so, but tell me what you mean? Certainly that might be where it finds an ethics, yes, but why would it have to be visible?

MS: Well, it wouldn't have to be visible at all – especially given the tremendous critique you direct at the visible, as we've already discussed, and the efforts you go to delineate the contours of the invisible, or the process of disappearing, of disappearance. But as a book that seems to be incredibly engaged with the difficulties of understanding the nature of visuality, and looking for ways in which the de-materialization of vision might be able to make certain kinds of possibilities available, if one is seriously taking as a starting point this particular axis, this point of convergence of the real physical matter of the performing body and the psychic experience of what it is to be embodied, it may well be that some kind of ethics of *visibility* can emerge too?

PP: That's terrific. You should write that book! I was not thinking of that. But yes I follow your point. I was trying to delineate a possible ethics of the *in*visible, but your idea is very rich and perhaps more positive. I wanted to talk about the failure to see oneself fully. This failure is optical, psychoanalytical and ethical. The wager of the book was to see if we could use this failure as a way to re-think what we mean by power, what we mean by representation, what we mean when we imagine our encounters with the other. I was suggesting that this central failure, instead of being constantly repressed by culture, might be something we could acknowledge and even embrace. If this were possible, I thought perhaps a different ethics, a richer encounter between self and other might become actual and actual-izable.

MS: Following up on these ethical matters, in *Mourning Sex: Performing Public Memories* [1997] you claim that 'it may well be that the theatre and performance respond to a psychic need to rehearse for loss, and especially for death' (p. 3). Would you tell us some more about the confluence of theatre, performance and death?

PP: Well, I started to take this question of disappearance really seriously! [laughs] Ultimate disappearance, as far as we know, is death, right? I became very interested in the ways in which theatre seemed to be obsessed with death. Currently I am writing a book about Andy Warhol and Ronald Reagan. They both were shot, they both were close to death and they both lived. Warhol said he heard himself pronounced dead and, characteristically, he says he heard this twice. For 18 years after, he said he didn't know if his existence took place on the side of life or death. Similarly, the announcement of Reagan's Alzheimer's disease in 1994 raises important questions about the assumptions we make about 'life' and 'consciousness' or 'subjectivity'. Is Reagan still Reagan if he does not know who he is? Is he alive in the sense that he is himself? Do we need to understand more clearly how life both needs and does not need consciousness in order to render a body a sense of liveness? Both Reagan and Warhol had explicitly pronounced theatrical worldviews and I am interested in how this worldview was challenged and either enhanced or rejected by these biographical and biological events. But to be brief, yes it is fair to say that the seeds of my new book, *Death Rehearsals* [forthcoming], were planted in that paragraph of *Mourning Sex*.

MS: Does *Death Rehearsals* have anything to do with your time at The Open Society Institute's Project on Death in America from 1997–99? As far as I can grasp what the Society does, it aims to 'understand and transform attitudes about dying and bereavement through research in the humanities and the arts, as well as to foster innovations in care, education and public policy'. How did you get involved, what did you do there, and what, as we say in this horribly bureaucratic age, was the 'outcome' of your time there?

PP: The 'outcome' is still to come! Yes, it's the forthcoming book, *Death Rehearsals: The Performances of Andy Warhol and Ronald Reagan*. The Open Society generously funded my work, enabling me to spend time reading in The Archives Study Center at The Andy Warhol Museum in Pittsburgh, Pennsylvania and in the Ronald Reagan Presidential Museum and Library in Simi Valley, California. My time in the Reagan archive was a mind-blowing experience on every level, but you'll have to wait for the book to read why. The Project on Death in America is now defunct, but it helped attract scholarly and pragmatic attention to issues of dying and death. Their work on palliative care has been especially successful and has helped increase the medical world's sensitivity to pain management.

MS: As a practitioner, and an academic, and a creative critical writer and as a performance writer, I was wondering if you'd say a little more about a project you worked on with the English Performance Studies academic, Adrian Heathfield, who is based at Roehampton University, entitled *Blood Math*, a performance piece via email on love, loss, memory, the body, the act of giving, employing philosophical, psychoanalytical and anthropological models of gift giving as a way of beginning a particular kind of exchange. In a similar vein, another of your projects is an imaginary dialogue with Jacques Derrida entitled 'P.S.' in which you write as 'P.S.', a pseudonym and/or acronym of/for Plato/ Socrates and/or Performance Studies. You also contrast the P.S. with the P.P. punning both on your own initials and Freud's *Beyond the Pleasure Principle*! [laughs] Would you speak about the multi - faceted nature of your commitment to performance?

PP: In *Mourning Sex* I was experimenting with what has come to be called performative writing. It's a way of bringing back to critical theory a certain *affective* emotional force. I was very interested in that. I was also concerned by a persistent separation between critical imagination and creative imagination: I wanted to foster a way of writing that would enable me to respond more completely, more emotionally I suppose, to art. And so it seemed logical, as a next step, to become a writer of performance. I first wrote 'Eat Crow' which was performed in 1997. It was originally written as a radio play. I was invited to the International Women Playwrights' Festival in Galway, Ireland in 1997, and

I worked with the actress, musician and scholar Lucia Sander on it. We performed it there and it was a fantastic experience for me. It inspired me to take my artistic ambitions more seriously.

I had been giving a lot of talks over the years, and after a while, I began to compose these talks as letters to the audience. As it happened, Adrian [Heathfield] heard a lot of them. I think he heard the first three or four. I became obsessed with the letter as a form. I was very interested in a direct address that I thought criticism was in danger of losing. Of course I was deeply influenced, if not obsessed, by Derrida's important book *La Carte Postale* (1987). Eventually I wrote two letters to Derrida that took up his book, and more particularly my meditation on his meditation on the P and the S central to his argument. For him, the P and the S stand for Plato and Socrates, the image on the post card around which he structures his book. These two figures also originate the textual structure of Western philosophy, hence their fascination for Derrida. I was interested in the P and the S as a way of thinking about Performance Studies, and we both were interested in the notion of PS as postscript, as that which exceeds the 'first' text and continues the text beyond its frame, including the frame of life. One of these two letter performances was published on the internet in a special issue of *Tympanum*, honouring Derrida's 70th birthday.[3]

When Adrian and I composed *Blood Math*, it was very much designed to be a kind of poor theatre piece – we used only music and slides. Most of my letter performances involved music and slides, and I know Adrian had often used video and slides in his talks. Even though my friends tell me to use PowerPoint and so on, I like the archaic nature of the slide projector; I even enjoy the stress of getting all the images in the trays properly. And there is nothing like music to create a mood and state of mind. Adrian and I began composing letters, almost all on email I believe, that would become the basic text for the performance. The text is about letters in the sense of epistolary correspondence and letters as in the alphabet. The performance plays a simple trick with letters that I won't reveal here! We performed it first in Chicago at the Goat Island Summer School, and then again at the Performance Studies international (PSi) conference in Arizona. The third and final performance took place at the London International Festival of Theatre (LIFT). The text, without the slides or music, was published in the journal *Cultural Studies* (2001).[4] Having now done these performances (and a few others), I have learned I prefer to let others perform my work. I am quite self-conscious and stiff, and when I am working with another person, I feel this awful burden and responsibility. I don't want to wreck the thing on their account. When I write my own texts and perform them myself, it seems to matter much less. If they are flops, I know I will survive and that I will try again.

MS: In the JD project you've just mentioned, you say 'Love, like writing, endures'. Could you say something more about the role that love plays in your thinking?

PP: I think that the older I get, the more I believe love endures. I think that when you're young, you have this idea that *you* are immortal and love is finite. And as you get older, you begin to develop a sense that *you* are mortal and *love* is infinite. I had been reading Derrida since 1981, and in the course of that 20-year long relationship my feelings about his work of course changed. But the practice of reading his writing endured. I wanted to address that element of love when I wrote to him on his 70th birthday. I was trying to write a love letter to someone not my lover but without whom my own love life would be less – what? – less well written! I'm kidding in a way, but I am interested in the ways in which writing and loving have always been entwined for me. The labour of critical attention I offer to the work of the other is a mode of love. A willingness to go out to the work of the other and respond to it with work of one's own is fundamental to critical writing. In this response, one writes, but one also loves. So love, like writing, endures.

Things of the Heart: Enjoy Your Symptom, Embrace Your Trauma

MS: I sensed that it might be fun to draw out some implicit themes, concerns and guiding impulses that I've discerned in your thought and writings over the years, and that we could play out a game of word association in a make-believe analytic situation? As the analyst, obviously, [laughs] I'll throw a word at you, and all you have to do is tell me the first thing that comes into your head. OK?

PP: OK.

MS: Community?

PP: I just moved to San Francisco and I don't yet have a community! Community is crucial. One of the things about living in New York I now see was how spoiled I was. I took for granted my intellectual, emotional and political community. In California, everybody drives cars – there is not that sense of spontaneous meeting in the street. I hope in time I will find an everyday community, but for now it is dismaying to miss it so much. Communities aren't always based on physical proximity of course. Some of the people I feel closest to don't live in the United States. Again, as you get older, you see the same people can be committed to a common project. It's very important. When you have this guy, George Bush in the White House, it becomes even more important to find a way to be sane and dissent. And sometimes you do have to do it in public, and get arrested. Sometimes you simply have to act. Having a community makes that a lot more fun, a lot more feasible, than it might otherwise be.

MS: Eroticism?

PP: I'm for it! [laughs] Eroticism and seduction, I think they go hand in hand. There's a certain kind of banal eroticism of the ubiquitous image of the good-looking, buff body that I'm happy to turn away from. I love Roland Barthes' essay *Camera Lucida*, where he speaks of the *punctum* in the image, which is really the space of the erotic – always traumatic. And I'm in favour of embracing the trauma. Enjoy your symptom, as Slavoj Žižek advises. [laughs] We need eroticism to keep us sane. And seduction, of course. Women's version of seduction – not Baudrillard's.

MS: Time?

PP: It's passing away. I'm really interested in the present. I say that as someone who lives in the United States and is incredibly embarrassed by the a-historicism of my native land. But I feel that that's a lost object for me, it's too late for me to become an historian! Beckett has this wonderful bit in *Godot* where Didi asks: 'Do you remember?' and Gogo says: 'I'm not an historian!' As I get older, I keep saying: 'I'm not an historian!' I think that we've either become obsessed with the future, which is what culture is always saying: 'It's going to get better...' or 'buy this and you will be ...' and so on. That's the imperative. Performers such as Stelarc and Orlan concern themselves with the future by radically revising the present surface of skin. Very important work for sure. And of course, many people as they get older fall in love with the past. But I really think we have to find a way to be present in and to the present. This is much harder than it appears to be.

MS: Intensity?

PP: I'm often told that I'm affectless, which I find very interesting. I feel myself to be intensely emotional, but I appear to be laid back, calm, and that gets read as affectless. But I'm pretty intense, and I'm interested in the intensity of others. I like extreme things, extreme art, intense emotions.

MS: Hesitation?

PP: Very useful. A discipline. I used to be extremely impetuous, but as I get older, I am becoming a fan of hesitation. It is useful because it allows you a moment to think. But it can be paralysing. So you have to say 'perhaps', and then do something. I think a lot of intellectuals get caught in the 'perhaps', and can't decide. I often suffer from this. Hesitation is a kind of humility that's worth practising. It's a discipline, but it's dangerous. Better not to fall in love with hesitation, but good to entertain it.

MS: Tenderness?

PP: There is a huge emphasis in contemporary culture on passion and hectic-ness towards desire. As I get older – god, I sound like I'm 90! – I feel gallons of tenderness towards my students and towards children in general. It's amazing. Tenderness is really beautiful and I want more of it – both to give it more and also to receive it more. And to trust it a little more, because especially with this war, we're in this unbelievably violent time, and I think the capacity for tenderness is especially worth cultivating now.

MS: Redemption?

PP: Redemption is more complicated! Redemption has such a theological canopy, it's hard to get out from under that. I do take my theology very seriously, but there is a spiritual overhang that I'm not always willing to engage. I did deal with some of this in my essay on Caravaggio's painting, The Incredulity of St. Thomas.[5] It begins with a meditation on Adorno's wonderful bit about redemption in *Minima Moralia* (1974 [1951]). I'm interested in that notion of redemption, the way in which one has to, as it were, think oneself past the dialectic, past the synthesis, into something we could call the after-thought. The P.S. or the after-death, the sense of survival that sometimes overtakes one unawares. I am interested in this kind of redemption, a consciousness of survival without expectation and without disappointment. I absolutely love Beckett. Beckett had a pervading belief, a pervading theology about failure. He has illuminated that brilliantly so there is no need to do it again. I'm interested in this other kind of post-Beckettian possibility, a post-theatrical age in a profound sense. The word 'beyond' isn't quite right – it implies a temporal thing, that you move through these things one at a time, but I don't mean it in that way. It's hard to express because our language is itself temporally bound in these ways. But I guess one way to say it is to suggest that there are some things that are conceptually 'after', that touch on, for lack of a better term, a kind of redemption. But it's not redemption in a sense of going to heaven ... It's more a sense of completion without expectation of response. A sense of having survived without needing any more experience to teach you what survival is. Something like this. It's not quite on the side of life, since it is in some fundamental sense 'after' desire, and it's not quite on the side of death because one still possesses consciousness, subjectivity, language, vision, touch and so on.

MS: You mean it's more like the 'something' that comes after the 'perhaps' of hesitation?

PP: Yes, perhaps.

Notes

1 Peggy Phelan in conversation with Marquard Smith, published in *Journal of Visual Culture*, 2(3), Winter (2003): 291–302. This interview took place on Friday 28 March 2003, days into the US/UK war on Iraq, on the eve of a conference – and series of events – co-curated by Adrian Heathfield, and Lois Keidan and Daniel Brine, Director and Associate Director respectively, of the Live Art Development Agency, entitled 'Live Culture: Performance and the Contemporary' at Tate Modern.

2 Auslander (1999) argues, contra Phelan, that in an effort to work against our desire to fetishize 'live' performance we must come to terms with the fact that 'liveness' itself is an effect of mediatization, and that it only comes to have meaning during or after the advent of its technologization: 'like liveness itself, the desire for live experiences is a product of mediatization' (p. 55).

3 This internet journal can be found at: http://www.usc.edu/dept/comp-lit/tympanum/4/khora.html

4 Peggy Phelan and Adrian Heathfield, "Blood Math", *Cultural Studies* (2001) 15(2): 241–57'.

5 Phelan (1997): 23–43.

References

Adorno, Theodor (1974 [1951]) *Minima Moralia: Reflections from Damaged Life*. London: New Left Books.

Auslander, Philip (1999) *Liveness: Performance in a Mediatized Culture*. London: Routledge.

Derrida, Jacques (1987) *The Postcard: From Socrates to Freud and Beyond*. Chicago: University of Chicago Press.

Lacan, Jacques (1981[1973]) *The Four Fundamental Concepts of Psycho-Analysis*. London: W.W. Norton & Company.

Phelan, Peggy (forthcoming) *Death Rehearsals: The Performances of Andy Warhol and Ronald Reagan*.

Phelan, Peggy and Lane, Jill (1998) *The Ends of Performance*. New York: New York University Press.

Phelan, Peggy, and Hart, Lynda (eds.) (1993) *Acting Out: Feminist Performances*. Ann Arbor: University of Michigan Press.

Phelan, Peggy (2001) *Art and Feminism*. London: Phaidon Press.

Phelan, Peggy (1997) *Mourning Sex: Performing Public Memories*. London: Routledge.

Phelan, Peggy (2001) *Pipilotti Rist*. London: Phaidon Press.

Phelan, Peggy (1993) *Unmarked: The Politics of Performance*. London: Routledge.

Schechner, Richard (1995) 'Transforming Theatre Departments', *TDR: A Journal of Performance Studies* 39(2): 7–10.

9

CULTURAL CARTOGRAPHY, MATERIALITY AND THE FASHIONING OF EMOTION

Interview with Giuliana Bruno

Introduction

Giuliana Bruno is Professor of Visual and Environmental Studies at Harvard University. She is author of *Streetwalking on a Ruined Map* (1992), *Atlas of Emotion: Journeys in Art, Architecture, and Film* (2002), and *Public Intimacy: Architecture and the Visual Arts* (2007), as well as numerous edited collections, articles, and catalogue essays. In this interview she speaks about her research and writing as it moves between visual, material, and spatial cultures. Here she concentrates on navigation – both thoughts as tools of navigation and how one navigates ones way through thought itself. In focusing on cultural memory, narrative, cartography, and the imagination – and in taking us from the mid-seventeenth century map of Madeleine de Scudéry to the psychogeography of the Internationale situationniste – she also considers the archaeological and genealogical importance of Warburg, Richter, and Benjamin's atlas, archive, and assemblage projects. Overall, Bruno draws our attention to cultural practices that mobilize thought and, in so doing, makes us all the more attentive to the materiality of the visual existence of life itself.

Interweaving Visual, Material, and Spatial Cultures

Marquard Smith (MS): I want to begin by asking you about your research and writing as it cuts across or reads between visual, material, and spatial cultures. You are one of the very few people mining and circling around this particular series of inter-disciplinary possibilities, and in very particular kinds of ways. I want to ask you some questions later on about the nature of the particular kinds of ways that you think about research and writing. But in the first instance, would you say something about the imperative to think across and between visual, material, and spatial culture?

Giuliana Bruno (GB): My work revolves around the relationship between architecture, visual arts, and film. As I grapple with sites of cultural geography, one could say that the centre of my research is space. I have a fascination for all things spatial but also for all things material, in the sense that space is usually a form of material reading, or, rather, a material condition. Space is not just simply created by architecture, which seems to have a hold on it; it is also created by the visual arts. I am interested in the space of the imagination and representation: the way in which we see things, we project things, and we imagine things in art forms as well as film, which have usually been considered not as spatial arts but as visual art. In my view, the distinction is not so separate. And when I say space, I do not mean necessarily only place but actually *espace*, in the sense that the French understand the word *space*.[1] For me this is a landscape that also involves an expanse of time, which in turn involves memory and everything that is created materially as one lives through and conceives of space. The construction of memory space is a function of the visual arts and of cinema, as well as of architecture, for they all shape the image of our built environment. So for me the intersection comes from being able to look across and in between all this, to imagine and understand a form of production of space that involves a temporal fashion – that is, the very fabric of time – and includes the ruins of the way things work, and to think about how all of this represents itself materially. So material culture and design are part of this cultural mapping.

MS: I'm glad you've mentioned material culture so early. I think you are officially the only person in this collection who is engaged quite explicitly in what we might call material culture. It is one of those wonderful points where Visual Culture Studies as an area of inquiry slides into design and design history, bleeds into architecture, which in turn opens itself out to something we might rather clumsily call spatial culture.

Material culture is a strange thing. Certainly in the United Kingdom. In the UK there's a real division between the scholars who, for decades, have been working out of design history and into material culture, and those who, much more recently, have been working in an expanded field of Anthropology that, by way of an ethnographic or empirical turn, have found themselves as scholars of (usually popular or vernacular) material culture. UCL's Department of Anthropology is exemplary here.

A great deal of significant historical work has come out of the first trajectory. Here I'm thinking about research by the likes of Barry Curtis, Guy Julier, Pat Kirkham, Victor Margolin, Penny Sparke, Anne Wealleans (née Massey), and many others of course. (And it also seems to me that a subsequent generation of scholars sometimes working through or by way of design history and material culture have taken this kind of thinking to the next level – and here I have in mind for instance Anna McCarthy's writings on televisuality or Laura Marks' work on the skin of the film, as well as your own cultural cartographizing.)[2] I have numerous colleagues at Kingston that work at the interface between design history and material culture: Penny and Anne, but also Trevor Keeble's writings on domesticity and Alice Beard's research on fashion and 'the new', and between them they've overseen and are overseeing a really interesting cluster of PhD students working on anything from nineteenth-century pub interiors to the profound superficiality of wood veneer.

The second trajectory, out of Anthropology, seems less interesting to me. And yet, despite the recent emergence of this trajectory, they're much quicker to claim the term 'material culture', in fact to the point where they've wrestled it away from its origins in design history and thus away from the ways that this discipline had carefully nurtured it.

Is there a question there? Maybe it has something to do with design history, material culture ... and fashion ...

GB: I do not look at visual culture as being only visual, a mere product of the eye. When you think of the visual arts as a field that is not only involved with the optic but has to do with the haptic – a space that can be almost in fact touched, that is apprehended not only by way of sight but by way of a certain form of contact – this space becomes a form of tactility, which is really the province of material culture. In this haptic sense, it becomes natural for me to think of architecture, design, and the visual arts as materially connected.

One of the things we know about objects is that they are there to be touched, used, and even 'consumed'. If one thinks of this fashion of using space theoretically, space becomes a material form of living. If one thinks of 'haptic' in the Greek meaning of 'coming into contact with', something that is an extension of touch becomes also a form of communication, in a fundamental sense. And that communication involves a kind of closeness to the object in the way that Walter Benjamin, as a critic who did not have an aversion to architecture or design or objects, or even fashion, understood reception. All these forms of representation are connected and brought into the equation when we employ a different way of looking at the visual that acknowledges this form of haptic contact with the object. This form of material communication has become much more prominent in contemporary visual arts and contemporary architecture, especially when we consider how much design is involved in the intersection of both. But this material form of reception also goes all the way back to the origin of the museum, to the cabinets of curiosity, if you think about it. The objects of a collection exposed in the museum, what were they? Were they mere art works? Or objects, in the sense of objects of design? They were objects framed for vitrines, designed to put us in touch with their material existence. So collection is also a form of the recollection of things.

Objects, things, material things ... And fashion enters into the equation in many different ways. First of all conceptually. One of the things I like about the

English language is that you can say that space is fashioned. The way I think about space concerns the very fashioning of the space: space being made, fabricated, and having itself a texture, a fabric. So another reason why design enters into the equation of thinking about architecture, art, and film is because, to me, the visual has a texture.[3] The more flattened the flat screen becomes, the more I think about this idea of the texture of the visual. When you think about texture in visual fabric, you think about the plasticity of forms. You become aware of all that it is involved in the making of the actual thing, in the fabrication of the object. But what is more important, you become sensitive to the fold of things. You expose layers and uncover strata, peel out coatings and veneers – that is 'films' – but you also look for such residue as a fabric of memory. In film, for example, it is the texture of light where this all comes into play. Thinking of the fabric of the visual in this way, one can relate the fabrication of film as an object and the making of an object in art to an actual object in design or in fashion.

After all, architectural space is akin to fashion as something we come into contact with epidermically. It is very clear, even from Condillac's eighteenth-century idea of the senses, that as beings moving into space we apprehend space haptically.[4] And this is not just about the hands. Of course the hands are what touch the objects, the things, but it is the entire being that is in touch with space. Everything, even our eyes have skin on them. So the skin is our first coating, our first dress, and then fashion becomes our second skin. Fashion is the way we decorate our epidermic selves. As such a spatial ornament, fashion is truly a form of design. By way of dress we actually 'fashion' our own selves, which also means our identities; we design our stories and tailor the way we project ourselves onto the world. And then architecture becomes the third skin. Architecture is the third fold of space we come into contact with. It is an enveloping space, a tactile extension of this way of designing ourselves – addressing our identities as we are dressing ourselves. So architecture and fashion are to me very much interactive as a social form able to project and share an imaginary, and to communicate the making of the self across visual fabrics. It is not by chance that some of the great architects were interested in fashion. And today the two fields are very much connected, not only because there are architects who design clothes. Clothes designers such as Hussein Chalayan, say, make this connection clear when making dresses that are basically architecture, that are chairs, constructions, or things that move. His clothes are objects, literally objects of design, and they really are an extension of furniture, in a sense, on a woman's or a man's body. So the two are interacting in a way that is very visible in our culture today.

And film fits into this fashioning of space, because it is also a 'projection'. For one thing, film is an object already; it is used and consumed, and it circulates as such substance. This art form is deeply involved in the fabric of things and the design of the self. Film is actually a very material object that makes visible something that is invisible, including our imaginary and mental space: atmospheres and moods. Through forms of light it basically creates and is able to transmit everything that belongs to the fashioning of everyday life. At the same time, it can be read itself as a textural surface. Equipped with a screen that used to be an actual sheet of fabric, it is a celluloid texture that absorbs things and can project all kinds of visual fabrications. If we look at it this way, we can see that at the root of the actual object of film is a kind of fashioning. We can even argue that the origin of film is fashion. After all, a film is a series of still images on a strip, which used to be cut and sewn just like dresses were cut and sewn. When you look at Vertov's *The Man with a Movie Camera* and you watch the woman editing the film, you realize it is very similar to making a dress. You have this form that you are putting together, that you are suturing really – tailoring – in the same way you would design a piece of clothing. There is much fashioning in the cinema, in many senses.

I am interested in cinema not just for the text of the film but also for the way the entire apparatus involves materiality, in the form in which it is made and projected. Film's fashioning of space includes a spectator who lives in that space, becomes part of this imaginary site, and is transported by its moving fabric within the space of the movie theatre. Cinema becomes a part of you in the sense that you 'suit' your own self into it, in an inside out form, in a double movement. In film, you constantly travel from an outer landscape to an inner landscape, and you go back and forth and in between these two forms. So this idea of the inside out is very much about fashion as well. The one thing the fabric knows is the inside out. Hence it all folds together in this kind of architexture, for fashion, architecture, and film are able to refashion in visual folds and permeable textures the way we look at the world.

MS: And the same is true of language? The kinds of words that you have been using ... I don't know where you pluck the words from ... but you manage to find a way of conjuring up an incredibly evocative and rich use of language that allows you to play around with words and phrases: 'collections' and 'recollections', 'dressing and 'addressing', the 'fashioning of space' and the 'spacing of fashion'. And tailoring. I think you used the word tailoring a couple of times ...

GB: 'Suiting' as well.

MS: Yes. So this is a question about the materiality of language, your use of the richness and texture of language ...

GB: Whether it comes directly from my inner thoughts, the unconscious, or from being a foreign speaker I am not sure. I think that the latter has something to do with it. When you learn a foreign language, when you are writing in a language that is not your mother tongue, there is a certain moment of pleasure that comes when you can actually play with it. Seriously, I care for all things material, that is, objects, things, and material forms. For me, language is one of these. The materiality of the way one writes is very important to me. I make an effort when writing – and it is not easy writing in a language not my own – to convey thoughts by way of the form of language itself, by way of the flow of words and the sheer unfolding of sentences. I take pleasure in using metaphors as means of transport, in finding words that evoke forms or shapes, and in twisting them, even in making them up sometimes. I probably made a few up along the way. But English can sustain this game – it is a fantastic language to actually suit your thoughts in.

Every material object offers you the pleasure of touching it. Language has this ability too ... it really touches you and me. In English, we can say this – words are touching or pictures are touching. So if one wants to write about the fashioning of space and think about materiality and fabric, one has to look for a fabric in language suitable to conveying these sensitive ideas, and has to tailor one's style accordingly. Furthermore, as a material object, language also allows you to go deeply into it, to excavate its mould. Another thing that I like about language is that it allows me to perform a kind of archaeology. This is part of my method, of the way in which I construct all of these connections: deeply excavating into words, I look for almost geological forms, strata of meaning that make ideas connect together. Language has this ability because it has a history. Sometimes in a word that used to mean something it no longer does, you actually find a way to retrace a notion and reinvent its meaning. I use etymology often this way, and sometimes doing this almost surgical operation on language has allowed me to find what I was looking for. There are moments of great serendipity, like when I was trying to express my ideas about a relation between motion and emotion in cinema, and it was the etymology of the word *cinema* that made it all evident, for cinema comes from the Greek *κινεμα* – well, the ancient Greek, long before cinema ever existed – and this word means both motion and emotion. It was perfect. This gave me the impulse to continue to play, of course. In the end, this kind of digging is more like an 'archaeology of knowledge': in the way Foucault talked about a genealogy, it is not about the origin or authenticity of the word but more about being able to make connections (Foucault, 1972/1969). It enables you to circulate meaning, to move with the fluidity of language, which holds strata of different knowledges within its history, and can therefore allow for multiple readings.

MS: And, like your example of the etymology of the word cinema, if it's already there, even better!

GB: Sometimes you discover things in this fashion, so to speak.

MS: It's that you have a sense, a feeling, that it might already be there without actually knowing. And if it's not ...

GB: ... then that is fine. It's not like we are proving anything. It is up to you to use language as part of the interplay of creating a field of work; so using words, in a sense, is a way to move through things. If they have it within themselves so much the better and if not, reinvent them!

Cultural Memory, Archives, Atlases, and Assemblages

MS: All of this talk of archaeologies and genealogies and excavating puts me in a position to ask you a question about archives, and the role that they play in your research and writing. Archives are on my mind at the moment because of the conference I'm programming with Michael Ann Holly that's taking place later this week at the Sterling and Francine Clark Art Institute entitled 'What is Research in the Visual Arts? Obsession, Archive, Encounter'.[5] They're also on my mind because I've been rereading your stuff in preparation for this interview. So, now, I'm thinking about layering, the ways in which you've been speaking about language, and the nature of the materiality of language, and the different ways in which this material is woven together, and that this weaving is very much like a genealogy, in the Foucaultian sense: an interlacing of contingencies, surprises and accidents, discontinuities, ruptures, truths and origins, facts and fictions, and of emergence [*entstehung*] (Foucault, 1977/1971). The idea of the archive has a really different role in this context. In your book *Atlas of Emotion: Journeys in Art, Architecture, and Film* you go to/through a number of archival projects – from Annette Messager to Gerhard Richter to Walter Benjamin – as particular ways of thinking about what an archive is and does, and how an archive mobilizes thought ... (Bruno, 2002)

GB: I am very fond of this word and of the concept. But perhaps my work, especially *Atlas of Emotion*, is a place where a traditional notion of archive doesn't work. I am attracted to particular kinds of archives, or certain kinds of methods, as it were, of collection – modes of collection that allow for different forms of recollection. We mentioned a few, and most of these are not conventional ways of thinking in certain quarters. But in others they are; it depends.

MS: It's shocking, and I'm afraid to say they'll *remain* unknown in these quarters.

GB: Yes, it's astounding. The other notion that applies, that goes with these figures that you mention, is the atlas. And to me an atlas and an archive are not far apart, partly because I understand the archive itself as a form of cultural memory that has a materiality, and also as a form of collection that allows multiple ways of recollection, which is to say, as a form of passage. Like an atlas, an archive can be navigated. It contains things that need to be explored and discovered. And, just like an atlas, it encourages you to be guided through its terrain.

To me, an archive is a territory to be unearthed, to be discovered, archaeologically dug up. Those operations are not necessarily linear. Just as an atlas allows you to move in time and space, across different territories, my kind of archive does not entail a prescribed journey; it is something that is an invitation to journey.

MS: Aby Warburg employs the word *orientation*.

GB: Orientation is a perfect word. Warburg is probably the main methodological influence in this way of thinking, especially his *Mnemosyne Atlas* (Warburg, unpublished), which is fantastic. Conceived towards the end of his life, his unfinished atlas of memory was very visual and very material. Here was an art historian who was in a sense making assemblages as he constructed a montage of disparate images, ranging in subject from art to science to the everyday, that were to be exhibited on panels. His kind of archive documented the relationship between states of mind and corporeal expression and made a geographic history of visual expression. In a way, these were collections of pictures that were in his mind, inner images being projected outwards for exhibition, and recollection. Before anyone was thinking about this notion of visual culture, Warburg was able to put together visual documents and material representations of the movement of life. His assemblages of life in motion, for example, would have exhibited on the same panel a great piece of artwork alongside the physical movement of a person, the flow of a dress, an image of travel, or the design of a room. His version of 'elective affinities' was inventively wide-ranging. As he surveyed the entire spectrum of vital kinetic manifestations in different forms of representation, he paid particular attention to affects. Warburg searched for 'the engrams of affective experience', and pursued a 'pathos formula' to be able to map living experience.[6] So the sort of communication established across these different forms in the atlas would touch upon the materiality of the visual existence of life and its very fabric, which was living in his archives. And the trajectory of art historical knowledge inscribed in this heterogeneous assemblage did not shy away from the emotional involvement of empathy. This archive was a living museum.

Walter Benjamin is another ... I mean I *still* love him. There are all these incredible ideas in his work that you think you have read and then you go back and rediscover them in a different way. Take the *Arcades Project*, his unfinished work, a real endless archive (Benjamin, 1927-40/1999). His form of archive is infinitely fragmented, a montage made of a palimpsest of quotations, segments and fractions, pieces and sections, all fluidly rambling. The fragmentary nature is important to me, probably because this idea of the assemblage of fragments in a way comes from film. Film is the most fractured form because it is nothing but a language of fragments, shots where time and space are compressed into units that are assembled in sequence. And Benjamin's arcades project is like an enormous movie.

And it is also the kind of book you can open at any point and stare at a sentence or two and then connect it to an entirely different part of the work, as if you were a film viewer. It is an object, like a video object, the book that allows you to flip through it and relate in your own way. Benjamin's form of writing is truly a conceptual image of modernity. And of course his archive of knowledge included a pioneering understanding of cinema, of the city, and even of fashion. All these modern manifestations are displayed in *The Arcades Project*, which is a veritable gallery of modernity's visual culture.

And then there is Gerhard Richter, an artist who has made another type of atlas, an ongoing work that began in 1962, consisting of photographs, collages, and sketches mounted on panels (Blazwick and Graham, 2004; Richter, 2007). Richter's *Atlas* is his own peculiar type of archive, which again is not an encyclopaedia. I like the fact that this kind of archive is always unfinished and does not wish to be all-encompassing. It gives no definite form to the knowledge it presents. Here, there are fragments set in motion in an orderly fashion but with no systematic or systematizing logic. The work is boundless, and yet bound. New images are constantly incorporated; and they can change the form – the territory – of the ever-growing atlas. Given its nature, this work can be endlessly disassembled and then re-assembled in another way, and so it is always exhibited in different forms and permutations. This also allows for multiple voyages of interpretation, which become an actual traversal of the terrains of the atlas, whose fragmentary trajectory includes the viewer.

If the figure of the fragment is always present in this kind of archive, I think it has something to do with ruins, and with loss. The fragment is melancholic by nature. I am very attracted to ruins – fraying fabrics of history. It started way before *Atlas of Emotion*, with my first book, *Streetwalking on a Ruined Map* (Bruno, 1992). This was basically written on a ruined landscape. For one thing, there was nothing there but fragments. I was exploring a territory that involved the work of a woman, Elvira Notari, who made sixty feature films and over a hundred documentaries between 1906 and 1930, of which only three remained. So there might have been no book to write, except that I am always attracted to being able to figure out how you can piece together the few remaining traces of a suppressed culture. So I went on a series of inferential walks through Italian culture, interweaving examples of cinema with architecture, art history, medical discourse, photography, and literature to render the visual and material world this woman film-maker depicted. It was a portrait of the city, at the cusp of modernity, set on location, right where the cinema, the railway, and the shopping arcade intersected to transform our ways of seeing. It was all about motion pictures as part of the emotion of modernity and of the metropolis. And while unreeling this modern, fragmentary cityscape, I constantly reflected upon the ruins of modernity. To draw the landscape of cultural memory in this way is not a matter of seeking origins or authentification of something that is lost. It does not become a job of preservation but is more like an art-historical type of restoration where you still sense the fragment, visible in the fabric of the (analyst's) work of intervention. Take the way frescoes are restored now: although the picture may appear seamless, on closer observation you become aware of the different textures of the reconstructed parts.

The trace of the passing of time on objects – the life of material objects, including films, books, works of art or architecture – is inherent in the creation of the archive in *Atlas of Emotion*. And, in different ways, Richter, Warburg, and Benjamin, whose archives are in a way cinematic, become models for thinking about mobilizing the fabric of time. I am fond of objects such as film, which is always in ruin. As André Bazin understood a long time ago, cinema suffers from a 'mummy complex'; that is to say, it is a plastic art, and, like the casts of the dead bodies in Pompeii, it creates a plastic image (Bazin, 1945/1967). Cinema is an heir of the plastic arts and represents the most important event in their history, for it both fulfills and liberates art's most fundamental function – the desire to embalm. As it captures the moment, film freezes it. But the second you fix something on celluloid, it is already gone, it does not exist anymore. Furthermore, film constantly moves. I think that cinema – a moving, ruinous kind of assemblage – has become today's archive. To make a play on words, we might say that *cine*mas and *cine*res are connected. From dust to cinemas. In other words, films are the ashes of our time. But the history they preserve is always shifting in motion.

MS: Death at 24 frames a second.[7]

GB: Yes, exactly. And you see this in art today. Many artists who are making moving-image installations about film, like Douglas Gordon as a classic example, are exhibiting this process. In general, this archive of moving images has become very important for art, and there are constant reworkings of cinematic cultural memory in art installation. Just think of Stan Douglas, Isaac Julien, Doug Aitken, Mattias Müller, Steve McQueen, Mark Lewis, or Jane and Louise Wilson, to name a few artists who all do it in different ways. Think in particular of the latest works of Tacita Dean, *Kodak* (2006), *Noir et Blanc* (2006), and *Found Obsolescence* (2006), about the closing of the factory in France that made 16 mm film, a work that is a wonderful meditation on the kind of archive that cinema is. As her work on obsolescence makes clear, film is our memory. It is our mental space, and it projects how we think. You see this clearly in the way Anthony McCall makes cinema into an art of mental projection in his art installations. This is how we imagine ourselves, how we think of ourselves, how we think of a culture – cinematically. Even anthropologists, not to mention historians, have come to terms with cinema as a history.

But art, in particular, is the place where this moving, filmic culture of memory is being reinvented. In the art gallery, the archives of cinema are constantly exhibited and reimagined. In many ways, cinema exists for today's artists outside of cinema as a historic space – exists, that is, as a mnemonic history that is fundamentally linked to a technology. Walking in the gallery and the museum, we encounter fragments of this history. Filmic techniques are reimagined as if collected together and recollected on a screen that is now a wall. In the gallery or the museum, one has the recurring sense of taking a walk through – or even into – a film and of being asked to re-experience the movement of cinema.

And thus, as I show in my book *Public Intimacy: Architecture and the Visual Arts*, we confront a mobile cultural memory as film exits the movie theatre and returns to the museum.[8] This return is not surprising or upsetting to me, for the contemporary interaction of art and film is a phenomenon that has a long history. What is happening in the contemporary art galleries and in the museums is only a reminder of how cinema itself emerged. Historically, cinema was born with the museum and emerged from its way of allowing experience of a visual work in forms of 'public intimacy'. A product of the same epoch of modernity, cinema shares with the museum a spectatorial mode. In a way, pictures – both paintings on the wall and images on the screen – were perceived, looked upon both subjectively and collectively, and traversed in similar fashions. Think about the archive of the museum: the pictures don't move but the viewer moves from one to the next and puts together her own montage of these gestures, of these memories, as Warburg understood in the way he assembled images together. Film also displays objects that are assembled together in time and space and, even if the spectator doesn't move, she makes imaginary movements, or projections into time and space, putting together her own assemblage.

Film itineraries *are* museum walks, and vice versa. And now moving image installations are exposing this double process as an actual itinerary. I am happy to observe this return of cinema into the museum, because the two started together as a (re)collection of images, open to viewing, and are now reinventing this process in renewed, refashioned forms of interaction. The cinema and the museum are archives that are converging in hybrid ways, in moving installations that mobilize the very nature of cultural memory. And it is cinema's own obsolescence today, its own ruined moment, that is making it return to life, because things that are dead, as cinema in some way is, are very much alive, and can be reborn in another form.

MS: All of which raises so many questions! I was going to interject at various points, it was hard not to. One of the things I wanted to say had to do with the idea of the assemblage as a 'living methodology'.[9] In teaching, and thinking through things, I often foreground Warburg and Benjamin and Richter, along with Borges' *Chinese Encyclopaedia* invoked in the introduction to Foucault's *The Order of Things* (1966/1996) – another unconventional encyclopaedia – as examples of living methodologies, living methodologies that are building blocks in the emergence of Visual Culture Studies before the fact. So much of the more creative, imaginative ways of thinking about what we do is already there in those models, as living methodologies.

I like them all very, very much. Theirs are practices that mobilize thought, thinking. But I sometimes wonder what it means to be using these living methodologies as *living* methodologies? They're 40, 70, 80 years old! What does it mean for, say, Benjamin in the 1920s and 1930s to be writing about nineteenth-century Paris, and for that to be a way we can make best sense of the early twenty-first century? This makes me nervous sometimes. I don't know if I've ever voiced that. But it does make me nervous. At the same time, it does make such good sense of certain ways of thinking about contemporary culture – although I recognize that its melancholic archival impulse might be a retreating from as much as a recognition of our global consumer capitalist age of empire. This aside, they offer a sensibility. It has something to do with the nature of these particular kinds of intellectual projects as assemblages. I think that's what it is. I think you've absolutely hit the nail on the head. It's the assemblages that still work ...

GB: I see what you are saying and I have often wondered about this myself. Benjamin to me still makes sense because he understood something about the origins of modernity, which we have had a century to play with. And, in the context of his understanding of modernity, he perceived the nature of the assemblage as a cinematic concept. After all, he was one of the earliest theorists to fully recognize the importance of cinema, not just as a way of changing our ways of seeing but also as a transformative spatial medium. Cinema became equal to architecture in the use and transformation of space, as a form of tactile appropriation of sites. And when he makes that analogy between the surgeon and the magician, as cameraman and painter respectively, he shows he understands not only the assemblage of the medium, its 'cutting' ability, but how it is deeply involved in the transformation of the material (Benjamin, 1936/1969). We are talking about metamorphosis, operating by way of these assemblages of modernity. In intellectual adventures this also means the possibility of transitioning along and in between ideas, connecting objects that are epochs of times or even mediums. This notion of moving across and along is again a cinematic concept, because it is within montage that you have reached this possibility of juxtaposing two things that generate a third, not just in the object itself but in the mind of the spectator. Hence the way Benjamin performed 'operations' upon this material of modernity is still speaking to me. It is a 'living methodology', indeed, living in forms of reinvention.

Sergei Eisenstein also understood this process, and he, too, saw cinematic montage as reproducing the transformative movement that occurs in architectural space.[10] Eisenstein understood montage in film to be an architectural promenade, a way to make you move across a space, and not just physically but mentally and emotionally. You become able to make jumps, imaginative leaps, in places that involve going back into the future or forward into the past, and to perform all kinds of operations that are science-fiction-like because of this ability that space has to evoke the past, the present, and the future, all intersected, almost geologically, in living space. So this goes back to the idea of lived space as also having layers – sediments and strata, residues and deposits – that is, as being a living fabric.

Cultural Cartography, Spirals, and Sensibilities

MS: Well now I completely understand your book *Atlas of Emotion*. Because what you've just said, *that's* at the heart of it, right?

GB: Well, yes, it's all in there.

MS: Turning to *Atlas of Emotion*, I was going to ask you a question about cultural cartography, and what it means to you. You've touched on it already, every now and then. *Atlas of Emotion* is absolutely the work of a cultural cartographer – whatever that might mean. It just struck me that you were talking about being able to move, or be moved, between time and space, between different historical moments and geographical places, possibilities. I marvel at how in the book you manage to somehow be in a seventeenth-century cartographical landscape and at the same time very much in the twenty-first century. You write and embody and enact the nature of the project at one and the same time, which is quite incredible! It has something to do with taking charge of the material. I'm picturing *Atlas of Emotion* next to these assemblages, and it's not an assemblage in the same kind of way as Warburg's *Mnemosyne Atlas*, or Richter's *Atlas*, or Benjamin's *Arcades Project*. I mean, it is *like* them, and *of* them, in terms of its sensibility, but at the same time there's a different sense of ... I keep wanting to use the word 'ownership'? That can't be the right word ... but there's a kind of ownership that *Atlas of Emotion* has of itself: that it gives itself up to things, but at the same time it also makes a decision about how to tell a story. Maybe that is the thing about the cultural cartographer, that they both give themselves up to things, to the shape and nature of things, and at the same time have to navigate a path through such environments?

GB: My work is very much about navigation; it is about routes, and process. And that is why the image of the map, which has sometimes been terribly demonized, is dear to me: because it offers your inner senses an instrument of guiding, which can take both the author and the reader through rugged and ruined terrains. The book was written as a kind of journey of palimpsest-like assemblages. There is a trajectory there, so it is not a random accumulation of things. As I moved through different layers of material, often I wondered, 'Am I all over the map? In which ways? How do I keep this navigation going?' The method of the navigation is important to me, and I prefer the kind of charts that one takes on a journey with oneself, that unravel as you go on the journey so that they are part of the voyage. And this journey is also a narrative itinerary, for I am concerned that a book tell a story, a specific kind of story.

Narration is historically part of cartography, which, after all, concerns the story of a place and has at times even embraced fictional forms of representation. In the seventeenth century, for example, the art of mapping was an imaginary cartography – it was not simply a charting of real places, although real places were portrayed, but it understood the relation between a real place and an imaginary one. In my type of cultural cartography, I touch upon that form of liminal connection that is so deeply important to the visual arts and to film, which do address reality but also dress it in fantastic forms. When you write about visual culture, you have to be able to navigate this story, the relation between the inner imagination and the outer expression, and move in between these two forms.

The map that most inspired *Atlas of Emotion* and its *'journeys in art, architecture, and film'* was *la Carte du pays de Tendre*, literally the map of the land of tenderness, designed way back in 1654 by Madeleine de Scudéry. This map of the land of affects is interesting because it is a very open map. Like a film it has a frame, but things keep falling off screen. At the edge, the sea would flow on the one side, the river on the other. This is a map of a specific place but also represents the place of imagination. And it is a map that wants you to navigate it, that needs somebody to actually enter the territory and move through it rather than form a single image of a place. You would constantly work on the border, around edges, to try and imagine what was behind the boundary of the frame, and your curiosity would pull you towards some *terrae incognitae*. So this was an important model to me in the creation of this kaleidoscope of different cultural sites and in thinking of how space becomes this repository in which I could move in time but also across different kinds of media.

This map was also important because of how it visualized affects and how it represented an itinerary of emotions, specifically, in the form of a landscape. In Scudéry's map there was a vast terrain punctuated by little towns, and one was supposed to move from one to the other, and that motion provoked an emotion. This mode of representation became a guide in my way of theorizing the relation between motion and emotion in the visual and spatial arts, and especially in writing about film's own emotion pictures. This map allowed me actually to visualize how within space itself there are different materials, textures, and fabrics that form the various itineraries you follow as a critic, and that includes the affects.

Speaking of other cultural cartographers, it is significant that the Situationists were inspired by Scudéry's map, which was reprinted in the *Internationale situationniste* in 1959. This form of mapping becomes, in a way, the model for the kind of psychogeography that rethinks spaces in relation to fluid assemblages, and to psychic montage. In this cartography, for instance, you can connect places in a city or on a cultural map not by way of real distances but by way of events that have been experienced in the imagination and in the reality of the people who have lived through them in the space. You can see motion in culture as deeply related to living space and lived temporality. And you can also understand that emotion itself is a movement, and then movement is something that touches a person, touches something profoundly deep within the person, which enables a deeper social transformation. In this way you can understand the work of affects beyond physiognomy, and emotion not just as one single image or state of mind but as the possibility of moving across different states of mind, creating diverse, mobile forms of connections to the world.

MS: Madeleine de Scudéry's map reminds me of a project published a couple of years ago by the magazine *Cabinet*.[11] As a project entitled 'A Slight Mismap', they reproduced François Jollain's *Nowel Amsterdam en L'Amerique* (1672). Exploiting Europeans' interest in the New World and their ignorance of it, Jollain's map is a fictitious bird's-eye view of Manhattan Island that's copied from a sixteenth-century view of Lisbon!

But Jollain's cartography is a lie. *You're* speaking about something quite different. What you're articulating is exactly the point where the experience of the thing itself and the imaginative possibilities of that thing come together. You're struggling with how the map can be used to mobilize your understanding of what it is you're needing to do. It's about the journeying, it's about the 'getting there', not the getting there.

GB: What is most fascinating about the journey is the process itself, not the beginning or the end product. Quite often, what is most important are the stops along the journey, the arrests and standstills that generate another way to go. Sometimes the journey begins on a personal note and takes a personal form, for, as a cultural cartographer, when you move through different geopsychic fabrications you are also moving through your own personal imagination and your own emotions. In this sense, critical theory can be understood as a journey in lived space. You traverse this huge territory and sometimes you even discover something that makes you want to go back within yourself. But this 'analytic' journey is not really a going back. It is almost as if you have moved through a spiral, which represents a different, more productive kind of circularity. I am fond of spirals and of spiralling ways of thinking. The spiral form is not the circularity of the ending, but it is a circularity that allows you to make motion, and even allows you to circle backwards while going forward.

I have been very fond of this idea of movement for the longest time (it spirals in different ways from *Streetwalking on a Ruined Map* to *Atlas of Emotion* to

Public Intimacy). And, in this respect, there was something I held very dear for a while, which was a concept that James Clifford expressed: 'to theorize, one leaves home' (Clifford, 1989). Which has to do with departure, and separation. As he writes, *theorein*, the Greek term, is a 'practice of travel and observation', so theory itself, from the beginning, is 'a product of displacement, comparison, a certain distance'. In my case it was even literal – I left my home country, my mother tongue. I left to find my own way to theorize, and possibilities became opened to me in New York, at a specific moment in time, to take on this theoretical journey.

Over the course of time, I have also realized that this kind of journey, this love of motion, has very little to do with speed. It actually has a lot more to do with slowness and with duration, and this is especially desirable in an age where we are deprived of the time itself of thinking. Rather than having this constant fascination for restless movement, I then became more and more interested in meditating on forms like spirals, which allow you to revisit things. Spirals enable a certain revisiting of territories, and even allow you a form of return. In fact, having taken this route and journeyed along this path for a long time, I finally discovered that to theorize one cannot really leave home behind. Ultimately, one must accept the risks, theoretical and otherwise, involved not only in leaving but in attempting a return.

So it is not by chance that the last chapters of *Atlas of Emotion* are devoted to Naples, the city in Italy that I am from, revisited with the eyes of someone who has left it behind. This is a virtual journey of return, in which I am not physically going back and through which I have become a different person along the way. This return is not about reclaiming roots, origin, or identity, but it is really about the nature of displacement and about what this motion means, culturally, to individuals like myself, who are now a type of cultural hybrid, existing across and in between cultures, people who not only have elements of different cultures but have also transformed themselves along the way.

Ultimately, this critical expedition is a real cultural journey, for it is its own journey of migration through territories. To connect this back to what we were saying about the materiality of language, I further discovered while working on *Atlas of Emotion* that the word *emotion* contains in itself not only motion but has, in its own roots, the cultural notion of migration. The Latin root of the word *emotion* speaks clearly about a 'moving' force, stemming as it does from *emovere*, an active verb composed of *movere*, 'to move', and *e*, 'out'. The meaning of emotion, then, is historically associated with a moving out, migration, transference from one place to another. This 'moving out' is exactly what one does as one crosses a border, which can be the territory of a nation, or a culture, a language, or even an emotional territory. It is a going out of oneself, in the sense of being able to push one's own limits and one's own borders. So this cultural journeying of migration, this moving from one place to another, is a cultural cartography deeply steeped in the pleasure and malaise of our time, a method created by new migrants, cosmopolitan workers who question their own territories. This is another way to understand the emotion of motion, as the affect brought about by all senses of migration, theory included, which is an actual emotional 'transport'. When you re-turn to theorize this way, and you go back, by way of writing, you make this kind of spiralling journey of understanding through the straits of material culture, while you are yourself being transported and transformed.

MS: This all leads me to ask a question about 'environment', or, rather, about Environmental Studies. It is, in a sense, a question that takes us back to the beginning of the interview, to matters of the university, disciplinarity, and so on. You are based in the Department of Visual and Environmental Studies at Harvard University. It's a title I love! When I first came across the name, it confused the hell out of me! I always understood the 'visual' bit, but on first viewing the 'environmental' part of the department's name seems to have something to do with ecology, sustainability, protection agencies, and so on. But everything that you have been talking about, everything you do in your research and writing, makes sense of a Department of Visual and Environmental Studies. You couldn't be in a more appropriately titled Department!

GB: I love this title. I like it even because it is confusing. I know a lot of people can get confused, because 'environment' has come to mean something different; but the origin of how it came about, in terms of the genealogy of this place, is perfect, and it even touches on a notion of the ecology of the image. The Department was founded over forty years ago, way before the concept of the 'built environment', which is its origin, was as theoretically relevant as it is today in terms of a culturally built space, that is, a representational landscape. In some way, the philosophy of this Department of Visual and Environmental Studies came out of a post-Bauhaus notion of connections among all the arts, and again that is where design also enters into it.

MS: With the Carpenter Center for the Visual Arts itself ...

GB: Yes, with the Carpenter Center for the Visual Arts, because there were some architects and also designers who were exiled from Europe during the Nazi era and World War II whose ways of thinking led to this. The idea was to create a building that might house a department that would not be just of architecture. The concept was broader, with the sense that the visual arts could have a place within design, or, rather, as we see it today, within a visual architecture, and that included even graphic design. The seeds of the birth of this place are contained in this idea of the creation of an architectural home for the art object, which was widely conceived, with all the arts represented along with architecture.

MS: And the fabric and materiality *of* the building and the nature of the experience of being *in* the building ...

GB: Yes, this is crucial, because Le Corbusier was given the commission to build this fantastic building that houses the Department of Visual and Environmental Studies, which is actually the only building of his in North America. The Carpenter Center is very different from the rest of the Harvard campus, and, as the artist Pierre Huyghe showed in his *Huyghe + Corbusier: Harvard Project* in 2004, a work produced for the fortieth anniversary of the building, a part of the institution was concerned about its modernism, for which the architects among the faculty had advocated, and there were letters in the archives fearing a white whale was to rise in the middle of campus. The concrete and glass structure of the building is almost like a pianoforte: it looks like two sides of a piano. This is a perfectly rhythmical place, in many ways, especially because you enter it through a ramp. So the door is already a place of motion – the passage between inside and outside is already a trajectory, an idea that suits me perfectly well. Also, there is no difference between entrance and exit: the way you enter the building by the ramp you can also exit, without even going inside, for the ramp cuts across the whole body of the building. It is a fantastic metaphor for what I have been thinking about for a while.

The Carpenter Center for the Visual Arts is also a building you cannot hold in your mind as a single image. I have taught there since 1990, so it is seventeen years, but if I close my eyes, as when I think about New York in my mind's eye, I am not able to recall it in a single image. There is no single vision that holds it; the building is full of fragments, a fractured place that is seen by way of lighting, that changes according to how the light reflects and refracts, that is all about windows that are cinematically 'cut' and that traverse the building. This building is really an assemblage, in some way, and one that can only be experienced in motion, for it comes to life only as you move through it. Le Corbusier, after all, was the architect who theorized and practiced the idea of an 'architectural promenade' (Le Corbusier and Jeanneret, 1964).

The first thing that attracted me was the potential of this edifice, and the extent of its conceptual expanse. The particular fabric of this building enfolded a visionary concept and had within itself the seeds of a very interesting history. I love this notion of an integrated study of visual culture, and the idea that this place housed architecture and design along with painting, sculpture, drawing, printmaking, photography, animation and film, and now also video art and art installation, in both theory and practice at the same time. This building is a kind of laboratory of ideas, and I was thrilled that I could actually find a place where I could expand across the horizons of everything I am passionate about, which was already contained in some form in this imaginary assemblage. Of course, the concept and the connections had to be reinvented, for, by the time I got there, naturally, the original founders were aged or retired, and their critical tenets could no longer hold in the same way. The Department's vision had to be rebuilt theoretically under the new tenets of thinking about visual culture. For me, a key to this is to work with the history, with the idea of an architectural container for objects of visual representation, understanding it as a theoretical architecture – an architecture of the visual that can extend from the art object all the way to the object of design. It is this material object that has the potential to cut across and connect all the visual arts, and to link them as well to the spatial field in a wide-ranging way of thinking about visual space. In this sense, Visual and Environmental Studies is about a broad sense of spatiality and how the visual arts themselves make space.

Many different roads can be taken from there. To stay with your original question about the environment, when thinking about the 'built environment', for example, the treatment of architecture can become an understanding of landscape. To speak of cityscape or streetscape says a lot more about the urban than mere architecture, which tends to be tectonic. The built environment is a place in motion, a landscape of movement. And when you think about the creation of this 'scape', of a built environment that is a representational landscape, landscape itself can be understood as something made up. There is nothing natural, after all, about a landscape. It has been framed and painted, over and over again, so that it has become an image; just think of the Renaissance or the Picturesque. And now it also is constantly photographed and filmed. This kind of complex, interactive, imaginary landscape is very much part of the fabric of how we think culturally and of how images are created and circulated. There is a real relation in visual life between art, architecture, and the moving image, which intersect in creating even our own scape. So the name of the Department of Visual and Environmental Studies is indeed very meaningful, and this was and is the perfect place to be able to develop my ideas. *Atlas of Emotion: Journeys in Art, Architecture, and Film* was born while walking up and down the ramp of Corbusier's building, and it grew through a number of seminars that I taught with students who are very inventive and willing to take a journey with you, something I cherish about this place of intellectual adventure. And the place continues to grow, and more colleagues have come in, and so it has become much more possible to share these ideas and further expand not only their horizon but also their impact.

Another important thing, institutionally – and this is something that I hope will expand to other places – is to rethink the place of film studies, to reposition it in relation to the history and theory of the visual arts and of architecture. The birth of film studies as an academic discipline in the institution was generally connected to literary theory and semiotics, at least in the United States, and cinema studies was regularly located in literature departments, often as an offshoot of English departments. Then it became its own place, though you still find literature programmes functioning as institutional homes for the study of film. But what has not been really tapped into, and I think there is a tremendous archive of possibilities, is its relation to art history as well as architecture and urban studies, which can open up a wealth of new research. To me, the idea of locating a graduate programme in Film and Visual Studies in a Department of Visual and Environmental Studies is a chance also to reinvent film studies, positioning it much more in relation to the traditions of thinking visually and spatially that exist in the history of art and architecture, and especially in contemporary art. Just think of art installation today, or go back to modernism or the origins of modern visual culture. I mean, how can you be an art historian and not know anything about the moving image, and vice versa?

The cross-pollination of these disciplines is crucial to creating new methods and new ideas, and to moving on into a different form of theorization of the moving image that can treasure the whole trajectory of the history of representation by delving into the visual archives that belong to the visual arts and architecture as well as into their cultural histories. There is tremendous energy in this interaction. Just to give you an example, my students in architecture are the cinephiles of our era, they are obsessed with film. And you can see why, in terms of the architecture that is being constructed, because architects have been struggling for a while with wanting to mobilize the object itself of architecture, this thing that doesn't move. So of course they are attracted to cinema. And then there is the connection between the two in terms of the creation of a living space, of a space of circulation and transition where fabrics of histories and stories are written on the walls, as they are in houses or buildings, which breathe the history that has been lived through them, or as they are projected on the screen, which also absorbs the fabric of life.

I think it is important for film studies to dig into these archives of art and architecture to be able to rethink its own medium, and vice versa. And film, this syntethic, hybrid art form, can be, and has been, tremendously important to these other disciplines in opening up their own frames of mind in different directions. The moving image is the centre out of which other journeys can take place. And more will come of these crossovers. Artists and architects already understand the power of the moving image. It is clear every time you walk into a gallery or look at architecture, even if sometimes academia takes longer in catching up with the ideas. Such is the nature of academic institutions. And so a lot more can still be done creatively within the institution to revitalize film studies by linking it, historically and theoretically, to the visual space of architecture and the mode of representation of the visual arts.

MS: In the end, when it comes to these questions of interdisciplinarity, one both thinks about and doesn't worry about the links between, say, Film Studies, and Geography, and Visual Culture Studies, and so on, and so on. It matters and it doesn't matter. One does what one does because it is important for it to be done, and then every now and then one thinks about what it means to reposition this or that in relation to this or that.

GB: I just do what I do.

MS: And they will come. People didn't come to the Bauhaus in the 1920s and 1930s because it was in Weimar or Dessau or Berlin. People didn't come to teach and learn at Black Mountain College in the 1940s and 1950s because it was near Asheville, North Carolina. They came because of a ...

GB: The word really is sensibility. A common sensibility. For myself, this is just the way I think, an attraction to all forms of representation of space. In the end, it is the passion and fascination of what one does that counts. I am not exactly an institution builder, in the sense that I didn't make a programme first; what I needed to say I needed to write, because I am a writer first. But the book is a building block. Books create a foundation by their very existence, and I am happy if *Atlas of Emotion* can function in this way. But to work in this *espace*, and in between textural fabrics, does not mean I do not have respect for the disciplines. It is actually much more difficult work to do, this transdisciplinary voyage. People sometimes misunderstand what it takes to do visual culture or material culture. You need to know a lot more, several fields, and be a lot more careful and sensitive to certain things – you have to know both the objects and the borders. It is tremendously rigorous work. The balance between the confines of the specific field or object you are tackling and how to cross over to make them speak in a different way is quite delicate. Perhaps, in the end, that's why I am attracted to cartography, because to map is to construct through close engagement with material objects – with method and fluidity, which have to work together if one is to move with sensitivity and elasticity across the terrains one is traversing and the materials one is interweaving.

Notes

1 See, for example, Henri Lefebvre, *The Production of Space* (Donald Nicholson-Smith, *trans.*). Oxford: Blackwell, 1991 [1974]; and Michel de Certeau, *The Practice of Everyday Life* (Steven Rendall, *trans.*). Berkeley: University of California Press, 1984.

2 Anna McCarthy, *Ambient Television and Public Space*, Durham: Duke University Press, 2001; Laura Marks, *The Skin of the Film: Intercultural Cinema, Embodiment, and the Senses*, Durham: Duke University Press.

3 On visual fabrics, and the relation of architecture and film to fashion, see, in particular, Giuliana Bruno, 'Pleats of Matter, Folds of the Soul', *Log*, no. 1, Fall 2003, pp. 113–22. An expanded version of this text is to be published in David Rodowick, ed., *The Afterimage of Gilles Deleuze's Film Philosophy*, Minneapolis: University of Minnesota Press, forthcoming 2008.

4 See Étienne Bonnot de Condillac, *Treatise on the Sensations* (Geraldine Carr, *trans.*). Los Angeles: University of Southern California, 1930. Originally published as *Traité des sensations* (1754).
5 The conference took place on 27–28 April 2007. The proceedings, edited by Michael Ann Holly and Marquard Smith, will appear in 2008 in the 'Clark Studies in the Visual Arts' series, published/distributed by the Sterling and Francine Clark Art Institute/Yale University Press.
6 Aby Warburg, 'Introduzione all'Atlante *Mnemosyne*' [1929], in *Mnemosyne. L'Atlante della memoria di Aby Warburg*, Italo Spinelli and Roberto Venuti eds., Rome: Artemide Edizioni, 1998; see especially pp. 38–43.
7 This is an allusion to the argument at the heart of Laura Mulvey's *Death 24x a Second: Stillness and the Moving Image*, London: Reaktion Books, 2005.
8 Giuliana Bruno, *Public Intimacy: Architecture and the Visual Arts*, Cambridge, MA.: MIT Press, 2007. See, in particular, chapter one, 'Collection and Recollection: On Film Itineraries and Museum Walks'.
9 This is a phrase that comes up in the interview with Susan Buck-Morss in this volume.
10 See Sergei M. Eisenstein, 'Montage and Architecture' [c. 1937], *Assemblage*, no. 10, 1989.
11 *Cabinet*, Issue 18, Summer 2005, 'Fictional States'.

References

Bazin, André, 'The Ontology of the Photographic Image' (1967, [1945]), in *What is Cinema*, vol. 1 (Hugh Gray, ed. and *trans.*). Berkeley: University of California Press, p. 9.

Benjamin, Walter (1936/1969) 'The Work of Art in the Age of Mechanical Reproduction', in *Illuminations*, Hannah Arendt (ed.), (Harry Zohn, *trans.*) New York: Shocken Books, pp. 233–34.

Benjamin, Walter (1999) *The Arcades Project*, Rolf Tiedemann (ed.), (Howard Eiland and Kevin McLaughlin, *trans.*). Cambridge: Belknap Press/Harvard University Press.

Blazwick, Iwona and Graham, Janna (2004). *Gerhard Richter Atlas: The Reader*, London: The Whitechapel Gallery.

Bruno, Giuliana (1992) Streetwalking on a Ruined Map: Cultural Theory and the City Films of Elvira Notari, Princeton: Princeton University Press.

Bruno, Giuliana (2002) *Atlas of Emotion: Journeys in Art, Architecture, and Film*, London: Verso.

Clifford, James (1989) 'Notes on Travel and Theory', *Inscriptions*, 5: 177.

Corbusier, Le and Jeanneret, Pierre (1964) *Oeuvre complète*, vol. 1, ed. Willi Boesiger, Zurich: Editions Girsberger.

Foucault, Michel (1966/1996) *The Order of Things: An Archaeology of the Human Sciences*. Poris: Gall. Mord.

Foucault, Michel (1972/1969) *The Archaeology of Knowledge*. (A. M. Sheridan Smith, *trans.*). New York: Pantheon Books.

Foucault, Michel (1977 [1971]) 'Nietzsche, Genealogy, History', in Donald F. Bouchard, (ed.), *Language, Counter-memory, Practice: Selected Essays and Interviews* (Donald F. Bouchard and Sherry Simon, *trans.*). Ithaca: Cornell University Press, pp. 139–64.

Gerhard, Richter (2007) *Gerhard Richter: Atlas*, New York: D.A.P,/Distributed Art Publishers.

10

VISUAL STUDIES, HISTORIOGRAPHY AND AESTHETICS[1]

Mark A. Cheetham, Michael Ann Holly and Keith Moxey in Conversation

Introduction

This dialogue is an opportunity for Mark Cheetham, Michael Ann Holly and Keith Moxey to speak together in print for the first time since their edited collection entitled *The Subjects of Art History* (1998). Concerned, in that volume, with the prospect that 'art history, like many other fields in the humanities, has entered a post-epistemologi-cal age', the three editors wrote opening 'position papers' outlining, respectively, their concern for the (Kantian) philosophical imperatives of/in art history, how the spectres of context haunt the writing of the history of art, and on the historiography of art history as Hegelian. Overall, their collection was a chance to reassess the role that the philosophies of history of Kant and Hegel and other philosophical, semiotic, queer, postcolonial, psychoanalytic and museological traditions concerned with 'history' have played, and continue to play, in art history's efforts to legitimate its past and predict its future. In many ways, then, *The Subjects of Art History* was an attempt, from within the discipline of art history, to picture that area of inquiry in an expanded field that we may continue to call art history or might be more usefully designated as visual studies.

The dialogue is an opportunity to continue that conversation. Specifically, it is a chance to rethink the question of the place of both 'aesthetics' and 'history' in and through visual studies. As such, this dialogue seeks to address questions such as: how might visual studies rethink what we thought we already knew? Are both critics and supporters of visual studies right to believe that 'aesthetics' has nothing to do with visual studies? Why might they be right, or wrong? (And if they are wrong, how does visual studies offer us an occasion to engage with aesthetics in new ways?) What status do or should the philosophies of history of Kant and Hegel, say, have in visual studies? How does visual studies affect such models of history, or what does it mean for it no longer to believe it needs History at all? Or, to put it more kindly, is there something that visual studies can teach us about Kant and Hegel and subsequent historiographical thought?

By no means looking to resolve these questions, this dialogue is motivated by an urge to problematize in productive ways the accusation that visual studies does not do, care for, take into consideration, or otherwise understand 'history'. It hopes to indicate why visual studies has to deal with history, however conceived, if for no other reason than at least (and most importantly) that it can attend necessarily to the genealogies of the study of our visual cultures.

Keith Moxey (KM): The idea of a conversation on some of the issues raised in *The Subjects of Art History* (1998) is a provocative one. Among many other things, the essays in that volume raised questions about the nature of 'history' and 'aesthetics' – the Scylla and Charybdis of art-historical historiography. There have been moments when art history threatened to dissolve into the morass of contextual detail that inevitably surrounds the creation of what we call 'art', so that its 'autonomy' either went unremarked or was assumed, and times were when all that mattered was an internal history of the object that insisted on its freedom from cultural entanglement. I suppose that in saying this I am opposing Erwin Panofsky's 'iconology' and Michael Baxandall's 'social history of art', with, say, Heinrich Wölfflin's notion of 'style', Alois Riegl's 'Kunstwollen' and Clement Greenberg's 'flatness'. History and aesthetics might be said to be the poles around which the discipline has organized its activities and negotiated their relation to one another to constitute what we mean by art-historical writing. Every time the profession decides to favour one of these poles, the other suffers and vice versa.

Mark Cheetham (MC): Yes, the alternation of paradigms seems still to be with us, if we define ourselves as art historians active in a broad, but nonetheless mappable, field. Of course, as you and Michael both know from your conference (2001) and publication (Holly and Moxey, 2002) from the Clark Institute entitled *Art History, Aesthetics, Visual Studies*, as well as numerous earlier activities, coordinates do seem to change once we add 'visual culture' to the conversation. There is a challenge both to history and to aesthetics, traditionally conceived. I wouldn't want to say prematurely what these challenges are, but from a visual studies perspective – really from all of the perspectives under scrutiny here – clearly we need to rethink the objects of inquiry, both their status within a western canon and perhaps especially those that come from other traditions. Traditional aesthetics, that is practiced by self-identified philosophers, to me remains often too pure a discourse, one that assumes (or wishes) that ideas can be compared and improved upon, more or less in a vacuum. Visual studies (and much art history) of course challenges this way of working. I doubt that art history alone would have made these discrepancies in method so apparent. How does the profession 'decide' to move in any direction? I would like to think about how we decide as putative individuals, how we choose our research topics, conference papers, grant proposals and what we will teach. What I should say here is that Michael and I disagree about the nature of the 'decision', as to how exactly one comes to one's research. While I acknowledge our lack of autonomy or volition, I still try to take a more sociological point of view of how it is that we do what we do.

Michael Ann Holly (MAH): The Scylla and Charybdis dilemma in art history is not one that troubles me. In fact, I revel in its capacity to unsettle. Even supposing that we could do without either history or aesthetics (as some of the most glib [mostly student] work in visual studies does mistakenly presume) or even disabling just one of the poles would be to disarm completely one of the most venerable (ha!) disciplines in the humanities. Do we take the art out of history, or the history out of art? If we managed to perform that surgical operation, we would have much more to lose than to gain. I'm a historiographer through and through. Responsibility to both *questions* about aesthetics (not only when or where aesthetics comes in, but what it is at that moment of interpretation, etc.) and *questions* about history (for whom, to what purpose, what evidence, etc.) dog us relentlessly, but that doesn't mean scholars of the visual arts will ever escape the need to turn around and confront them. In fact it is in the confrontation that entirely novel insights arise. When we composed *The Subjects of Art History*, we asked each essayist to take an explicit approach from the 'new' art history and rub it up against an 'old' object and see what happens. I don't think we could ask for the same naive approach now, but it seemed to work then. And one more matter, gentlemen. When we choose our corner of the scholarly terrain, we cannot forget that it is also the case that the terrain (or at least the kaleidoscopic shake-up of it today) chooses us – time changes questions that the artwork puts before us, different objects call to different subjects at different moments, new political angles make new objects come into view. So the 'deciding' is always a see-sawing enterprise. Mine is more a phenomenological conviction, Mark, as compared to your sociological view.

KM: Yes, that see-sawing is certainly evident. However, the situation is perhaps singularly fraught with difficulty at the moment because there is little agreement as to how either of the poles might be defined. Our traditional confidence in a Hegelian model of history, with its reassuring evolutionism, its inspiring teleology and its reliance on the concept of genius, has been shaken beyond repair. Georges Didi-Huberman's *Devant le temps* (2000) and Mieke Bal's *Quoting Caravaggio: Contemporary Art, Preposterous History* (2001) have demonstrated the inevitable anachrony of the art-historical enterprise. In drawing attention to the role of the present in the construction of history, they pose the old question: 'What is to be done?' Are there any principles according to which history is to be told, or should we recognize once and for all that history must depend on the nature of the interpreting subject? If this is indeed the case, then what is it to identify history as a genre that would distinguish it from, say, fiction?

MAH: Perhaps because it should have an ethical commitment, a dose of intellectual rigour, a temporarily accepted protocol of investigation, a clear delineation of argument, etc. – and more, Keith.

MC: I agree that the Hegelian model of evolution has been challenged frequently and powerfully, but – and I never thought I'd echo Ernst Gombrich in print – I also think that we have to watch carefully for examples of this sort of thinking still holding sway. I was at a symposium recently on the topic of 'Making History'. A prominent curator spoke passionately about the spirit of the times driving artmaking and its critical response. I objected strenuously to these potentially misleading mystifications, but I sensed that many people in the audience felt quite comfortable in abdicating any sort of agency or responsibility for the art history that most would agree is made, rather than motivated from within. We have to take responsibility for our choices as art historians, critics and curators. On the other hand, we aren't always even partially aware of why we do, what we do, and no doubt many of our 'decisions' are the result of institutional conditioning. I don't see that we can step outside this cycle and I do not believe that a 'critical' position requires that we do so.

MAH: Or as Gombrich would say in his well-known rant against Hegel, dispense with the metaphysics and concentrate anew on the critical choices and their relationships. But how do we know what choices? What criticality? Consider Horkheimer:

> Critical theory appears speculative, one-sided and useless – it runs counter to prevailing modes of thought ... Those who profit from the *status quo* entertain a general suspicion of any intellectual independence. (1972[1968]: 218, 232)

But of course that would also include Gombrich.

So, how do we proceed? Shouldn't the protocols of interpretation be often ironic, turning one thinker (past or present) round another, twisting one idea (past or present) inside another? That's genuine 'intellectual independence', the kind that you hope will help the interpreter (or his or her students) think anew, producing new knowledge rather than reproducing the old.

MC: I agree, and I believe that this was very much the purpose of *The Subjects of Art History*. It wasn't naive to ask contributors to our collection to put their methods into proactive contact with art-historical subject matter in a more or less practical demonstration. It worked and it still does. Some form of history (if not historiography): this idea came to us about 10 years ago, even though the collection appeared in 1998. It seemed like a good plan for the target audience and was suggested by Cambridge University Press, which was keen to present the book as a useful 'text', which it has been.

KM: If traditional notions of history have been placed in question, as we've already begun to outline, is the situation any clearer when it comes to aesthetics? As a consequence of the long reign of 'objectivism' that art history went through following the Second World War, it became incumbent on art historians to conceal the nature of their aesthetic relation to the works they discussed. The social history of art has perpetuated attitudes developed during the heyday of iconography and iconology, in which the last thing expected of the historian was the subjective expression of his or her aesthetic response. The result has been the deep naturalization of Kantian and Hegelian ideas. It is perhaps the modernist field, with its investment in the criticism of contemporary art, that has demonstrated the greatest creativity in the application of the Frankfurt School aesthetic theory of Adorno, Benjamin and others, as well as the phenomenological traditions associated with the work of Heidegger and Merleau-Ponty. Yet, even this field must find its certainties challenged by an ever-increasing awareness of the artistic production of those parts of the world not usually identified with the modernist tradition. How is contemporary African art to be evaluated? On what grounds are aesthetic discriminations to be made? To what extent will the stories we have been telling ourselves about the quality of artistic objects apply in these circumstances? Should we begin to think in terms of 'aesthetic communities' rather than in the universal terms usually associated with the idea of aesthetic value?

MAH: Neat idea, but doesn't that stretch the word beyond all recognition? Or maybe you're right – we can just burrow inside the concept and inhabit it in a new way. Its appropriation then becomes part of a new politics of recognition. But, then again, how can any one scholar understand, much less question, even a minority of the 'aesthetic communities' of the world? To be unaware of even a few of them jeopardizes what any one of us might wager to say about her or his own chosen community.

MC: I like the notion of more localized, specialized interpretive communities. I think that's what we have, however universalist our fantasies may be at times. I've just given an example of the naturalization of Hegel that Keith notes, but on the other hand, there is now and has been for some time a widespread denaturalization of the philosophical elements of art history. What I'd like to see is avid rereading of these texts (in addition to others, and with no special priority) so that, say, new 'Kantian' ideas can be put into play in the fields concerned with the visual arts. I tried to do this in my book on Kant and the visual arts (Cheetham, 2001) by reading Kant's autonomy aesthetic against itself and against its social and political contexts of creation and reception. He becomes less important as a formalist when we think of his powerful example in the political arena c.1800 or his obsessions with bodies, notably his own. To be frank, I wasn't thinking explicitly about the expansion of the discourses around the visual made by visual studies. My approach was deconstructive in many ways. But I felt then (in the late 1990s when I was writing) and believe still that art history has become an increasingly capacious and flexible field over the past years. Perhaps there is a point at which for some art history shades over into visual studies because of the approach or the work in view, but I have tended to blithely assume (as a way of insisting) that we can go ahead and call this art history if we so desire.

MAH: May I interject something here – your and Keith's references to the almost unconscious hold that Kant and Hegel have on art history remind me of Fernand Braudel's quest

> to convey simultaneously both that conspicuous history which holds our attention by its continual and dramatic changes – and that other, submerged, history, almost silent and always discreet, virtually unsuspected either by its observers or its participants, which is little touched by the obstinate erosion of time. (1966[1949]: 16)

Is that what you're advocating: a recognition of a submerged history that cradles the eruptions and disruptions of surface perturbances – which today might be called visual studies?

MC: Yes, I like this formulation. Lately I've been thinking about Bruno Latour's *Politics of Nature* (2004), which also seeks to recognize crises rather than regularities.

But as I anticipated, argued and have had confirmed by the reception of my own work on Kant and art history, disciplinary assumptions still get in the way of this sort of open exchange. A lot of philosophers have felt the need to defend Kant against my supposed criticisms of his place in art history. What I haven't articulated fully in my published work, but would like to entertain here, is that we take Kant seriously when he calls in his political writings for a 'cosmopolitan' relationship among interlocutors. Could we productively move his ideas on geopolitical interaction to the arena of conflict – and cooperation – among art history, aesthetics and visual culture? My own answer is 'yes' and my tactic, again, has been 'just' do it (although this is a poor excuse for my passivity in the debates about these disciplinary changes). For example, I devoted the final chapter of my Kant book to a consideration of his 'image', including obscure miniatures from his own lifetime, phrenological photographs of his skull, mail art disseminations of his famous head and the role that Kant statuary plays in the current realignment of national identities in the Baltic region. The result was not normal art history because I discussed almost no canonized works of art or well-known artists. My own sense is that I explored the visual culture of Kant's head, though others may see the work differently.

KM: Very much in keeping with Mark's account of his recent work, paradoxically enough the development of visual studies may allow students of the visual to address both 'history' and 'aesthetics' in a more flexible and creative manner than has been possible hitherto. Far from rendering the concept of aesthetics obsolete, for example, the study of visual culture as a whole may allow us to see more clearly the discriminations we make when we separate 'art' from the rest of the realm of visual artifacts. Instead of falling back on aesthetic principles that have animated art-historical writing in the past, instead of talking about 'pleasure', 'originality', 'disinterested contemplation', 'complexity', 'coherence', 'freedom', 'beauty', 'transcendence' and the 'sublime', it may be possible to perceive the very different kinds of value that not only different classes and age groups belonging to a single culture ascribe to those objects they seek to privilege with the name 'art', but it will be interesting to learn the value with which analogous objects are invested in other cultures. Not only does the death of modernism allow us to see the artificiality of the borders that were once built around 'art' to keep it 'pure', but also the rise of postcolonialism and the process of globalization enable us to see the power relations that guaranteed the dominance of its historical narrative. All this brings us to the very interesting question of the 'value of value'. What might be the point of finding exceptional interest – philosophical fascination – in some objects rather than others? It is here that Hal Foster's concept of 'strategic autonomy' (Foster, 2004), recalled in an interview in a recent issue of the *Journal of Visual Culture*, is relevant. Far from drawing the conclusion that the death of the grand narratives brings the age of aesthetic autonomy to an end, it seems to me that it complicates and enriches the question of autonomy in interesting ways. It recognizes that there can be no 'essential' definition of what autonomy might consist of, and places new stress on the responsibility of the historian or critic to articulate the grounds on which autonomy is claimed.

MAH: Good point; I would even expand it. The value of visual studies is that its historians and critics often find themselves in this position of 'responsibility', defining and redefining core concepts such as aesthetic autonomy, or conceptions of the artist, or definitions of art, or characterizations of the public, not to mention many others. And can't one genuinely make the claim that for over 100 years, traditional art history has gained its 'legitimacy' over and against repeated challenges to the assumptions or values on which it is grounded? Keith, Norman Bryson and I were being too short-sighted when we claimed in the introduction to *Visual Culture: Images and Interpretations* (1994) that: 'During the past fifteen years or so, the ideas about which we think and write have seemed at odds with the traditional canon in which many of us were schooled'. Leave it to the young and brash to think they are reinventing the wheel. We not only gave too little credit (although we did give some) to the role of feminism and Marxist social history (e.g., Nochlin and Clark) 15 years before we were writing, but to ignore the role of writers such as Benjamin, Kracauer, Riegl and (for me especially) Warburg was historiographic heresy. Warburg has been invoked constantly in the last decade as the 'founder' of the 'expanded field' of contemporary visual studies. At the time I believed that he was the perfect intellectual sponsor for a variety of new developments in art history that are now loosely connected under the rubric 'visual and cultural studies', and I still partially subscribe to a good part of that genealogy. The study of art was for him a serious study of history and the power of history to shape contemporary consciousness. In his quest to discover meaning in the past, he excluded nothing: from salt boxes to altarpieces, from Native American rituals to Renaissance murals. His erudite eclecticism is precisely what continues to appeal to postmodernist art historians, even if we have lost the sense that there is any meaning there to be discovered. The problem sets in when we try to enlist Warburg as an intellectual predecessor and patron in more than the most general genealogical line. As much as I admire them and have devoted my intellectual life to these figures from the past, I have grown increasingly skittish about the insidious ways in which this compulsive return to earlier theoretical art historians – say Warburg, Riegl or Panofsky – is contributing to the disparagement and dilution of genuinely novel thought. Just at the moment when all sorts of new subjects and approaches are coursing through our field, we seem to have succumbed to a conservative urge to revisit earlier authorities, as though to emphasize that this sort of thinking has been part of art history for a very long time. Invoking precedents in order to tame the untamable. In other words, the past sometimes gets in the way of the present, something Nietzsche recognized long ago. One of the most serious issues raised by the current practice of art history is whether its cultural foundations in a particular intellectual milieu flourishing at least three generations ago can sustain the usages and practices derived from it. In the United States at any rate, there's a great deal of significance in changing the name 'art history' to 'visual studies'. For the latter refers more to an intellectual attitude than a field of study. It names a problematic. It's the banner that proclaimed 10 or 15 years ago that 'the times, they are a-changin''. But of course we only recognize change if we study, historiographically, where we have been. So what am I saying? I don't think that there has been a major theoretical shift recently, but rather a working out of the implications of an earlier seismic one that occurred a couple of decades ago, rather than a century. The theoretical shift of the 1960s and 1970s – which reached art history most fully in the 1980s – has been followed by the practical application of these earlier ideas. In other words, developments in visual culture now would be inconceivable without Foucault, gender theory, deconstruction, postcolonialism, etc. Our mothers and fathers, rather than our venerable great grandfathers, should be held most directly accountable for our behaviour.

MC: Michael, these are provocative questions. Your query was to Keith, but I want to ask if Warburg was a predecessor – now rediscovered – or an influence?

Like you, I've heard a lot of papers on his work recently, but he seems to be taken more as a model for a certain kind of creative and conceptual thinking-through of questions concerning the cultural history of art history and visual studies and not examined historiographically as such. Do those looking back at Warburg and others see them as part of a traceable lineage, or as examples to be emulated but without a continuous historical effect between their time and ours?

Going back to Keith's point about autonomy, Modernism is in part defined by the autonomy topos, or the rhetoric of autonomy, whichever specific strain one articulates. Whatever else we may say, many species of that paradigm seem to be past, which means that we can now understand the modern as a period and set of tendencies with a beginning and end. But of course many scholars would disagree – for example, Arthur Danto and Thierry de Duve – which at least proves the point that modernism in some way continues to hold sway.

MAH: By the way, following up on the matter of Warburg and historiography and historiography in visual culture, I always wonder why 'visual studies' equally cannot refer to a new theoretical understanding of old art – of the Renaissance, for example? Why is modernism always invoked? Just a question (or a desire to return to Warburg!). When the term 'visual culture' was first nominated by Michael Baxandall in *Painting and Experience* (1972) and seconded by Svetlana Alpers in *The Art of Describing* (1983), it was, after all, about Renaissance images and Dutch visual culture and thereby ripe for a re-energizing of early period studies.

MC: Modernism comes up so often because so many of us work in this period and, perhaps more importantly, because we wonder if the modern is indeed somehow over. I think it's past in an historical sense but remarkably influential still as a set of paradigms. I'm also bemused by the increasingly frequent bashing of postmodernism, often from a conservative position in the sense that it asserts the ongoing primacy of modernist paradigms. I'm thinking here of much of Thierry de Duve's writing and the visual production of Jeff Wall. There was a paper delivered at the recent CIHA (Comité International de l'Histoire de l'Art; Hadjinicolau, 2004) conference in Montreal that sought to dismiss the importance of pretty much all French poststructuralist thinking on the study of the visual arts. Thankfully, Keith spoke to this elision. I really don't know to what extent these debates involve visual studies. But to respond to you directly Michael, I think that we can always find earlier and earlier examples of a paradigm recently identified. What's the purpose of such a quest for authenticity in origin? But you've shown the positive side of such archaeology: many pay overdue attention to Riegl and many others now. I'd really rather use texts and ideas and images than say who got to what and where first, which strikes me as disciplinary posturing. It's likely true that there is more emphasis on modern and contemporary art than on other areas, as you say, but again I think the reasons are sociological and institutional.

KM: Even if visual studies follows its ancestor cultural studies in dedicating itself mainly to synchronic analyses of contemporary cultural production, the concept of history seems inescapable. Not only will the passage of time need to be acknowledged in one way or another, but the historicity of the analyst's own position will figure either explicitly or implicitly in any narrative. In both cases it is possible that the encounter with visual traditions whose pasts have been shaped by forces distinct from those traditionally associated with the history of art, as well as the development of new subject positions from which to view them, will offer opportunities for creative new solutions to the problem of 'artwriting'.

MC: For me as well, it is imperative that art writers – whatever their focus – have a working sense of their own historicity and those objects or themes that they explore. We must instill the sense that the past was different but that our access to it, our writing of it, posits a connection *in the present*. There is no time travel, but there is what we call time and we must account for its role in the changes we seek to account for in art.

MAH: Back to an old art historian. I cannot help myself (despite my suspicions of a few minutes ago), for there is where the philosophical grappling with the assumptions of art history seems so frequently to reside. Riegl (1982[1903]) already worried about this conundrum in his essay on monuments. Drawing a distinction between 'historical-value' (that which elucidates the past) and 'age value' (that which imbricates the viewer in his own ruminative sense of the past as no longer), to which should we be more responsive in the practice of artwriting (*pace* Carrier, 1987)? Historians or poets? And do philosophers fall in-between? Why have we abdicated the 'pasts' of art history for the 'presents' that studies of visual culture give us? What have we sacrificed? What about the act of writing itself? What change of commitment and direction in research would it take to say that in visual studies we work towards more understanding than 'proof'? Even more 'poetry' than analyses?

MC: Your question reminds me of Richard Rorty's (1981) vision of analytic versus continental philosophy and what counts for truth. A few more thoughts: perhaps we could each comment on how we teach material related to our collaborative edition now, your recent course at MIT, for example, and mine upcoming at the University of Toronto. What do you have people read? What do they look at? Do they find this sort of programme useful, and how so? And have you both changed at all in what you teach and what you think? Another way to put this: if we were doing *The Subjects of Art History* now, what would we change, roughly 10 years on? I haven't taught 'theory in art history', as we call it, for several years. The last time, I used our book in conjunction with Donald Preziosi's excellent *The Art of Art History* (1998). But *Subjects* has sold its print run and is unavailable in English. One needs to be able to read Korean to get a copy now – 2000 copies of a Korean translation will be published soon – which is perhaps indicative of where art history is going, in a positive sense. My sense is that the demand for this sort of book – a methods and theories of art history book – still exists among students. I do not subscribe to the argument that 'theory' has been so absorbed by our discipline that to teach it separately is to ghettoize; most who float this line do so from a conservative position. So, I'm using Preziosi as a main text with *Subjects* available on library reserve. I'm also making a new book available: Robert Williams' *Art Theory: An Historical Introduction* (2004). But what will still be missing in my students' readings will be a sustained reading of the debates over the terrain of visual culture. I will bring this up as an issue.

And what about your research, any changes in direction or desire since the advent of visual studies? What would you write now if there were no institutional restrictions, if you had no other obligations? Personally, I would curate more contemporary art. Why? Because I believe that working with contemporary artists (aside from all the other reasons that it is exciting and worth doing) opens one's eyes to some of the debates exercised here. This is my other answer to Michael's question about why there is such a modern or contemporary focus in visual studies. To be polemical, one finds out more about the motivations and intricacies of visual culture from its practitioners than any other source.

KM: In attempting to answer Mark's important question, I'd like to return to the issues of history and aesthetics with which this conversation began. Both seem to depend on universal structures of thought born in the Enlightenment that have proven both empowering and distinctly inimical to the way in which we approach non-western cultures. Partha Chatterjee's *Nationalist Thought and the Colonial World* (1993) and Dipesh Chakrabarty's *Provincializing Europe: Postcolonial Thought and Historical Difference* (2000) have shown how inappropriate western notions of historical development are to the analysis and interpretation of Indian history. As fruitful as subaltern studies have been in rewriting the history of British India, for example, the Marxist model on which this was undertaken had its distinct limitations. Having never experienced capitalist industrialization nor seen the rise of a bourgeoisie – the necessary conditions for proletarian revolution – subaltern historians often characterized Indian history as incomplete and deficient. India's peasant culture allegedly condemned it to play a backward role in contemporary historical developments. In Chakrabarty's terms it is necessary to 'provincialize Europe' if historians are to do justice to the unique qualities of Indian history.

However, what does 'provincializing Europe' amount to? Chakrabarty is not utopian enough to suggest that the understanding of the Indian past can do without the theoretical models of the Enlightenment, but that these cannot be applied uncritically to historical and cultural circumstances for which they were never intended. Inevitably, the theoretical structures developed by the dominant cultures of Europe and the United States will continue to inform every attempt to contest them. As valuable as the construction of new and alternative identities may be in the assertion of cultural difference, their strategic value will be obviated if their contingency is not recognized.

In terms of teaching, it seems important to me that we recognize the power relations that have shaped – and continue to shape – the nature of our discussions of visual culture. We live in the shadow of modernism and it would be hard to insist that artistic developments in, say, a major city in a non-western culture receive the same amount of attention as those taking place in New York. Currently, we can recognize that it is the economic, military and cultural power of the industrialized nations of Europe and the United States that supports their claims to aesthetic superiority – rather than, say, 'manifest destiny'. This allows us to relativize the dominant narrative so as to gain insight into its claims on our attention. We can see through the fabled 'autonomy' of the western artistic tradition to the cultural interests that motivate it. An awareness that aesthetic value is situational and local makes us leery of universalizing claims to transcendental value. It makes us appreciate the philosophical strategies on which claims to autonomy actually rest. As a consequence, I think that postcolonial studies and the globalization debate are necessarily embedded in the visual studies curriculum. The important authors here would be Edward Said, Homi Bhabha, James Clifford, Fredric Jameson, Arjun Appadurai, Gayatri Spivak and García Canclini. Said, Bhabha, Clifford, because they are canonical to postcolonial thinking and Jameson, Appadurai and García Canclini, because they represent radically different approaches to the project of understanding globalization, Spivak for both reasons.

MAH: Keith and I just finished co-teaching a graduate course this past semester in the History, Theory, Criticism Program at MIT that we rather pretentiously entitled 'Art History After the "End of Art"'. In it, we addressed the aesthetic traditions that have animated the history of art history, posing the question: 'What does aesthetics still mean for art history today?' The choice of readings, from Kant to Benjamin to Bürger to Belting and beyond, was prompted by our shared sentiment that if art history was ever to become philosophical again (as the best work in visual studies needs and urges it to be), it would be on the basis of questioning not only what we mean by 'history' today, but what we mean by 'aesthetics' as well. Watching the foundational concepts for our discipline metamorphose through author, time and cultural location may not provide singular definitions, but that was the point. Intellectual history goes a long way to making us all think anew.

KM: While we live with historical models more subtle and more sophisticated than either Hegel or Marx, we should be aware that even a Foucauldian notion of 'epistemes' may have little relevance for our understanding of certain cultural circumstances. While the notion of time- and culture-sensitive epistemologies is of enormous assistance in thinking about knowledge in an age of globalization, we should never forget that the very tools we use to understand the clash of epistemological systems bears the imprint of the culture in which it was developed. We thus live in the age of paradox, one in which 'both/and' and 'either/or' reign supreme. As sophistic and unsatisfactory as it may be to assert continually the limitations of our understanding, we may be too much aware of the dangers of epistemic universalism to do anything else.

Much the same may be true of aesthetics. While the power of this idea has enabled the artifacts of the world to be collected and appreciated under the rubric of 'art', it has also tended to erase the very distinctiveness that made these artifacts fascinating in the first place. The profound sadness resulting from a walk through the galleries of the Louvre last summer, where the creative works of radically different periods and places were reduced to sameness by means of an exhibition policy that implied that they were somehow equivalent to one another, was quite depressing. While the walls of this great museum are still dedicated to the 'history' of western Europe (including those geographies that have been annexed to its story so as to enhance its transcendental significance: for example, Egypt, Mesopotamia and Greece), a gesture has been made to the rest of the world by including a selection of works from Africa, Oceania and the Americas. We are informed that this is a prelude to a much more systematic representation of world 'art' in a renovated Musée de l'Homme(!). Whether or not the drabness inflicted on diverse cultural artifacts because of their categorization as 'art' will be avoided in this new setting remains to be seen.

It is perhaps because of the failure of the ideology of modernism, our current reluctance to subscribe to an evolutionary view of artistic development, that allows us to rethink the heroic narrative of western art history in the twentieth century. It is now possible to pay attention to what had necessarily to be neglected if that narrative was to be accorded the power and privilege it demanded. For example, it is now possible to consider South African post-Impressionists and Brazilian surrealists without rejecting and subordinating them on the grounds of their alleged lack of 'originality'. There is a new generation of scholars at work attempting to understand the significance of western-inspired artistic forms developed in non-western circumstances. Often their stories have an 'Alice in Wonderland' quality to them. We go through the looking glass as we realize that what had one kind of meaning in Paris or New York had quite another in Johannesburg or Rio de Janeiro. Even if the scholars engaged in this project happen to be, say, South African or Brazilian, they encounter the histories of the art of their own cultures through a lens imposed on them by the dominant story of Euro-American modernism. The value of the new work is that it serves to demonstrate that the success of the dominant story depends on power relations between industrialized and non-industrialized nations rather than on rational necessity. Another important dimension of this work is that it allows us to gauge the extent to which artists active at the hegemonic centres of the western narrative were aware of artistic developments in other places, even if this knowledge was often repressed. The value of these developments, it seems to me, lies not in replacing one type of history with another, but to complicate and relativize what we once regarded as 'the' story.

Just as the passing of a modernist aesthetic allows us to tell new and different stories about the aesthetic histories of the non-western world, so the introduction of visual studies enables us to pay attention to forms of visual creativity that previously have been ignored due to art history's dedication to the canon of 'high' art. Even if the 'new art history' extended the art-historical canon by attending to overlooked artists and works by insisting that the variety of subject positions from which the history of art might be told mattered, much of its energy remained focused on those works to which traditional art history had dedicated its attention. The arrival of visual studies in a context of aesthetic relativism means that art historians can no longer fall back on an inherited canon to guarantee our professional activities without betraying a lack of self-awareness about the nature of what we do. While the construction of local and specific 'aesthetic communities' characterized by their unique characteristics seems a necessary dimension of what aesthetics might currently mean, these communities still exist in the context of aesthetic judgments that have the backing of the dominant artistic institutions of the West. While it may now be possible for us to do justice to the aesthetic potential of what Garcia Canclini calls the 'industrialized arts' of television, advertising and the new media, the traditional canon of painting and sculpture may still be assigned a privileged status, within art history at any rate, in relation to other forms of visual culture.

The real opportunities of our current situation (and this is where these ideas are affecting both my teaching and writing) seem to lie in the way in which revised notions of both history and aesthetics allow us to rethink the nature of our scholarly work. Non-Hegelian philosophies of history (Benjamin, Foucault) and non-universalizing approaches to aesthetics (Bennett (1987), Shohat and Stam (1998)) invest the study of the visual with new philosophical and political relevance.

MAH: One of the insistent issues that has been perplexing me in my role as director of a research institute is: 'What does *research* in art history today mean anyway?' The scientific paradigm that once-upon-a-time kept art history focused on empirical data is undeniably bankrupt when it comes to its legitimation as a discipline in the humanities. Consequently, the concept of *research* needs some investigation so as to elicit its philosophical implications and commitments. The same goes for visual studies.

And something more besides. What worries me most is that the scurrying about in the name of *research* that goes on in visual studies, as well as art history, loses something along the way. Heidegger once put it this way: 'Art historical study makes the works the objects of a science ... In all this busy activity do we encounter the work itself?' (1971: 40). The manipulations and manoeuvers of any research paradigm can contribute to the process of stripping the work of its awe, the awe that makes art still matter. I guess what I am still troubled by is the loss of wonder in the writing about the visual. I hear you challenge me: 'Doesn't research resist, by necessity and necessarily so, the "wonder" that is at the heart of the aesthetic experience?' I understand that question. Just so that we don't envelop ourselves in the pernicious haze of art appreciation, we need to ask those insistent questions about why? For whom? According to which archive? etc. On the other hand, I sense that some of contemporary visual studies so willingly seems not only to have found the glib route to answering these serious questions, but also to have sacrificed a sense of awe at the power of an overwhelming visual experience, wherever it might be found, in favour of an easy identification of the 'political' connections that lie beneath the surface of this or that representation. To me, that's neither good 'research' nor serious understanding. All I am saying is that there are many times when I yearn for something that is 'in excess of *research*'. But 'what is that wonder?', I hear you ask. And where did it go? Can we get it back? Why do we want it back? How do we generate the very conditions for 'wonder' to take place – whether it's a more philosophical or a critical 'wonder' at the character of archives, art objects, artifacts, whatever, in their specificity and singularity, how they work, mean, fail to be intelligible, etc.? These are undoubtedly incisive questions, ones that cut to the pulsating heart of art history. The art of art history. The romance of research. The recreation, in words, of a thoroughgoing visual encounter. Hasn't this visual 'pull' also something to do with aesthetics? Does the act of writing in either art history or visual studies yearn towards a recreation of a visual 'aesthetic' experience, even if there is little or none there to be found? Is the desire to write about a subject the first 'aesthetic' choice? Or does it, rather, lie in our histories?

Notes

1 Originally published in *Journal of Visual Culture*, 'Visual Studies, Historiography, and Aesthetics', by Mark A. Cheetham, Michael Ann Holly and Keith Moxey, April (2005), 4(1): 75–90. This exchange took place via email. To structure the conversation, I asked Cheetham, Holly and Moxey a number of questions; requested that they open out or clarify their comments here and there; and encouraged the dialogue in one way or another. In the end, with three people already contributing to the exchange, we decided that my role as interlocutor should be absented.

References

Alpers, Svetlana (1983) *The Art of Describing: Dutch Art in the Seventeenth Century*. Chicago, IL: University of Chicago Press.

Bal, Mieke (2001) *Quoting Caravaggio: Contemporary Art, Preposterous History*. Chicago, IL: University of Chicago Press.

Baxandall, Michael (1972) *Painting and Experience in Fifteenth-century Italy*. Oxford: Oxford University Press.

Bennett, Tony (1987) 'Really Useless Knowledge: A Political Critique of Aesthetics', *Literature and History* 13: 38–57.

Braudel, Fernand (1966[1949]) *The Mediterranean and the Mediterranean World in the Age of Philip II*, Vol. 1, Siân Reynolds, *trans*. 2nd edn. New York: Harper & Row.

Bryson, Norman, Holly, Michael Ann and Moxey, Keith (eds.) (1994) *Visual Culture: Images and Interpretations*. Hanover, CT: Wesleyan University Press.

Carrier, David (1987) *Artwriting*. Amherst, MA: University of Massachusetts Press.

Chakrabarty, Dipesh (2000) *Provincializing Europe: Postcolonial Thought and Historical Difference*. Princeton, NJ: Princeton University Press.

Chatterjee, Partha (1993) *Nationalist Thought and the Colonial World: A Derivative Discourse*. Minneapolis: University of Minnesota Press.

Cheetham, Mark A. (2001) *Kant, Art and Art History: Moments of Discipline*. Cambridge: Cambridge University Press.

Cheetham, Mark A., Holly, Michael Ann and Moxey, Keith (eds.) (1998) *The Subjects of Art History: Historical Objects in Contemporary Perspective*. Cambridge: Cambridge University Press.

Didi-Huberman, Georges (2000) *Devant le temps: histoire de l'art et anachronisms des images*. Paris: Editions de Minuit.

Foster, Hal (2004) 'Polemics, Postmodernism, Immersion, Militarized Space', *Journal of Visual Culture* 3(3): 320–35.

Hadjinicolau, Nicos (2004) 'Interdisciplinarity Without Disciplines', paper presented at the International Congress of the History of Art, Montreal, 26 August.

Heidegger, Martin (1971) 'The Origin of A Work of Art', in *Poetry, Language, Thought* (Albert Hofstadter, *trans*.). New York: Harper & Row, pp. 17–78.

Holly, Michael Ann and Moxey, Keith (eds.) (2002) *Art History, Aesthetics, Visual Studies*. New Haven, CT: Sterling and Francine Clark Art Institute/Yale University Press.

Horkheimer, Max (1972[1968]) *Critical Theory: Selected Essays* (Matthew O'Connell, *trans*.). New York: Continuum.

Latour, Bruno (2004) *Politics of Nature: How to Bring the Sciences into Democracy*. Cambridge, MA: Harvard University Press.

Preziosi, Donald (ed.) (1998) *The Art of Art History*. Oxford: Oxford University Press.

Riegl, Alois (1982[1903]) 'The Modern Cult of Monuments: Its Character and Origin' (Kurt Forster and Diane Ghirardo, *trans*.) *Oppositions*, 25(Fall): 21–51.

Rorty, Richard (1981) *Philosophy and the Mirror of Nature*. Princeton, NJ: Princeton University Press.

Shohat, Ella and Stam, Robert (1998) 'Narrativizing Visual Culture: Towards a Polycentric Aesthetics', in Nicholas Mirzoeff (ed.) *The Visual Culture Reader*. London: Routledge, pp. 27–49.

Williams, Robert (2004) *Art Theory: An Historical Introduction*. Oxford: Blackwell.

11

THAT VISUAL TURN: THE ADVENT OF VISUAL CULTURE[1]

Interview with Martin Jay

Introduction

Martin Jay is Sidney Hellman Ehrman Professor of the History at the University of California, Berkeley. Co-editor of *Vision in Context* (1996), his books include *The Dialectical Imagination: History of the Frankfurt School and the Institution of Social Research, 1923–1950* (1973), *Marxism and Totality: The Adventures of a Concept from Lukács to Habermas* (1984), *Permanent Exiles: Essays on the Intellectual Migration from Germany to America* (1990), *Downcast Eyes: The Denigration of Vision in Twentieth-Century French Thought* (1994), *Adorno* (1984), *Cultural Semantics: Key Words of Our Time* (1998), *Refractions of Violence* (2003), and *Songs of Experience: Modern American and European Variations on a Universal Theme* (2005). With a commitment that ranges from intellectual history and critical theory to cultural histories of vision, here Jay speaks about the need to take seriously as objects of scholarly inquiry all manifestations of our visual environment and experience; the reasons why it is important to take account of the differences between diverse kind of images and experiences; and a series of historical and philosophical questions relating to visuality such as natural visual experience, the art of describing, the optical unconscious, scopic regimes, glances, gazes, and surveillance.

Marquard Smith (MS): While *The Dialectical Imagination* (1976), *Adorno* (1984), and *Force Fields* (1993) – to name but a few of your earlier works – touch upon questions of aesthetics and/or vision in passing, it is not until *Downcast Eyes: The Denigration of Vision in Twentieth-Century French Thought* (1994) that you attend to matters of visuality in a more sustained manner. Why this passage from intellectual history and critical theory to what we might call a critical intellectual history of visual culture or a cultural history of vision?

Martin Jay (MJ): The work that links the two projects is, in fact, *Marxism and Totality*, the history of Western Marxism I published in 1984. In that work, I noticed that hostility to the concept of totality was often accompanied by scepticism about the possibility of a totalizing gaze, a God's eye view, of the whole. Sartre and Merleau-Ponty were its main critics, but Adorno also challenged the spectatorial premises of what he called 'peephole metaphysics'. Althusser as well, from a very different vantage point, had linked ideological mystification with the persistence of Lacan's mirror stage. It then became gradually clear to me that questions of philosophy and social theory, as well as those pertaining to the position of the critical intellectual, were closely related to the privileging of vision in Western thought. I did not, however, anticipate how varied and pervasive the critique of that privileging had been in French thought until I began my research.

MS: In 'Visual Culture and its Vicissitudes', your contribution to *October's* watershed 'Visual Culture Questionnaire' of 1996, you present yourself as an intellectual historian interested in discourses about visuality. Here, you suggest that advocates of visual culture have extended its scope not only beyond the traditional concerns of art history, but also further than what W.J.T. Mitchell called the 'rhetoric of images' to include, and I quote you here, 'all manifestations of optical experience, all variants of visual practice' (p. 42). In writing this, you claim that visual culture's democratic impulse, its sense of inclusivity, can happily and comfortably investigate anything that can 'imprint itself on the retina', including, you say, non-retinal ingredients such as the 'optical unconscious' (p. 42).

First, I'd like to ask you how serious you were in making this last claim at that time. That's to say, what does it mean for visual culture to be democratic? What are the advantages and the dangers too? It certainly seems the case that your generosity towards visual culture is tempered. If I hear this dissatisfaction – your wryness – correctly, then I'm in accord with it. I worry – putting aside the accusations of ahistoricism often directed at writings bearing its name – that visual culture is too habitually caught up in a form of political correctness that makes it impossible for it *not* to be democratic. I'm wondering if you, like me, are concerned by the restrictions in this that limit what it might be possible for visual culture to become, to do.

MJ: By democratization, I simply meant the growing willingness to take seriously as objects of scholarly inquiry all manifestations of our visual environment and experience, not only those that were deliberately created for aesthetic effects or have been reinterpreted in formalist terms (as was the case with, say, so-called 'primitive' ethnographic objects by aesthetic modernists). Although images of all kinds have long served as illustrations of arguments made discursively, the growth of visual culture as a field has allowed them to be examined more in their own terms as complex figural artifacts or the stimulants to visual experiences. Insofar as we live in a culture whose technological advances abet the production and dissemination of such images at a hitherto unimagined level, it is necessary to focus on how they work and what they do, rather than move past them too quickly to the ideas they represent or the reality they purport to depict. In so doing, we necessarily have to ask questions about the viewer as well, thus the value of Benjamin's notion of the optical unconscious recently resurrected by Rosalind Krauss, as well as the technological mediations and extensions of visual experience.

The danger in such an indiscriminate levelling, of course, is the loss of an ability to make distinctions among different kinds of images and experiences. Traditional art history with its canonical restrictions still has a lot to teach us about the ways in which optical virtuosi, those with the gifts and training to explore and extend the limits of visual experience, transcend the conventions of their visual environment and open up new worlds for our eyes. I am still enough of a follower of Adorno to want to maintain the vexed distinction between genuine works of art and derivative kitsch, high and low, avant-garde and academic art, at least as a way to avoid the promiscuous reduction of everything to the same level of cultural significance.

MS: As an enthusiastic reader of philosophy, as well as history, do you think that the recent ethical turn, if I can call it that, characterized by the writings of, amongst others, Jacques Derrida, Alan Badiou and Simon Critchley, and the extensive rediscovery of Emmanuel Levinas that underpins it, will have an impact on visual culture? Should it? Has it already? Will this ethical turn assist and advance the ethical imperative of visual culture, or is it already part of the problem that people identify with visual culture's democratic impulses? How can, say, a concern for hospitality, nourish the thinking, writing and practices of visual culture?

MJ: In the critique of the reifying power of the gaze, most extensively explored in Sartre's *Being and Nothingness*, there was already a powerful ethical moment, which was given added impetus when feminists like Luce Irigaray and Laura Mulvey stressed its gendered character. The Jewish emphasis on hearing as opposed to the Greek stress on sight, which Levinas tied to the relative importance respectively of the ethical and the ontological in each tradition, increased still further the ethical stakes in discussions of visual culture.

Perhaps the real task these days is not so much to rehearse these now familiar connections, but rather to probe the ways in which the sense of 'looking after' someone is just as much a possibility as 'looking at' them in *le regard*, and 'watching out for someone' is an ethical alternative to controling surveillance. I remember very well a conversation I had in the mid-nineties in Berlin with the poet Allen Ginsberg about the 'gaze of the Buddha', in which he demonstrated for me the non-dominating, benign way in which looking takes place in that religion. Perhaps it is time to look for comparable examples in traditions a bit closer to home.

Questions for the Academy

MS: In particular ways, Visual Studies very clearly emerges specifically out of disputes in recent art history, film studies and cultural studies, born of questions, often historiographical in nature, of politics, ethics and practice. At stake are the vital matters of democracy, recognition, identity, inclusivity and difference to name but a few. How much of this is of Visual Studies itself, rather than adopted from elsewhere? That's one question. Another is this: How much do these pre-occupations of Visual Studies jar or confirm, in your experience, with the more wary accounts which suggest that the field of study is first and foremost an administrative contribution to the further professionalization of academia and academics, a chance for some to make an academic and commercial profit from what otherwise might primarily be an intellectual matter? That's to say, is Visual Studies any more than rhetoric, in the most straightforward sense of that word?

MJ: No new field emerges full-blown without debts to what preceded it. We shouldn't be surprised to find it borrowing some of its methods and concerns from neighboring or antecedent disciplines and intellectual formations. There are furthermore perennial questions, such as those you mention, which need to be addressed again and again, no matter in what idiom or with what tools of analysis. So I am not really troubled by the parasitic nature of much of what passes for Visual Studies. From new combinations, however, potentially new answers can follow, so it remains to be seen how fruitful the institutionalization of the new field will be. As for professionalization itself, I am not cynical in an a priori way about the careerist and even commercial exploitation of visual culture. Those of us who earn our livings by inhabiting established fields, which can pretend to have always existed rather than being themselves products of historical struggles for legitimation, have no right to look down on emerging formations, which are compelled to be more forthright in their attempts to gain respectability and recognition.

MS: In 'Vision in Context: Reflections and Refractions', your introduction to the collection co-edited with Teresa Brennan entitled *Vision in Context: Historical and Contemporary Perspectives on Sight* you say that the volume includes a 'welter of competing interpretations of the meaning and implications of vision and visuality' that don't 'provide a sovereign overview' (p. 10). I too support the need for Visual Studies to be richly varied and for it to offer rival accounts, explanations, speculations. It's imperative that it not be reducible to one dominant model. My question then is how you think this lack of a sovereign overview is both a strength and a weakness.

MJ: To argue for a single dominant approach seems to me problematic in the extreme in any intellectual endeavour. What, for example, would the result be if we were to have only one way to make sense of that extraordinary thing we call 'language', or to assume that all languages were somehow subvariants of a single ur-model? Would we get rid of, say, hermeneutics, or grammatology, or ordinary language analysis, or structural linguistics or sociolinguistics, all in the name of one master discourse? Making sense of visual experience demands no less a willingness to tolerate different, sometimes complementary and sometimes contradictory, approaches. Certain questions are perhaps more fruitfully addressed by one approach than another, but we can always think of new questions that demand fresh analytical tools.

The Experiences of Practice

MS: Your work is testament to the value of melding, working with and through the confluence of the historical and the present. Such a convergence makes it possible to account for and direct our thinking towards the indeterminacies that are made available by re-definitions, competing interpretations, meanings, and so on, when it comes to practices of looking, or reading, or doing history. Much of your research and writing over the last 30 years has been tied to this kind of complex historical and philosophical convergence as it takes place in and can be drawn out from the concerns of German and French thought, of intellectual history. Your work on Adorno, Benjamin and the Frankfurt School, and *Downcast Eyes* – on vision in twentieth-century continental thought – is testament to this. Your most recent work seems to be directing its gaze onto a specifically American genealogy. I'm wondering about the reasons for this shift, and its implications.

MJ: My current project, which examines the discourse of experience in modern theory, necessarily has an American component because of the extraordinary attention paid to the concept by pragmatists like William James and John Dewey. But anyone who is interested in twentieth-century European thought has to recognize that the Atlantic has become a very narrow body of water (sometimes, in fact, much narrower than the English Channel!). That is, the current of ideas that went largely from Europe to America in the eighteenth century and much of the nineteenth – with some exceptions like Poe and Emerson, who had an important influence in Europe – began to become a reciprocal flow in the early twentieth century. Pragmatism itself is an example, as figures like Bergson, Schiller, and Papini learned a great deal from James. Works like James Kloppenberg's *Uncertain Victory* (1988) have shown us how integrated the Western intellectual world already was by the 1880s. By the time of the intellectual migration from Nazi Germany, much of the most creative thought in Europe was in exile in America and elsewhere, and when it went back, either through personal returns or intellectual exchanges, it was powerfully changed by its experience abroad. The well-known shift of avant-garde art's centre of gravity from Paris to New York reinforced this tendency. By the time Richard Rorty was finding parallels between Heidegger, Foucault, Derrida, and Dewey, the old distinctions between American and European thought were in large measure overcome.

Or to put it differently, a complicated process of creative misreadings of different national traditions and idioms is now going in both directions with enough vigour to undercut any simple notion of centre and periphery (a point that would be complicated still further, if we acknowledge the global cross-fertilization of ideas outside of the NATO cultural region). As an American intellectual historian of mostly 'European' ideas, I recognize that I come to them with the prejudices of my formation, but I also understand that my formation is always already filtered through ideas that have a European accent. So I guess it was only a matter of time before I was compelled to read a little more seriously in American sources and compare the results with what I had learned from a lifetime of reading European ones.

MS: A question about experience: in *Downcast Eyes* you are already attending explicitly to the *experience* of vision. For instance, you consider questions of natural visual experience, the art of describing, the optical unconscious, scopic regimes, enLIGHTenment, the optics of temporality, epistemological vision, phenomenological perception, glances, gazes, spectacles, and so on. And you consider these questions as experiential or phenomenological rather than theoretical questions *per se*.

Your forthcoming book continues to be concerned with the question of experience. As a thinker for whom experience has played such a central role – in your preoccupation with intellectual history, the study of culture, and the matter of the visual – how do you think that this new book will impact upon our understanding of the necessary difficulties of experiencing something called visual culture?

MJ: *Songs of Experience*, as the new, still unfinished book will be called, focuses on the discourses about experience in European and American thought rather than on something that one might directly call experience itself. Its goal is to clarify the assumptions that underlie our appeal to experience, whether they be in epistemological, religious, aesthetic, political, or historical terms. It also seeks to understand the attempts made by many twentieth-century thinkers to revive a more robust and all-encompassing notion of experience, often one that transcends the traditional subject/object dichotomy. To the extent that the eye is implicated in one way or another in virtually all of these modalities, I hope that by increasing our sensitivity to the historical complexities of the concept of experience itself, we will become more aware of how mediated our visual experiences are by the discursive contexts in which they appear.

MS: As historians of visual culture, how do we respond to the events of Tuesday 11th September 2001 and its aftermath?

MJ: It is perhaps too early to draw definitive conclusions from the events or even to begin talking about their 'aftermath'. That is, the war they initiated, and I'm afraid that is an accurate term to use to describe what is now happening, is a long way from being over. Having said that, I would only add that one immediate result is that the long-standing assumption of much cultural studies, visual or otherwise, that the hegemony of global capitalist culture must be 'subverted' or 'transgressed' in the name of a more progressive alternative is now very hard to maintain in its naive form. Insofar as the hijackers hijacked the vocabulary of anti-globalization for their own not very progressive ends, it is necessary to recognize a new political/cultural landscape in which some of the old conventional wisdom no longer holds. I was at a conference a short while ago at the University of California, Davis on 'Visual Worlds' in which radical artists using media like the internet to produce acts they had once called 'cultural terrorism' were beginning to engage in a painful rethinking of more than just their rhetorical strategy. This is not to say that the chilling warnings of what has come to be called 'patriotic correctness' in the United States against any form of dissent should be heeded, just that it is no longer possible to revert to the late twentieth-century premises of cultural studies, which in any case were beginning to get a bit too stale and predictable.

Notes

1 Interview with Martin Jay, originally published in *Journal of Visual Culture*, 'The Visual Turn: A Conversation with Martin Jay', 1(1), April (2002), pp. 87–92.

References

Brennan, Teresa and Jay, Martin (eds.) (1996) *Vision in Context: Historical and Contemporary Perspectives on Sight*. London: Routledge.

Jay, Martin (1984) *Adorno*. Cambridge, MA: Harvard University Press.

Jay, Martin (1986[1984]) *Marxism and Totality: The Adventures of a Concept from Lukács to Habermas*. Berkeley: University of California Press.

Jay, Martin (1993) *Force Fields*. London: Routledge.

Jay, Martin (1994[1993]) *Downcast Eyes: The Denigration of Vision in Twentieth-Century French Thought*. Berkeley: University of California Press.

Jay, Martin (1996[1973]) *The Dialectical Imagination: A History of the Frankfurt School and the Institute of Social Research, 1923–1950*. Berkeley: University of California Press.

Jay, Martin (2006) *Songs of Experience: Modern American and European Variations on a Universal Theme*. Berkeley: University of California.

Kloppenberg, James T. (1988) *Uncertain Victory*. Cary, NC: Oxford University Press.

12

POLEMICS, POSTMODERNISM, IMMERSION, MILITARIZED SPACE[1]

Interview with Hal Foster

Introduction

Hal Foster is Townsend Martin, Class of 1917, Professor of Art and Archaeology at Princeton University. Internationally regarded for his provocative writings on twentieth-century art practice, and as an Editor of the journal *October*, Professor Foster is the author of *Design and Crime (and Other Diatribes)* (2002), *The Return of the Real* (1996), *Compulsive Beauty* (1993), *Recodings: Art, Spectacle, Cultural Politics* (1985) and *Prosthetic Gods* (2004), and editor of the defining *The Anti-Aesthetic: Essays on Post modern Culture* (1983), among other books. Recent and forthcoming books include *Art Since 1900*, a co-authored textbook on twentieth-century art, as well as a survey of Pop Art. Here he speaks about these and other things, including polemical thought, cultural criticism, immersion, Visual Culture Studies, and design, architecture and urbanism.

Polemics, Cultural Criticism and Art Writing

Marquard Smith (MS): You obviously like polemics. The second section of your 1985 book *Recodings: Art, Spectacle, Cultural Politics* is entitled '(Post)Modern Polemics', and a recent book *Design and Crime (and Other Diatribes)* begins: 'This book is a polemical account of recent changes in the cultural status of architecture and design as well as art and criticism in the West' (Foster, 1985a, 2002: xiii). A commitment to the idea of the polemic persists throughout: in your thinking, in your writing, and in the mode of your engagement that has at its heart a certain kind of fractiousness. It is very much in keeping with the etymology of 'polemic' – war – that offers us a sense of the polemic as an art or practice of conversational discussion and controversial attack. Disputation. It is a mode of argumentation, a way of thinking and seeing and writing that is at war with itself.[2] I'm curious to know how you feel about polemics in general. More specifically, I'm wondering how much the polemic has to do with your attention to the political, aesthetic and ethical implications of historical ruptures, epistemic breaks and notions of transformation, contradiction, demise: paradigm shifts, or, better perhaps, turning points.

Hal Foster (HF): I hadn't thought about the militaristic etymology of 'polemics', though it's certainly there in other terms we use too – like 'tactics', 'fronts' and 'avant-garde'. But, yes, I like to be polemical, though not agonistic: some intellectuals thrive on antagonism, and I'm not one. As Nietzsche says in *The Geneaology of Morals*, too much criticism is driven by *ressentiment*. It might be that some resentment is irreducible in critique, but too much makes the whole business bitter, and almost nothing is worse than contempt masquerading as criticism. Foucault says somewhere that scholarship was first developed by scholastic monks whittling away at one another, with the world receding behind a pile of nasty missives and marginalia, and there's a little of this solipsistic infighting still in the academy. There are benefits, of course, in the testing of research and the refining of ideas, but all the divisiveness is dispiriting.

Foucault (1984 [1971]) also says somewhere that knowledge is made not only for understanding but for cutting. That's the key to polemics for me – clarifying stakes, advancing positions. And that's what drew me to criticism in the first place: the task of cutting through, clearing up, connecting, opening out. (I know that sounds grand, but why not?) Early on I was a graduate student of Edward Said, who always insisted on the worldliness of criticism, in the sense not only of cosmopolitanism but of commitment. This points to another etymological relation – between 'criticism' and 'crisis' – which leads back to your question about 'breaks' and 'ruptures' as well ...

MS: So that cutting is part of an opening out, a way of being able to imagine or envisage a field or a question or a debate, to actually see something clearly enough? One has to be blinkered enough in one's polemic to be able to see something clearly enough! [laughs]

HF: Well, if not blinkered, at least focused – focused enough to see the problem at hand, to pressure it, to open it up historically. I've never seen critical work in opposition to historical work: like many others I try to hold the two in tandem, in tension. History without critique is inert; criticism without history is aimless – a bumper sticker, I know, but one I believe. Sometimes, of course, this connection prompts trigger-happy declarations of the end of this, that, and the other thing. My generation was very seduced by such pronouncements of rupture; for one thing, it seemed to promise an avant-garde continued by critical means, an avant-garde of criticism. But then, for many of us, critical theory *was* the most vital part of the culture, more vital than art, literature, music, dance – maybe only film could compare. People suspicious of 'theory' today forget that, never knew it, or can't imagine how heady it was. (Or, perhaps worse, they try to pick it up again, in an abstract, neo-radical sort of way, as if nothing had changed in the meantime.)

MS: Let me just backtrack for a minute. This distinction, or lack of a distinction, this imbrication, you've brought up between historical work and criticism is significant, and something I was hoping to ask you to consider. It raises a couple of questions for me, or maybe one question in two parts. The first part has to do with the difference between the kind of writing, and the kind of thinking, you do in your Art History writing *and* how this is distinct from your art writing or art criticism – if at all. Could you draw out some of the differences between the imperatives of, or the particular *kinds* of tasks involved in, writing as an art historian on, say, seventeenth-century Dutch still-life painting or Primitivism or Surrealism or contemporary art practice even, *and* writing contemporary art or cultural criticism (Foster, 1985b, 1993, 1995)? The second part of the question has to do with 'History' itself, and I wonder if it feels to you that your more art historical writings are more concerned with a reconsideration of the past in the present, while art criticism seeks to delineate the present on behalf of the possibilities of the future?

I ask this question as someone involved in Visual Culture Studies who cares about history, or the problem of 'history'. In light of the accusations of ahistoricism so often directed against it, if for no other reason, I'm provoked *to have to* think through the question of history very, very seriously. History is not 'dealt with' as an issue, as some say. It can't simply be put to one side! [laughs] To do so demands such wilfulness ...

HF: I began my intellectual life as a critic in New York in the late 1970s, a time when intellectuals could still be semi-independent. Today most critics are bred and born in the academy, at least in the States, and often they stay there too. This is a not a dig at the academy, which remains a partial haven of necessity, but a lament for the dissolution of that semi-mirage called 'the public sphere'. Yet back in the days one could survive as a critic in the interstices of institutions – writing for magazines (I wrote for *Artforum* early on), doing the odd catalogue for a museum, giving a lecture or a seminar here or there – there were still pieces of a critical space to hold on to. By the mid-80s, however, the squeeze was really on: the market began to swallow the art world almost whole, the klieg lights of the media were turned on it as well, and I made the move back to the academy then. I had been senior editor of *Art in America* along with Craig Owens, and for a time its pages were open to critical work; then things shifted, with artists like Jeff Koons, dealers like Mary Boone, collectors like the Saatchis, and museum directors like Thomas Krens, and that niche closed. The last thing those people wanted was critics; I mean *really*...

Of course, I made my move back to the academy also for reasons internal to my work: criticism had opened up historical projects for me and for others in my milieu (Craig, Benjamin Buchloh, Douglas Crimp...). In different ways most of us felt a connection between critical theory and postmodernist art that led us to historical practices. I came to contemporary art by way of Minimalism, and sooner or later it brings you to Constructivism, a movement that was still occluded in most accounts of modernist art. Like many others, I was also struck by feminist work, by its questioning of sexuality and representation, and eventually it led me to look into Surrealism. And so on: the tracks differed, but the impetus did not: contemporary work opened up historical practices, which in turn fortified us in the present. Personally I was also taken by the example of three disparate critic-historians a generation ahead of me: Michael Fried, Rosalind Krauss, and T.J. Clark. Each had a contemporary stake that grounded historical inquiry but also made it cut in motivated ways – late-Modernist abstraction for Michael, Minimalist and Postminimalist art for Rosalind, Situationist critique for Tim.

So I came to alternate between contemporary criticism and Art History. *Recodings* (Foster, 1985a) was a collection of criticism mostly written for *Art in America* and *October*; *Compulsive Beauty* (Foster, 1995) was a book on Surrealism, originally my dissertation; then I turned back to postwar art with *The Return of the Real* (Foster, 1996). I raised an abiding concern in its first chapter where I attempted to refashion the opposition drawn by Peter Bürger (1984) between prewar historical avant-gardes and postwar neo avant-gardes. Burger had connected the two forcefully, but also to the diminishment of postwar art as a farcical repetition of the prewar. I wanted to reframe, but not to undo, the connection between historical and neo avantgardes. What troubles me now is the apparent disconnection of much practice from *both* avant-gardes. As a result, I have come to attend more to continuities than to discontinuities; I don't think we can assume the value of 'rupture' anymore. Like *Design and Crime* (Foster, 2002), my book, *Prosthetic Gods* (Foster, 2004), ranges across the last century.

MS: Talking of the 1980s, you were involved centrally, and thus implicated in, the delineation of Postmodernism. I'm thinking here not just of the crucial edited collection, *The Anti-Aesthetic: Essays on Postmodern Culture* (Foster, 1983), but also of your own writings in journals, anthologies and books (Foster, 1984, 1996). At this moment in time, how would you account for the demise or turning away, implicitly or otherwise, from discourses of Postmodernism that we have witnessed in the last few years? I also wonder to what extent you think recent writings that are critical of Postmodernism, and, even more significantly, of 'theory' in general – culminating in, say, a book like Terry Eagleton's *After Theory* (2003) – have not only had a profound effect on the withering of Postmodernism *per se* but also seem to be intent on papering over theory's awkward, necessary, productive cracks. Which is to say, such debates often suggest that their rediscovery of ethical imperatives draws attention to the ways in which critical theory always already denied the 'big questions' of love, of evil, death, metaphysics, religion and so on. I don't recall critical theory ignoring these things, quite the opposite. But by asking 'the big questions', the questions that we've all been accused of ignoring for years, are these more recent discussions offering ways out of what seemed like the often suffocating ecstasy of Postmodernism or, rather, presenting us with gleeful, condemnatory sleights of hand that allow their authors to slam almost 35 years of critical thinking, as well as earlier traditions, in one fell swoop? Or, alternatively, is the whole caboodle a knee-jerk response to the events leading up to and including September 11th, 2001, and their aftermath...

HF: I never understood the term 'theory', or rather, I always understood it as a reification, a reduction used first as a rallying cry and then as a whipping boy; it functions mostly as a term of abuse today. Of course there is no 'theory' as such; there are 'only' philosophical models, theoretical methods, critical interventions, different resources used in different ways at different moments. And of course you can't just pick and choose – you have your own formation, your own investments – but you can use the different tools you have as pertinently as possible.

Again, for my generation critical theory was a very lively arena; there was a displacement of energy there not only from art but from politics too (both had lost their way a little in the 1970s). It was lively; it was also crowded – maybe that's why some onlookers lumped it all together as 'theory'. In the States, the reception of the French masters – Barthes, Derrida, Foucault, Lacan, Althusser, Irigaray, Kristeva ... – overlapped in part with the reception of the Frankfurt School, especially Benjamin and Adorno. This was a mixed blessing: on the one hand, it made for an amazing array of concepts that could be tested against film, literature, mass culture, art and architecture; on the other hand, these concepts were often thrown together. (That's another thing 'theory' means to its common sense enemies: messy thinking, bad writing. Often these charges are defensive gestures against difficult thought or, worse, contrarian politics, but sometimes they are warranted too.) Moreover, one could hardly match the brilliance, let alone the ambition, of most of the masters; for many of us it was hard enough just to understand them. And yet in-between the confusion and the intimidation there were critical elaborations: for example, the way that *Screen* put into play different figures – Brecht, Althusser, Lacan ... – to think through developments in cinema, questions about subjectivity, new political formations, or the way that *October* motivated Poststructuralism to theorize Postmodernism, and the Frankfurt School to periodize both. These elaborations were not only about tweaking imports, as is still often claimed: in the States and in Britain, 'native' innovations – pragmatist philosophy, Marxist cultural studies, feminist theory – were also developed. The theorizing of Postmodernism is where all these different projects came together for some of us; and, even as our Postmodernism was set against one formalist account of Modernism, it opened up other readings. As a result *both* Modernism and Postmodernism have long seemed like incomplete projects to me, not dead ends that we can now ditch for the paradise of beauty and spirituality or the big questions of good and evil. Modernism and Postmodernism can't be dismissed any more than 'theory' can be dispensed with.

The rest is just people getting bored and moving on to other, hipper scenes, or beating up on caricatures of their own making. This is not to play down the consequences of either: the first produces a know-it-all/know-nothing fatigue that affects everyone; the second can spread a real pall and do great damage (if this sounds paranoid, log on to a neo-con site like 'Campus Watch' some time). Of course, people on the Right have long beaten up on us decadent Postmodernists; it's sad when some on the Left do so as well, and downright scary when the two attacks converge, as they sometimes do now. Of course, certain aspects of all these 'post's – Postmodernism, Poststructuralism, Postcolonialism – are easy enough targets; they can appear morally relativistic and politically irresponsible. But why throw out all the babies with the bathwater?

Certainly the bashing got a lot worse after 9/11: open season was declared on 'pomo' and 'poco' in particular, which were cast as the twin sources of our intellectual, ethical and cultural rot, to be cauterized if we were to prevail in the 'clash of cultures'. It would all be hilarious if it were not so deadly serious. Remember the old *New Yorker* cartoon, showing a cocktail party on the Upper East Side, with a fashionable lady saying to a scruffy young man: 'Oh, you're a *terrorist*. Thank God – I thought you said you were a *theorist*!'? Well, after 9/11 some people didn't bother with that distinction much any more. As for Terry Eagleton, I can't say what his motivations are (besides burnishing his self-image as the Only Truly Left Critic in the World); but these attacks are not new to him. In any case, some of what he demands – questions of ethics, questions of responsibility – have *already* returned within the very critical theory that he is keen to expose as shiftless and apolitical.

Immersion: Between the Avant-Garde and the Spectacle

MS: Autonomy, as part and parcel of conversations around the avant-garde, is obviously essential to the determining of modernist aesthetics. It has been a matter of consequence throughout your writings, most noticeably in the early sections of *The Return of the Real* (Foster, 1996). In *Design and Crime*, you say that:

> for many of us 'autonomy' is a bad word – a ruse in aesthetic discourse, a deception in ego psychology, and so on. We forget that autonomy is a diacritical term like any other, defined in relation to its opposite, that is, to subjection. (2002: 102)

Is it the case for you that the veracity of art, of the art object, of the art viewing subject and of Art History turns on or distinguishes itself by the question of autonomy?

HF: It's not simple: some avant-gardes claimed autonomy, some attacked it, some did both at the same time. Closer to the present, the question of autonomy returned in the debates about Visual Culture and Visual Studies. For me, those terms signify an expanded field of art and Art History, respectively, in some respects expanded *beyond* them as well. And I wonder if, for all the gain here, there might not also be some loss. In the shift to Visual Culture – what I called an 'anthropological turn' in *The Return of the Real* (Foster, 1996) – many artists began to work more synchronically, more horizontally, moving from site to site, problem to problem, discourse to discourse. And in some cases this emphasis on the horizontal appeared to diminish the vertical axis, the historical repertoire of forms, devices, meanings, positions within each art. The post-war work that I value the most was able to keep the two axes in contact, in conversation: questions posed by the culture at large were articulated with problems presented by past art, the one brought to bear on the other. So my little role in the Visual Studies debate was simply cautionary: to urge that the resources of Art History not be foreclosed, and that we not participate unwittingly in the general desublimation of art in the culture at large. (Part of me still believes, with Carl Andre, that 'art is what we do, and culture is what is done to us'.) And at the end of the day I do believe that any art, any discipline, is differential, defined in its connections and disconnections with other practices. That's one reason why, for me, autonomy is always 'semi'; it's provisional, and at times it can be made strategic...

MS: OK, but to what end? Why? Is this meant to be a political thing, purely and simply an effort to try recreating or extending the political potential of art, for art, from the moment of the advent of the historical avant-garde, or a way of trying to make sense of the contemporary avant-garde, or of this contemporary Visual Culture industry, and to see ways out of it?

HF: Why not both – recreating the political potential and clarifying the contemporary condition? It's not as if the two are exclusive; in fact they are intimately connected. Of course, one problem is that the term 'autonomy' is such a bogeyman: it calls up all kinds of nasty associations: the imperious subject of Kant, the liberal subject with its reflexive ego that can somehow stand apart, and so on.

MS: In a sense, *semi*-autonomy gets you far enough along to be able to do whatever it is that you need to do ...

HF: Maybe, but it often seems a hedge too. Certainly the autonomous subject is mostly gone, even as a fiction, and gladly so. But the alternatives are not always so appealing: there's the schizoid subject associated with Postmodern culture, the networked subject associated with information society ...

MS: The tired subject! [laughs]

HF: Yes, the subject multi-tasked to death. Dr Evil had only one 'mini me' to watch over; the rest of us seem to have a whole brood ...

Right now, the question of autonomy – or its lack – concerns me most in relation to the heightening of distraction in our media/web world. And this concern has led me to rethink my own take on some art after Minimalism – to think about how it might participate, knowingly or not, in this distractive condition. Twenty years ago, I wrote a text titled 'The Crux of Minimalism' (Foster, 1996: 35–70) where I argued that, in its break from the frame of painting and the pedestal of sculpture, Minimalism opened up a line of work in which actual bodies and actual spaces were tested, defined, demarcated. Along with many others, I thought that line – the line of process and body art, of site-specific and institution-critical art, and so on – was of primary significance. Yet it is now clear that the Minimalist opening allowed not only for a progressive differentiation of bodies and spaces, but also for the partial dissolution of those terms. Think of the 'light and space' art of Robert Irwin and James Turrell: it seems phenomenological, but its phenomenology is somehow *faux*, already mediated. And this faux-phenomenological art was further technologized in the video projections of artists like Bill Viola – work that wants to overwhelm bodies and space, to produce a kind of techno-sublime. Today this seems to be the desired effect of much art – digital pictorial photography, say, as well as projected image installations – so much so that this secondary line of art after Minimalism now appears to be the dominant one. And people love it, of course, in large part because it aestheticizes, or rather artifies, an 'experience' already familiar to them, the intensities produced by media culture at large. For the most part, such art is happily involved with an image space that goes beyond the distractive to the immersive.

That's a story I think needs to be told, and recently in London I tried. The occasion was the Donald Judd retrospective at the Tate Modern, which revealed, to me at least, how much his art was always bound up with the very illusion that it purported to banish. Concurrent with the Judd show was an immense Olafur Eliasson installation, 'The Weather Project', with a mirrored orb like some otherwordly sun set atop the Turbine Hall, and again people loved it: in the middle of winter they bathed on the floor, basking in its faux-phenomenological glow. The juxtaposition of the Judd and the Eliasson almost made the argument for me about this post-Minimalist line involving illusion and distraction. Anyway I sketched this account at the Judd conference,[3] and afterwards a young woman in the audience said in effect:

> Essentially I agree with you: this expanded field of art has hooked up with an expanded field of media, but to pull back from it as you do under the cover of terms like 'culture industry' and 'spectacle' isn't satisfactory anymore; that response's too easy, its judgment too automatic. Can't you think of other ways to consider this mediated illusion, this immersive experience, if indeed, as you suggest, it is a principal experience that the culture gives us today?

That question (I've fleshed it out here) has stuck with me, and I'm working on a response now.

We are in the midst of a new twist in spectacular media; certainly the 1960s witnessed one too, as did the 1920s before that. At that moment, critics like Benjamin and Kracauer confronted the full effects of photographic reproduction and cinematic training, and they didn't flee to the high ground of modernist art: they examined the effects, explored how this condition might be reworked. Think, for example, of how Benjamin speculated about tactility and distraction in Dada, architecture and film. And Kracauer went further: he saw, more clearly than Benjamin, the deleterious effects of new technologies on social life – as evidenced in the (ir)rationalization of 'the mass ornament', for example – but rather than pull back, he asked *why not go through*? That is his famous 'go for broke' wager: what might these technologies render on the other side of their capitalist deployment? Others like Gramsci asked the same thing – even though 'the other side' turned out to be mostly an abyss. So how might the question, translated to the present, be phrased? Is there another side to this culture of immersive experience? Might there be a cultural politics that doesn't leave it to our masters to control every aspect of these terms? Of course this immersion is much more total in its effects than distraction faced by Benjamin and Kracauer, and both terms seem completely other to critical consciousness, and so we often fall back on the model of the autonomous subject as a crutch. But there are other ways to address the problem ...

MS: So, following the audience member's question at Tate Modern, *how to* make more of immersion, make something else of it, to try imagining how immersion might have the potential to work outside of those terms that come before it?

I'm reminded of my visit to New York in April, during which two things happened to me that are relevant here. The first is that I got 'lost' in a Richard Serra sculpture at DIA Beacon, which was quite an amazing, vertiginous experience. The second is that I stumbled into Robert Irwin's *Varese Scrim* (1973) at the Guggenheim's exhibition 'Singular Forms (Sometimes Repeated): Art from

1951 to the Present' – I was so busy trying to look through it I failed to see it! I began to think about what I called 'the trouble of walking into art', and I said jokingly to myself, I'm going to write a book entitled *Walking into Art*, and it's going to be about all the ways one can literally 'walk into art', and it's going to include chapters on accidents, disorientation, labyrinths, losing one's way, mistakes, vertigo, confusion.

As I walked away from Irwin's *Varese Scrim*, with the security guard's scolding still burning my ears, I was reminded of the need to find discrete tropes, modalities, *the right ways of figuring* 'immersive' experiences that are 'proper' to the particularity of the works themselves.

Of course, Eliasson's installation that took up every square inch of the Turbine Hall at Tate Modern and whose solar glow, its mist and hum, spilled out through the building's windows and doors was a very singular instance of what happens when you walk into art, and it reminds you that immersion can be completely all-embracing, comforting even. I'm not talking about digital arts, or VR, or the kind of immersion orchestrated by technology-enhanced interactivity but, rather, an interactive art that is born of site-specificity, of place, of location and of a phenomenological affect. During Eliasson's installation, it's true that the audience – rather participants – were very happy to pretend to sunbathe, to run around as if they were at the beach, to lie on their backs looking up at their reflections on the mirrored ceiling, moving their arms and legs in an effort to make simulated snow angels. Here's a kind of immersion that's very pleasurable, comforting, as I've already said, but this installation, and these feelings, are in no way complicit *in principle* with the culture industry or the society of the spectacle as such. There's also a *generosity* in that piece that I like.

So, I'm wondering about distinctive types of immersion – or at least the points at which a moment of liminality gives way to immersion: what happens when you immerse yourself in, say, digital art like many of the pieces on show at the San Francisco Museum of Modern Art's 2001 exhibition '010101: Art in Technological Times', or the Eliasson, or *inadvertently* immerse yourself in a Minimalist art work or sculpture in its purest form? You've mentioned the Judd to Eliasson trajectory, and it's a really nice one. Surely each instance in that changing trajectory, as well as a whole series of other non-artistic immersive encounters, from the Diorama and the Panorama in the nineteenth century to the IMAX cinema or 'surround sound' in the twentieth century, offer themselves up in their historical, technological and conceptual particularity?

Incidentally, the first time I understood Barthes' and Foucault's discussions of authorship, more than 10 years *before* I read them, was when, as a kid, I inadvertently stumbled into, thereby modifying, Carl Andre's bricks, *Equivalent VIII*, at the old Tate. That was a moment of understanding how art making takes place, and how meaning making takes place. I'm not a clumsy guy in general, but I've obviously got a long history of stumbling into art, I hadn't realized! [laughs]

HF: 'Walking into' is different from 'stumbling into', and both are different from 'being immersed'. Minimalists like Andre confront you; they don't immerse you. Judd is a little different, and Dan Flavin even more so. I think many of us read those 'literalists' too literally: we took them (and especially Judd) at their word, found their writing too readily in their work, and thought their art did banish illusion outright, when really it played with it all along – in the colours and surfaces of Judd, in the luminous effects and spatial washes of Flavin. At the same time, they did change the terms of illusion, and it is never simple immersion: Judd always gives you a bolt, and Flavin a fixture, to fasten down the illusion of the Plexiglas sheet or the fluorescent light. Each time they bring you back to the materiality of the object, the limit of the space, and a sense of your own bodily relation to both. In some ways, Richard Serra pushes this dialectic further: his work is evermore immersive and defining at once. As you wend your way through his ribbons, spirals and ellipses, the space wraps around you in a way that is as psychological as it is physical. An almost intrauterine space is set up that is nothing if not also materially actual.

For me, the recent Guggenheim show marked the culmination of the historical reversal I mentioned earlier: the contemporary triumph of the secondary line out of Minimalism, the one that recoups it for the pictorial and the illusionistic, for light and space effects, for projected images and immersive spaces. With Serra you're made reflexive in your immersion; you're not virtually obliterated by the experience. With the world of Turrell, Viola *et al.* you are: you're somehow lost in relation to your body, and you stumble not only into the work but through it as well. It's an effect, beyond distraction, of disorientation, of being lost in space, and one has to wonder about its ideological effects – that is, beyond its sheer aestheticism, which is what attracts people, for again it gives the rush of media intensity with the surplus value of art.

MS: Which is why the question of the specificity of medium persists, and why questions of mediation, remediation and discussions of the post-medium come to the fore...

HF: Sure. Which is not to say that specificity is tied to any particular set of materials or precedents. The point is not to delimit what can count as art; rather it is to differentiate between experiences and effects. Now when I say 'faux-phenomenological', I don't mean to imply some prior state of perceptual purity. Our sensorium is now so mediated that such a state would be impossible to recover even if it ever existed in the first place.

MS: In a sense, it's a phenomenological response, or a faux-phenomenological response to the *im*materiality of material...

HF: What do you mean?

MS: That there is a resurgence of interest in phenomenology at the moment across the arts and humanities, and I never thought about the resurgence in this way but it may well be not just an effort to try reaffirming a certain kind of contact with the body, the body of the viewer, the spectator, the participant, but that that effort to reassert or reaffirm contact comes absolutely as a response to these concerns over *de*materialization, or the *im*material, or the kind of immersion that we were just discussing in which art and media converge. And that one's contact with works of art, along with so many other encounters, is mediated and remediated to such an extent that perhaps a little bit of old-style, clunky, phenomenology is absolutely necessary both as a way to remind oneself of oneself *and* to think through the implications of the damage, or the pleasures that are done, and done to us, by such immersion. And how to get out of it, around it, through it! Maybe we're just caught in another playing out of that earlier moment of immersion – distraction ...

HF: Yes, one term is bound up with another that it opposes. And there is such a dialectic of de/materialization in art after Minimalism, and a stress on the phenomenological does recur whenever the object in question – the art, the body, the space – seems to be too virtualized. That dialectic is already active in Minimalism and Pop – I said as much in 'The Crux of Minimalism' (Foster, 1996: 35–70). In the 1990s it was again in play in abject art, which insisted, in the face of cyberspace, on the untranscendability of the body, which it often figured as traumatically fixed. And it's there in the present too, only now the 'phenomenological' term is more social, a sort of being-together in the space of art – hence all the talk about 'the relational' and 'the interactive' today. When artists go on about 'the space of art as the site of community', I don't know whether to laugh or to cry, but I understand the impulse.

October, Visual Culture and that 'Questionnaire'

MS: Can I take you back... I have a question or two about the now legendary, watershed 'Questionnaire on Visual Culture' that appeared in issue 77 of *October* in 1996. The 'Questionnaire' appeared at a time when Visual Studies was becoming institutionally both constituted and legitimized in the US academy. What were the reasons behind presenting the 'Questionnaire' at that time – was it an effort to further strengthen or frustrate the prospect of Visual Studies? In your opinion, what were the repercussions of the 'Questionnaire' in the American academy, and beyond? And what image of Visual Studies did the *October* editors have in mind that led you collectively to ask the questions posed?

HF: There are a few things one should know about 'that' questionnaire. First, Rosalind Krauss and I cooked it up, not the *October* editors as a group. Second, we meant it as a provocation (that much worked); obviously no one person could hold all the positions presented – some contradicted others – and in any case they were offered only as points of departure, as so many ideas – some 'received', some reasonable – to pick apart. That said, Rosalind and I were suspicious, in different ways, about certain aspects of Visual Studies as it was framed at the time (this was 1996). I've stated some of the reasons, and others in my contribution to the issue.

One thing to stress here is that, in some sense, Visual Studies is always already bound up with Art History, even internal to it, at least in Art History at its best moments (think of Semper, Riegl, Warburg, the early Panofsky, to name only a few, or in our own time Michael Baxandall, Svetlana Alpers, Jonathan Crary...). It's a little like what I said about the relation between Modernism and Postmodernism in criticism, or vertical and horizontal axes in art: there is a dialectic of Art History and Visual Studies, too, in which the latter term opens up the former, while the former term keeps the latter rigorous. Isn't that what interdisciplinary work does, that is, if it is truly 'inter' *and* 'disciplinary'? In any case I don't see Art History and Visual Studies as quite as antagonistic as they were presented then; and even then I felt there were resources for Visual Studies within Art History and vice versa.

The *October* issue was driven by two primary concerns. The first was the way in which Visual Studies was too taken by the visual, by a fixation on the image, a fixation long questioned in advanced art. (Maybe we drew the line too quickly from 'the visual' to 'the virtual', but it seemed Visual Studies had done so for us.) The second had to do with the anthropological turn I've mentioned, and the atrophying of the mnemonic dimension of art as a potential result. The responses of the more reactive parties in both camps were not very helpful, and in any case there's a partial *rapprochement* now. In the end, not only is Visual Studies often internal to Art History and vice versa, but so is visual culture in art: some of the greatest moments in Modernism are openings to new or neglected visual cultures.

MS: That helps clarify things for me, thanks. Let me pick up on one point you've just made: this matter of artists, or academics for that matter, working horizontally, or moving across the present. This is another way of articulating what you earlier called 'the anthropological turn'. It seems to me that this is also the difficulty at the heart of accusations of ahistoricism directed against Visual Culture Studies. This is in part also to return to your first concern, just noted, of the *im*material dimension of the visual – and I do believe questions of ahistoricism and immateriality are connected here.

I never quite understood why the study of visual culture was, is, at root, considered intrinsically ahistorical and anthropological. And it often seems to me that *this very idea* of Visual Culture Studies as ahistorical and anthropological, and not only the dissemination of this idea, comes from the *October*

'Questionnaire' itself; not so much from the responses as from the questions themselves. I'm interested to know where this characterization of the study of visual culture came from?

Having now read *Design and Crime,* I think I have the beginnings of an answer to my own question. And it has something to do with Visual Culture Studies being or being seen to be the 'visual wing of "cultural studies"', as you call it (Foster, 2002: 90). Let me quote you back to yourself:

> As an academic subject... 'visual culture' is... maybe as oxymoronic as 'art history'. Certainly its two terms repel each other with equal force, for if art history is sustained between the autonomy implied in 'art' and the imbrication implied in 'history', then visual culture is stretched between the virtuality implied in 'visual' and the materiality implied in 'culture'. (p. 90)

And you continue:

> In general terms visual studies might be too quick to dismiss aesthetic autonomy as retrograde, and to embrace subcultural forms as subversive. Its ethnographic model might also have this unintended consequence: it might be encouraged to move horizontally from subject to subject across social space, more so than vertically along the historical lines of particular form, genre or problematic. In this way visual studies might privilege the present excessively, and so might support rather than stem the posthistorical attitude that has become the default position of so much artistic, critical, and curatorial practice today. (p. 91)

Your argument here is that the attention 'visual studies' lavishes on the contemporary, and on particular contemporary forms of 'visual culture' – the spectacle of visual commodities, technologies, information and entertainment, as you characterize it – is both born of and leads to subjective, interpretive and ethnographic practices – from psychoanalysis and anthropology – that are themselves in effect *de*materializing and *de*historicizing. (In its attention to the visual, it de-materializes art. In its attention to culture, it dehistoricizes history.) This is the case, you say, because 'just as social imperatives and anthropological assumptions have governed the shift from "history" to "culture", so technological imperatives and psychoanalytic assumptions have governed the shift from "art" to "visual"' (p. 92).

As I've already mentioned, while I've never been quite sure why *in principle* 'the visual' is open to accusations of dematerialization or why 'the cultural' is charged with a will to dehistoricize, I understand the argument itself. And it's a relief that someone has finally explained this to me with quite so much precision and clarity. So after all that, my question is quite straightforward: is it simply the case that those committed to the study of Visual Culture, or Visual Cultural Studies, or Visual Studies need to attend to history, and historical formation, if they're not already doing so, as well as privilege the present? Or is 'Visual Culture' itself, because of its very etymology, destined to fail to respond to such an appeal?

HF: One reason why I was sensitive to 'the virtuality of the visual' in Visual Studies was that this was an effect also produced by the formalist reading of Modernism: Greenberg and company had valued Modernist painting as if it were a matter of opticality only, little more than a test of sublimatory eyesight – whether you could transcend your body through your vision. It seemed odd, to say the least, that Visual Studies, which was otherwise so opposed to such criticism, should reproduce its fetishism of the visual.

As for the charge that the anthropological is ahistorical, that was tendentious; but again my focus was on art and criticism that had taken up the ethnographic model of field work, that moved from project site to project site. I was concerned with its possible present-ism – that was all.

Design, Urbanism and the Architecture of Demoralization

MS: To end, I'd like to turn to *Design and Crime* (Foster, 2002). The second half of the book considers the art museum, Art History and art criticism, or cultural criticism, and we've already discussed some of these matters. But the first half of the book is, for want of a better phrase, design criticism. My question is that in *Design and Crime* you engage with a series of design-related matters: from Adolf Loos to subcultures; from Art Nouveau to branding and the media industries; from 'Bruce Mau Design' to Frank Gehry and Rem Koolhaas. You also touch on the designed nature of 'memory-structures', or *musée imaginaire*, such as Warburg's 'Mnemosyne' and André Malraux's 'The Voices of Silence' as a 'history-as-catastrophe'. This attention to architecture, design and the (more rhetorically driven) designing of things, such as history or memory, is not new to your work, but why has it come to the fore now?

HF: Because they have become more important in the culture at large, more important than art certainly, the status of which has seemed to diminish roughly in inverse proportion to the rise of architecture (in some ways the architect has assumed the old cultural role of the artist as visionary form-giver). As an inveterate party-crasher I wanted to weigh in on these matters, and to do so in a more public way than *October* (much of *Design and Crime* was first published in the *London Review of Books*). For early Modernists, of course, architecture and design could not be separated out any more than photography and film could be: they were all a part of the expanded field of cultural practice. So architecture and design were always within my bailiwick as a Modernist, however amateurish I was about it. (It's important, I think, to keep, to cultivate, a little amateurishness sometimes – both in the etymological sense of the love of the thing and in the common sense of non-professional status. The architecture world is full of insider trading and critics on the dole – it makes the art world look transparent by comparison – and it has made me cause some disturbance.)

I also wanted to pursue the trope of design in other arenas: designer genes, drugs, personalities, spaces ... The ramifications are immense for social life and political culture, to say nothing of the 'new economy'. But recently another aspect of the problem has come into focus for me as well. I suppose it was triggered by the last text of W.G. Sebald, *On the Natural History of Destruction* (2003 [1999]), which revisits the firebombing of German cities and the complicated silences that ensued. But it's also there every morning in the newspaper: the occupation of Iraq, the settlements in Israel (the wall there too), gated communities, 'homeland security', the control of space, the militarization of architecture and urbanism. More and more, war is waged in cities. War 'over there': the Pentagon sees the battle of Falluja as a paradigm of things to come, and it has begun to enlist architects and urbanists to model these spaces, these sites, to plan not only for their destruction but for their suppression, occupation, control. And 'war' right here: think of how our cities have changed since 9/11: the manipulation of the terrorist scare, the accepted talk of 'defensible space', the generalized deployment of surveillance from scanning your retina to scoping everything from satellites. Here are some topics for art, architecture and Visual Studies, alike.

Notes

1 Interview with Hal Foster, originally published in *Journal of Visual Culture*, 'Polemics, Postmodernism, Immersion, Militarized Space: A Conversation with Hal Foster', 3(3), December (2004), pp. 320–35.
2 See issue 11 of the cultural theory journal *Parallax* (Routledge/Taylor & Francis) entitled 'Polemics: Against Cultural Studies', April–June, 1999, as a fascinating enactment of such matters.
3 'Donald Judd: The Writings', at Tate Modern, Saturday, 28 February 2004.

References

Bürger, Peter (1984) *Theory of the Avant-Garde*. Minneapolis: University of Minnesota Press.
Eagleton, Terry (2003) *After Theory*. London: Penguin Books.
Foster, Hal (ed.) (1983) *The Anti-Aesthetic: Essays on Postmodern Culture*. Seattle: Bay Press.
Foster, Hal (1984) 'Re: Post', in Brian Wallis (ed.) *Art After Modernism: Rethinking Representation*, pp. 189–201. New York: The New Museum of Contemporary Art.
Foster, Hal (1985a) *Recodings: Art, Spectacle, Cultural Politics*. Seattle: Bay Press.
Foster, Hal (1985b) 'The "Primitive" Unconscious of Modern Art, or White Skin Black Masks', *October* 34 (Fall).
Foster, Hal (1993) 'The Art of Fetishism: Notes on Dutch Still Life', in Emily Apter and William Pietz (eds) *Fetishism as Cultural Discourse*, pp. 251–65. Ithaca, NY: Cornell University Press.

Foster, Hal (1995) *Compulsive Beauty*. Cambridge, MA: MIT Press.
Foster, Hal (1996) *The Return of the Real: Avant-Garde at the End of the Century*. Cambridge, MA: MIT Press.
Foster, Hal (2002) *Design and Crime (and Other Diatribes)*. London: Verso.
Foster, Hal (2004) *Prosthetic Gods*. Cambridge, MA: MIT Press.
Foucault, Michel (1984 [1971]) 'Nietzsche, Genealogy, History', in Paul Rabinow (ed.) *The Foucault Reader*, pp. 76–100. London: Penguin.
Sebald, W.G. (2003 [1999]) *On the Natural History of Destruction*. London: Penguin.

13

THE OBJECT OF VISUAL CULTURE STUDIES, AND PREPOSTEROUS HISTORY

Interview with Mieke Bal

Introduction

Mieke Bal holds the position of Royal Dutch Academy of Sciences Professor. She is also Professor of the Theory of Literature at the University of Amsterdam and A.D. White Professor-at-large at Cornell University. A co-founder of the Visual and Cultural Studies programme at Rochester, Bal has written more than 25 single-authored books. These include *Narratology* (1985/1997), *Quoting Caravaggio* (1999), *Looking In: The Art of Viewing* (2001), *Louise Bourgeois' Spider* (2001), and *Travelling Concepts in the Humanities* (2002). *A Mieke Bal Reader* was published in 2006. Here Bal speaks about a series of institutional matters that include changes in the landscape of Visual Culture Studies over the last 20 years; the formation of the Visual and Cultural Studies programme at Rochester; self-reflexive methodologies in and the object of Visual Culture Studies; and questions of ahistoricism and historicity, as well as her own notion of preposterous history. Preoccupied by postcolonial and transcultural practices, she also considers issues raised by her recent multimedia/video installations and experimental documentaries such as Arab culture in the West, story-telling, love, homelessness, migration, and displacement.

Marquard Smith (MS): In 1989 you were co-founder with Michael Ann Holly of the graduate programme in Visual and Cultural Studies at University of Rochester in upstate New York. This is seen to be the first graduate programme of its kind. Would you tell me more about the genesis of this programme, the kinds of conversations that took place as it took shape, the pleasures you experienced in its realization, and its achievements.

Mieke Bal (MB): There is an official and an unofficial story to be told. For my point of view, they are both important. Unofficially, I just hit it off with Michael, we laughed until tears were streaming down our faces, we talked deep into the night, and we bore grief together. Intellectual friendship – of which I have written in the Afterword to *Looking In* – has been the most precious experience in my career (Bal, 2000). Within a friendship, everything can be said, dared. Conversely, intellectual engagement produces friendship.

But this friendship, consequently, is an intellectual friendship. Hence, there is no real distinction to be made between the two stories. At the heart of intellectual work, I realized in that collaborative project, lies what is best called 'intersubjectivity'. This is a concern that binds procedure with power and empowerment, with pedagogy and the transmittability of knowledge, with inclusiveness and exclusion. I picked up the concept and cherished it for its insistence on the democratic distribution of knowledge. I was interested in developing concepts we could all agree upon and use, in order to make what has become labelled 'theory' accessible to every participant in cultural analysis, both within and outside the academy. This concern was the driving force behind the writing of my first book, *Narratology* (1985 [1978]). Intersubjectivity is my standard for teaching and writing, discussing and collaborating with others. And then, beginning in Rochester, for friendship. And once I began making films – which is teamwork by definition – this preference came in good stead.

Under the influence of this excitement I became totally involved in what happens when concepts are taken seriously as the tools of intersubjectivity: they must be explicit, clear, defined in such a way that everyone can take them up and use them. Each concept is part of a framework, a systematic set of distinctions – *not* of oppositions – that can sometimes be ignored but never transgressed or contradicted without serious damage to the analysis at hand. Throughout my professional life, I have been fussy about them. Concepts, or those words that outsiders consider jargon, can be tremendously productive. They help articulate an understanding, convey an interpretation, check an imagination run wild, enable discussion on the basis of common terms, perceive absences and exclusions. For me, a concept is not just a label that is easily replaced by a more common word.

Concepts that are (mis)used as labels lose their working force. They are subject to fashion and quickly become meaningless. A few years ago, 'uncanny' was just such a label; then, 'cultural memory' and, more disturbingly, 'trauma', a concept with a precise, specific meaning, the understanding of which can actually be used to help people with serious grief, but not to meaningfully describe exposure to television news. Instead of reductive labels, concepts can become a third partner in the otherwise totally unverifiable interaction between critic and object, on condition that they are kept under scrutiny through confrontation with – not application to – the cultural objects one wishes to understand, are amenable to change, and apt to illuminate historical and cultural differences. This is why I fuss about them, not because of an obsession with 'proper' usage.

The *gaze*, a key concept in visual studies, is one such concept I find it important to fuss about. Norman Bryson's analysis of the life of this concept in feminist and gender studies, in the introduction to *Looking in: The Art of Viewing* (2000), amply demonstrates why it is worthwhile to fuss. He rightly insists that feminism has had a decisive impact on visual studies; film studies would be nowhere near where they are today without feminism. It would appear that to challenge concepts that seem either obviously right or too dubious to keep using as they are in order to revise rather than reject them is a most responsible activity for theorists. Interestingly, concepts that do not budge under the challenge may well be more problematical than those that do. So, as you see, my unofficial story has already blended with its counterpart.

Now, the more official story is related to this. We made an attempt at Rochester to hire Norman Bryson in Art History and Comp. Lit. To make the case, Michael and I started thinking about a common graduate programme. Before we knew it, we had it done. The times were ripe, the excitement spread out, and we managed to convey the urgency of radically innovating the way the Humanities think about visuality. Of course, there was a lot of bureaucracy and lobbying that followed, and these are not my forte, but the general thrust was very positive. You have to understand that nothing like this existed in any American university at that time. We had to make it up so to speak, but then, we had the freedom to do just that.

The first years of the programme achieved so much that soon it was overtaken by better-funded emulators. We got the best students, and they all landed great jobs, precisely because they had been trained in more than Art History alone. Theory – a general notion that I find problematic, by the way – was the buzzword of the day, and our students had that. We also had some very successful studio-theory combination students, for example, Walid Ra'ad who went on to become a really high-profile artist as well as academic. All this made the case for the kind of boundary-crossing endeavours this programme was meant to be – academic boundaries between disciplines, boundaries between academics and practices (not to forget curating, for example). Clearly, it needed to happen. I feel privileged to have been able to participate in this movement.

MS: Almost twenty years later, does the institutional situation and situated-ness of Visual Culture Studies seem more or less solid, more or less sturdy? This is the tricky, two-edged sword-type of question.

MB: As always, success has its downside. The programme has changed, and honestly, I am not sure I would recognize it anymore. None of the early-days principals are still there. More importantly, the concept that underlay the programme has been diluted considerably. I think Visual Culture Studies is ready for re-vision. It needs to be re-conceptualized beyond either the hip art history or the generalizations about images having taken over culture. Institutionally, I can't really tell what the situation is. This is probably different locally. In my country with very few exceptions there is barely a trace of change in art history, let alone an engagement with visual culture. The interesting developments are in anthropology and film studies. Here and there in modern art history.

Anthropology in the Netherlands numbers a good crowd of people inspired by visual anthropology – which is not so much interested in tracing iconographic traditions but in opening up visual culture as a serious 'text'. Patricia Spyer, for example, works on violent movements in Indonesia, and the visual material she brings back tells a story that dramatically nuances and revises the story we get from journalism and the media. And when I needed someone to help me film a mother in China (for my video installation *Nothing is Missing* [2006]) it was an anthropologist who volunteered, and understood exactly the ins and outs of the project. This matches the international situation. The handbook for cultural analysis that is currently produced by the Open University has a great mapping of the numerous aspect of visual anthropology (Bennett and Frow, 2007).

That film and media studies would be the avant-garde of Visual Culture Studies seems predictable. It is their job, so to speak. Since their subject-matter is itself at the heart of visual culture. It would have worked much better if art history had collaborated with and granted leadership to the people in those relative new fields. Thomas Elsaesser, for example, does work that 'goes places' – from exhibitions in the Centre Pompidou to DVDs and journalistic writing, without ever sacrificing depth to clarity. His younger colleagues – José van Dijck, who works on digital cultural memory, or Patricia Pisters, on popular cinema, phenomena such as Madonna or Hitchcock, from a Deleuzian perspective: these are the people who do it. I am hopeful for the next few years but it's too early (or too late!) to rejoice.

MS: To what extent do you feel that some of the changes we have seen on the Visual Culture Studies landscape are in part due to the particular kinds or the range of subjects and objects that scholars have chosen to pursue? Or, is it more a matter of how scholars have sought to conceive of their objects of study? I ask the latter question with your article 'Visual essentialism and the object of visual culture'(Bal, 2003a) very much in mind. This article published in *Journal of Visual Culture* in 2003 received a series of lively responses from Norman Bryson (2003), James Elkins (2003), Michael Ann Holly (2003), Peter Leech (2003), Nicholas Mirzoeff (2003), W.J.T. Mitchell (2003), and Griselda Pollock (2003) to which you replied (Bal, 2003b). For me, why the article is so crucial is because you claim that Visual Culture Studies is a movement that 'lays claim to a specific object and raises specific questions about that object' (2003a: 6). You go on to write that '[t]he object ... comes first' (2003: 7). That's to say, as you point out, because the object domain of Visual Culture Studies is not obvious, it must be 'created'. And here you refer to Roland Barthes' fundamental observation: that to do interdisciplinary work, it is 'not enough to take a "subject" (theme) and group several disciplines around it, each of which approaches the same subject differently'. Following Barthes, you conclude, '[i]nterdisciplinary study consists of *creating* a new object *that belongs to no one*' (2003a: 7). I'll be asking you a question about inter-disciplinarity in a while, but for the moment would you also say a little more about what it means for 'visuality' to be the 'new' object of Visual Culture Studies (2003a: 9), and why this is so key ...

MB: Let me begin by saying something about cultural studies as the movement from which Visual Culture Studies has emerged. First, while one of cultural studies' major innovations has been to pay attention to a different kind of object, as a new field averse to traditional approaches it has not been successful (enough) in developing a methodology to counter the exclusionary methods of the separate disciplines. More often than not, the methods have not changed. While the object – *what* you study – has changed, the method – *how* you do it – has not. But without the admittedly rigid methodologies of the disciplines, how do you keep analysis from floundering into sheer partisanship or being perceived as floundering? This is the major problem of content and practice that faces us today, which in turn creates more problems, especially in teaching situations.

Second, cultural studies has involuntarily 'helped' its opponents to deepen rather than to overcome the destructive divide between *les anciens* and *les modernes*, a binary structure as old as Western culture itself. This is unfortunate, for this opposition tends to feed an oedipally-based psychosocial mechanism that is unhelpful when it comes to changing predominant power structures. The problem is primarily a social one, but in the current situation, where academic jobs are scarce and hierarchies returning, it entails a tendency to a monolithical appointments policy that, under the name of backlash, threatens everything that has been accomplished. Whereas a book like this cannot change that situation at all, a recognizably responsible practice based on reflection on the problem of method may help to pave the way for a more nuanced academic environment.

Third, the inevitable consequence of the inadequate methodology and the reinforced opposition combined is even more mundane yet just as dangerous. At a time of economic crisis, the inter-disciplinarity inherent to cultural studies has given university administrators a tool with which to enforce mergings and cancellations of departments that might turn out to be fatal for the broad grounding cultural studies needs.[1]

Against this background, emphatically, all three aspects of it, we must consider what has happened to Visual Culture Studies and how it has been framed, sometimes trapped. The move or transformation from art history to Visual Culture Studies is not the only contributing factor to the development, and I am a bit regretful that it has been appropriated too much, to my taste, by that particular corner. When social and anthropological perspectives get integrated something like a new object – visuality as social process that includes but is not confined to, actual images – can emerge. To put it strongly, the power relations, in access, representation, performance, skills etc. are just as important in this object as the things we call images. And yes, the creation of a new object or object domain is what is key to inter-disciplinary thinking. I have experienced the urgency of this, at least in two moments.

The first was my increasing engagement with anthropology. Critical anthropologists – and my colleague Johannes Fabian is the one I know best as a brilliant instance – have a way of doing their research while questioning the concepts they bring to bear on their fields of study – *culture* being the first and foremost, and they will never sit down with satisfaction about it! The questioning – and this for me is key – occurs in conjunction with the actual analysis. A good anthropological study based on fieldwork will always also be a keen introduction to critical thinking about cultural things. When every one was carrying on about vision, Fabian wrote about listening, and about theatre. Theatre, by the way, is another of those fields that are by definition multi-media based and therefore compelled to think about the terms of analysis. For example, a brilliant study on theatre by Maaike Bleeker deeply engages Michael Fried, in ways that even the most critical art historians have yet to do (Bleeker, 2002). My somewhat grumpy article you mention published in *Journal of Visual Culture* was motivated by the sense that we, in visual analysis, didn't do that enough.

My second moment was when I started making films. Film-making is, in fact, making an object. That's why documentary versus fiction is the most unhelpful way of categorizing films. If you allow me to give a few examples, you will see that each film was an encounter with an entire field of analysis I didn't know was out there – because the library had not presented it. First, I made some films on art, documenting the responses viewers articulated in front of single art works. It was my resistance against the expert on television, explaining art. I claimed through these ArtClips (6-minute shorts) that people are their own experts. That they, literally, know better. I also made two exhibition-based films.

Then, something happened in my own environment that raised more profoundly social questions. In line with anthropology's inherent self-reflexivity, I became sensitized to the difficulty of storytelling when power inequity frames who can speak and who cannot, and who gets to decide what the next step is. In [the film] *Mille et un jours* (2004) we (a collective of filmmakers called Cinema Suitcase) celebrate the outcome of a long and intricate journey of the anguish, struggle, loneliness, and financial constraints of a young 'sans papiers' in Paris. Three days of the joyful celebration of his wedding establish the here-and-now of this documentary, which is organized through an Aristotelian unity of time, space and event. But from within that same event, pockets of history weigh in with darker times, tougher spaces. As if bound by elastic ties to the present of the festive moment in which the film is anchored, the characters descend into memories of fear and uncertainty, only to bounce back again and rejoice in the outcome.

Tarek (27) came to Paris from Tunisia in 1999 to get an education. Despite the difficulties of his status as 'illegal immigrant', he followed a course of study in computer science and obtained his diploma. As he was pursuing this double life of earning a living and studying, the French authorities tried to expel him. But they didn't succeed.

Tarek's is a long and complex story, which the film tells through the voices of the people concerned. After some 1001 days, his marriage to Ilhem (22), a young woman belonging to the second generation of Tunisian immigrants, finally establishes him in an ordinary life.

Like the collection of Arabic tales from which the film's title is derived, the film organizes a multiplicity of stories around a wedding. With celebrations in full swing, the politics of immigration remains present under the surface. While highly political, this is not a one-issue, one-position film. Instead, its political thrust is to solicit debate by enlisting the viewer to become acquainted with the characters and the ins and outs of their situation; to be guests at the wedding. Judgment is withheld. Through an intimacy with characters that is rare for documentary, we witness how four generations of Tunisian immigrants give shape, each in their own way, to dealing with migration, and the different opportunities and hardships they encountered. Tarek's obsession with time's frightening speed is cast against the shadow of his father's failure to cope with capitalist time as an earlier immigrant. Rife with bureaucratic violence but also with the characters' vitality, determination, honesty, and intelligence in outsmarting 'the system', the film's content and aesthetics together constitute a plea for an open society.

But, unexpectedly, this is also a love story. Or is it? Interwoven through the political machinations is a consideration of what is easily dismissed as an 'arranged marriage'. There is a picture of the social fabric of immigrant life, and a tender portrait of a young woman and her friends reflecting on the transformation of one of them from schoolgirl to adult woman. The profound grief of loving parents about to see their eldest child leave home and move to the city – a change they barely seem able to face – alternates with the happy anticipation of and preparations for a wedding that must give expression to their love for and pride in their daughter. Siblings, relatives and friends candidly express their opinions of Tarek and Ilhem, while the voices of an official and a 'faux' journalist pose contrary views that open up – rather than shut down by way of consensus and prejudice – the question of how the administration ought to deal with situations where rules and people appear no easy match.

It is in the framework of the literary legacy of Arabic culture in the West we see what is perhaps the film's most significant move against stereotypes: the play with masculinities. To be sure, there are ways in which Tarek is not only the main character of the story of his voyage to legitimacy, but also a rather macho type of man, who directs the production of the wedding-as-theatre with his eyes and his mobile phone. But in several ways, this macho image the Western cliché tends to attribute to Arabic men is constantly undermined. The most important moment when this happens is early on in the film, when Tarek follows what appears, from the back, to be an army of guys ascending the stairs to fetch the bride.

At first, this view might seem frankly scary: a dozen of young men about to 'take' a 21-year-old woman. But arriving upstairs, the shot is reversed, in a classical move to suture the people we see to what they face. And in that reverse-shot we see Tarek's face in all its gentle nervousness, biting his lips, looking at his friends for support and one friend patting his shoulder in encouragement. For me, this is one of the most touching moments, where I am confronted with my own prejudice and drawn into empathy with the other side.

Interspersed with other moments where men take on caring activities, this image stays with us throughout the film. An uncle combs the hair of Ilhem's young brother; at another moment, this uncle feeds a baby; Tarek's father helps his son dress for the traditional wedding in Tunisia. Meanwhile, Ilhem's brother comes up with a very ambivalent expression of gender politics when he emphasizes that his sister was allowed to marry whomever she pleased, by her father, without mentioning the mother's opinion at all. Yet, when a Western viewer might still be reeling over this double talk, he continues to predict that his father will be crying at the imminent departure of his daughter – as he might himself, as well.

Most strikingly, and perhaps unsettlingly, during one of many singing sessions in the apartment where the festivities are being prepared but already savoured, Ilhem's father lets his youngest daughter put a headscarf on his head. His somewhat shy but accepting and an affirming look at the camera shows that for him, being 'feminized' is nothing to be ashamed of. Yet, the scarf-wearing neighbour sitting next to him cannot bear it, and takes the scarf off him. Here, as in many other moments, reflection on cultural customs go hand in hand with reflection on the processes of cultural transmission, as well as collusion and contestation.

Together, then, these moments in which diverse forms of masculinity are enacted, shown, and subliminally evaluated are at the heart of the film's relationship to the dual tradition of the fairy-tales of heroism, eroticism, and adventure, and of prejudice, rigidity and contempt. As with the more overt political issues – of the confrontation with the law and of the arranged marriage – the visibility of the clash between these two traditions is facilitated, not imposed; its evaluation as well as the possibility to bridge the gap through empathy are rigorously limited to visual enactment, not commentary. Since the characters have no reason to reflect on what is their own 'natural' masculine behaviour, no spoken words are called for.

In *Access Denied*, (2005) a 30-minutes film also by the Cinema Suitcase collective, the issue was literally to gather information where this turns out to be impossible. Ihab (31), a Palestinian academic living in Amsterdam, is preparing to travel to visit his family in Gaza for the first time in four years, and do some fieldwork. Gary (28), an Irish artist also living in Amsterdam, intends to accompany Ihab and film the reunion with his family, the interviews with informants, and the progress of Ihab's project: to study the cultural memory in Palestine of *al nakba*, the catastrophe of 1948. While they prepare for the trip, Ihab and Gary become closer. But, once they arrive in Cairo airport, Ihab's arrest and deportation separates the two.

From here on, the film alternates between the backdrops of the two men's trip. While Ihab conducts his research with determination and commitment, Gary is flooded by his first encounter with Arabic culture. He turns around in circles, having nothing to do but wait until he can fly back to Amsterdam. Ihab, in contrast, works frantically, but cannot leave on the planned date, since meanwhile Israel has closed the borders.

This film uses the metaphors of travel and failed encounters for a meditative reflection on the intercultural encounter between Arabic and Western individuals eager, but not always able, to understand each other. By the way, this film got a follow-up when Ihab, two years later, wanted to visit his family again and had volunteered to shoot an interview with his mother for my installation project *Nothing is Missing*. The day before he was set to go, Israel invaded Gaza and closed the border. To my utter amazement, ten days later a film slid into my mailbox. Ihab's brother had organized the interview, and instead of Ihab, this brother is the mother's interlocutor. It tells you how eager people are to tell their story.

I also worked for a while with an Iranian artist based in Berlin, Shahram Entekhabi. Unfortunately, after some great projects his severe personality problems made further collaboration impossible. But if you look, for example, at the film *Lost in Space* (2005), there is an issue of language and accents that gives depth to Hamid Naficy's concept of accented cinema (2001). When asked, in an interview conducted in English, what he missed most about being away from home, an Iranian long-term asylum seeker burst into his native Farsi and said that of the sorely missed things, the primary one was language. This triggered the aesthetic of this experimental film.

The film about homelessness and displacement tears apart the different manifestations of language. First, in an extensive credit sequence, all speakers are shown saying exactly what they say in the film. But only their mouths and hands are speaking; no voice can be heard over the street noise that accompanies their visual speaking. When the film begins proper, it becomes clear that the visual remains severed from the voices. During the film we hear the voices and see, in yet a different manifestation of speech, the translated utterances in screen-filling typescript. The images of failed attempts to insure home and security are relegated to the background. Meanwhile, the discrepancy between what we see, read, and hear becomes a statement on language in the contemporary world of displacement.

Just now, in early Fall 2006 Cinema Suitcase has made a film entitled *Colony* (2007) on labour relations in a perspective of pre-posterous history (34 minutes). It's about the early multi-national Bata, crated by a Czech shoe manufacturer. Concentrating on the ruins of Batanagar, a Bata colony near Calcutta, the film weaves past and present together through the voices of those who were there when this colony was a thriving community. Meanwhile, an activist, an archivist, and others with a more oblique relationship to that idyllic but paternalistic past put critical footnotes to the time-travelling women.

All these films can be called experimental documentaries, if they need a genre label. I also work on more performance-based films. With Shahram Entekhabi, I made a series of short performance films, one-act, one-situation. In these films, the everyday life of the figure of a migrant is stylized and reduced to single acts: travelling, looking for work, intervening in public space, offering cake on his birthday, standing in the street with a bunch of flowers looking for someone to give them to, running away from suspicious urbanites who finally see him, and think he's up to no good. This conclusion is the equivalent of the loop that starts at the beginning, endlessly repeating entrance and exit, while conflating that social reality with the collapse of the look: looking as being-looked-at.

In an exploration of the media that have shaped our visual consciousness, the works show that the temporal looping that characterizes video installation is on a par with a multiple 'looping' that is visual, social, and mediatic. The films show a constant interruption, sometimes a failure of the action, sometimes a visual interruption of movement, as another way of creating never-ending stories. The films reflect (on) the medium in which they are made, sometimes to the point of interrupting the medium itself. At the same time, they reflect on the twin issues of the hierarchies among media, in particular, the prime position of painting in the Western artistic tradition since the Renaissance, on the one hand, and the lure images constitute for prospective migrants, attracted by blondes and cars, both equally flashy.

My favourite of these is the one that I proposed, and that generated the entire series. It's called *Road Movie* (2004). Depending on when one enters the gallery space, the film looks like a still photograph, evoking a traditional landscape painting, or like a film. The one-shot film *Road Movie* is 17 minutes long. On a four-lane highway, dangerously close to the cars, on the edge of a green median stripe of hollow road, a man walks. The man in the somewhat shabby, slightly out-of-style but very proper suit and black shoes just walks away, his back turned to us. He carries two old cardboard suitcases. He walks fast and disappears into the distance, into nothingness. He never looks up. Cars keep rushing by. Then for at least eight minutes nothing happens but more cars. Empty America.

Just when the viewer might get a bit annoyed by the narrative silence, something happens again. From very small to recognizable, the man comes back, as a relief of the tension emptiness creates. Was he sent back at the other end, refused entry or chased away by angry Americans-only types, or did he return because America has nothing to offer? Or did he return in belated acknowledgement of the viewer? At the end, he comes close enough to looks at us, but he doesn't ever look us in the eyes, because he is too busy walking on.

At this moment, I am most excited about a video installation I am doing on my own (with the help of many friends, of course). Visitors are invited to sit in armchairs or on sofas, around them four women speak to someone else. The interlocutors are people close to them, intimates, but the relationship with whom has been interrupted due to the migration of the women's children: a grandchild she didn't see grow up; a child-in-law she didn't choose or approve of; the emigrated child; in one case, three generations. The intimacy, but sometimes a slight uneasiness, is characteristic of the situation. Sometimes you hear the other voice, sometimes not.

Communication unfolds between the older woman and her relative, but due to the installation set-up, also between the women, and between the women and the visitors, all at once. The performative aspect on all these levels brings about a merging of these communications. The armchairs that can be moved or turned, as if one were visiting the women on the screen, concentrating on one or alternating their attention among the women.

The women are filmed in consistent close-up, as portraits. The relentlessly permanent image of their faces provides a modest monument to the women who suffered these profound losses. It also forces viewers to look these women in the face, in the eyes, and listen to what they have to say, in a language that is foreign, using expressions that seem strange, but in a discourse we can all, affectively, relate to.

Thus, this work pertains to 'migratory aesthetic'. There will be no narrative voice; only the mothers do the talking. Any sense of tourism is carefully avoided: while intensely visual, the films show neither monumentality nor picturesque scenery; no spectacle is offered to gratify a desire for beauty; instead, the films engage intimately with the individuals concerned. All sound is diegetic. Indirectly, the installation constitutes a monument to those mothers who were left behind, bereft of those they most cherished.

As you can deduce from my account of these film projects, they all broach issues that are hard or impossible to categorize, to put in a section of a library, or even under the umbrella of any discipline. I got hooked by these projects because of the enormous learning effect. I discovered things – nuances of emotions, affective interactions, the politics of personal life – that I didn't know enough about to even begin to inquire. Hence, my sense is that the films are so rich as research – regardless of the aesthetic character they also have – because there is always a collective, however provisional and temporal, that enables the generation of insight and knowledge.

MS: Fascinating. And moving – in both senses of that word. OK, so what's exciting or not exciting has something to do with scholar's initiatives, projects, and practices, and how we've gone about encountering or tackling or conceiving of or creating the objects, subjects, media, and environments of visual culture. To pursue this a little further, what if we look for another answer elsewhere? Have you felt, for instance, that studies in visual culture have benefited (are more exciting) or suffered (are less exciting) from the accusation that Visual Culture Studies is ahistorical?

MB: Criticism – not accusation – has always stimulated me to rethink what I thought was clear and certain. As long, of course, as it's not plain vulgar trashing. Of which I have a life-long experience. I think the criticism of ahistoricism is not justified. On the contrary, for me, art-historical historicism has tended to be historically naïve and unreflective. But to decide that, historicism itself needs rethinking. The thrust of Visual Culture Studies – to bracket elite art-only, and to look at power relations, economic and ethnographic factors, use and belief systems, etc. – has made a more sophisticated sense of history possible. One that does not deny the presence in the history of the present. Take Eilean Hooper-Greenhill's *Museums and the Interpretation of Visual Culture* (2001). I am convinced that her take on museums has greatly benefited from the centrality of the concept of visual culture. It got her out of the somewhat empiricist tendency of museum studies, it foregrounded analytical reflection, and yet it is profoundly historical. It is not necessary to repress the present and its concerns when one works historically.

MS: I think I came across this 'accusation' for the first time in 1996 in the *October* 'Visual Culture Questionnaire' which proposed provocatively that Visual Culture Studies leads to ahistoricism, as well as anthropologism and of a disembodying of the image.[2] For you, is this issue of ahistoricism an epistemological question: that we're engaged with the strained links that the emergence of Visual Culture Studies as a movement or field of inquiry has to a particular notion of history in a post-epistemological moment? Or is it simply a question of subject matter: that Visual Culture Studies and its proponents spend a disproportionate amount of time attending to the contemporary, to contemporary spectacles of visual communication, commodity circulation, information, digitality, entertainment, surveillance, the popular, the vernacular, and so on? (Janet Wolff has called this over-valorization of the contemporary a suspicion with a 'new kind of timelessness', [2002] and Adrian Rifkin has mocked its 'perpetual *nowness*' [2003]).

And, as a follow-up question, is your conceptualization of 'preposterous history' a response to this? Here I am of course referring to your idea of 'preposterous history' which demonstrates 'a possible way of dealing with "the past today", ... [a] reversal which puts what came chronologically first ("pre-") as an aftereffect behind ("post-") and its later recycling' (Bal, 1999). It's what Michael Ann Holly (2003) describes as crucial about your presentism: 'the awareness of the presence of the present in encounters with the past'.

MB: If you allow me to declare the 1996 Questionnaire irrelevant and out-of-date (it has been consistently overrated) I'd rather insist that what I have dubbed preposterous history is, precisely, an attempt to overcome both a naïve historicism and an equally naïve presentism. Preposterous history is still history. I consider it the only self-reflective and intellectually tenable conception of historical work.

I have been challenged to rethink my relation to history when my *Reading Rembrandt* became such a scandal piece (Bal, 1991b). I wrote *Quoting Caravaggio* in response to what I considered a misunderstanding of the Rembrandt book, not to renege but to further the argument. More radically than in the earlier book, I theorized history as *necessarily* anachronistic. There I simply put forward the notion that 'Rembrandt' exists in the present as part of popular culture. Look at Amsterdam this year, where the old master is abused to advertise virtually anything *and* help the project of uglification of the city, and I consider myself proven right. But in QC I developed my argument through engagement with contemporary artists.

I focused on works that simultaneously convey pleasure and sorrow, irony and emulation in an explicit relationship to the Baroque. We cannot read those works without a sense of the history into which the artist is inscribing himself. At the same time, I juxtaposed the contemporary works with paintings by Caravaggio – my case study. The baroque works gain a new dimension through the juxtaposition, as much as through the overwriting and the reworking in each of the contemporary works. But the juxtaposition also makes the older works recede farther into the past.

My ambition here could be conceived as a demonstration against that infamous, simplistic accusation of ahistoricism. Such re-visions of baroque art neither collapse past and present, as in an ill-conceived presentism, nor objectify the past and bring it within our grasp, as in a problematic positivist historicism. They do, however, demonstrate a possible way of dealing with 'the past today'. This reversal, which, as you say, puts what came chronologically first ('pre-') as an after-effect behind ('post') its later recycling, is what I like to call a preposterous history.[3] In other words, it is a way of 'doing history' that carries productive uncertainties and illuminating highlights. In that particular book, a vision of how to re-vision the Baroque.

But there is more, something that traditional history cannot do. I moved aesthetics and epistemology into the equation. I put forward the idea that the current interest in the Baroque acts out what is itself a baroque vision, a vision that can be characterized as a vacillation between the subject and object of that vision and which changes the status of both. To the extent that vacillation binds the contemporary to the baroque art, a certain coevalness between the two can be alleged. To understand this I can best draw attention to the insistence, in anthropology, on *shared time* as an epistemological requirement (again, Johannes Fabian's work is key here). My pursuit in this book similarly aims at establishing a coevalness between the contemporary subject, exemplified by the artists I am discussing, and the historical subject, in this case Caravaggio's paintings, through the notion of a 'shared time', defined by concerns that are both of today and of then.[4] It is a vision that integrates an epistemological view, a concept of representation, and an aesthetic, all three of which are anchored in the inseparability of mind and body, form and matter, line and colour, image and discourse. No baroque oeuvre makes a clearer case for the role of both precursor (or inventor) and product (or result) of this oscillation than that of Caravaggio. I gratefully took his oeuvre to not only make the point intellectually, but also make it sensible – in the sense of sense-based.

MS: How does inter-disciplinarity fit into all of this? It's something we've already mentioned in relation to the thought of Barthes. But what about its role in your own research and writings? While it's fair to say that many of your own books have come most directly out of disciplines such as Biblical Studies, Literary Studies, and Art History – and here I'm thinking of publishing projects such as *Lethal Love* (1987), and *Death and Dissymmetry* (1988a), *Narratology* (1985 [1978]), and *On Story-telling* (1991a), and *Reading 'Rembrandt'* (1991b), *Quoting Carravagio* (1999), and *Louise Bourgeois's Spider* (2001) – there's nothing discipline-specific about these books ...

MB: I actually think this is not true. They are very discipline-specific and only through that can they be interdisciplinary as I conceive of that notion. The point is, they are not confined to those disciplines. If you take *Murder and Difference* (Bal, 1988b), for example. That's one long plea for inter-disciplinarity. But the argument is conducted completely from within the disciplines (plural) of Biblical Studies. Three-quarters of the book are sustained critiques of how these disciplines fail their own premises, and how the disciplinarity makes the object of that discipline almost invisible. I would contend something of the same order with *Reading 'Rembrandt'* – I would boldly assert that my approach makes the actual images of the Rembrandt corpus more accessible to detailed interpretation. So, inter-disciplinarity is not the opposite of discipline-specificity, but rather a deepening of the possibilities the disciplines harbour, but are unable to fully exploit because of their conventional methodological hang-ups. In a marvellous article about the concept of the performative, Jonathan Culler cast inter-disciplinarity in the metaphor of travel. From that I got the idea for *Travelling Concepts* (Bal, 2002), my most sustained plea for inter-disciplinarity. He wrote:

> This point of arrival, with talk of a performative concept of gender, is very different from the point of departure, Austin's conception of performative utterances, but to make your fortune, as the genre of the picaresque has long shown us, you have to leave home and, often, to travel a long way. (Culler, 2000)

Culler's article, which traces the fortunes of the concept of the *performative*, travels first back and forth between philosophy – where the concept was first used – and literature – where it solved major problems, but at the same time challenged the limitations of the philosophical proposal – then back to philosophy, on to cultural studies, and back to philosophy again. His article stands out as a model for the kind of study of 'concepts as travelling' that I had in mind when I first contemplated this book.

The *field* of cultural analysis is not delimited because the traditional delimitations must be suspended; by selecting an object, you *question* a field. Nor are its *methods* sitting in a toolbox waiting to be applied; they, too, are part of the exploration. You don't apply one method; you conduct a meeting between several, a meeting in which the object participates so that, together, object and methods can become a new, not firmly delineated, field. This is where travel becomes the unstable ground of cultural analysis. Cultural analysis, like anthropology, does construct an object, albeit with a slightly different sense of what that object is. At first sight, the object is simpler than anthropology's: a text, a piece of music, a film, a painting. But, after returning from your travels, the object constructed turns out to no longer be the 'thing' that so fascinated you when you chose it. It has become a living creature, embedded in all the questions and considerations that the mud of your travel splattered onto it, and that surround it like a 'field'.

Inter-disciplinarity in the humanities, necessary, exciting, serious, must seek its heuristic and methodological basis in *concepts* rather than in *methods*. For myself, the most surprising realization has been that I was able to innovate disciplines from within, to begin with the Bible, simply by doing that methodological homework that anthropologists do routinely: question the self-evidence of methods.

MS: I take your point. Is it this inter-disciplinary impulse that figures the way you raise questions about specific objects and subjects? In so many ways, it is after all the way that these questions are raised that goes on to contribute so profoundly to the formation of new movements, disciplinary patterns, fields of inquiry, such as Film Studies or Cultural Studies or Visual Culture Studies?

MB: Partly. The object, for me, comes first, and this is where I connect well, sometimes even better, to traditional object-oriented fields. This was my advantage with the Bible crowd: I took the text seriously. Another part comes from the cultural changes, the desire for more social commitment, the politics of race and gender that have influenced the ways we think on more levels than one.

First, my position on the objects, whether they be canonical paintings or advertisements. In my view the counterpart of the concepts we work with is not the systematic theory from which they are taken, although that theory matters and cannot be neglected. Nor is it the history of the concept in its philosophical or theoretical development. And it is certainly not a 'context', whose status as text, itself in need of analysis, is largely ignored. The counterpart of any given concept is the cultural text or work or 'thing' that constitutes the *object* of analysis. No concept is meaningful for cultural analysis unless it helps us to understand the object better *on its* – the object's – *own terms*. Here, another background, or root, of the current situation in the humanities comes to the fore.

The turn to methodology already mentioned was partly a reaction to the cultivation of the object and its details, in critical movements such as the new, literary hermeneutics in Germany, the *explication de texte* in France, and the New Criticism in the Anglo-Saxon world. The general term *close reading* is still with us, but the practice of it, I am afraid, is not. This loss is due to practical changes, in particular, the reduction of programmes. But it is also due to the loss of innocence that came with the awareness that no text yields meaning outside of the social world and cultural makeup of the reader. This is where the social movements mentioned above join forces with the pull of the object. I have often had occasion to regret the loss of analytical skills that accompanied the disenchantment with the illusion that 'the text speaks for itself'. True enough, a text does not speak for itself. We surround it, or *frame* it, before we let it speak at all. We have learned this from the political movements, feminism, anti-racism, Aids-activism. But rejecting close reading for that reason has been an unfortunate case of throwing out the baby with the bathwater. For, in the tripartite relationship between student, frame, and object, the latter must still have the last word, simply because it justifies our attention to culture, images, or art.

Whereas this sustained attention to the object is the mission of *analysis*, it also qualifies the term 'cultural' or 'visual analysis'. It is well known that definitions of culture are inevitably programmatic. If 'culture' is defined as the thoughts and feelings, the moods and values of people, then 'analysis' is bound to a phenomenologically oriented approach that shuns the social that is culture's other. If subjectivity is the focus, then social interaction remains out of its scope. And if it is the mind that comprises the cultural fabric, then all we can analyse is a collection of individualities. These traditional conceptions have been abandoned or adjusted, but they continue to share the impulse to define culture in the abstract and general sense. This is the area of study the social sciences focus on. It would be presumptuous to pronounce on what 'culture' is, except perhaps to say that it can only be envisioned in a plural, changing, and mobile existence where power relations and networks operate.

The objects of study of the disciplines that comprise the humanities *belong* to culture but do not, together, constitute it. The qualifier 'cultural' takes the existence and importance of cultures for granted, but it does not predicate the 'analysis' on a particular conception of 'culture'. For, in distinction from, say, cultural anthropology, 'visual cultural analysis' does not *study* visual culture. 'Culture' is not its object. The qualifier *cultural* in 'visual cultural analysis' indicates, instead, a distinction from traditional disciplinary practice within the humanities, namely, that the analysis of the various objects gleaned from the cultural world for closer scrutiny are analysed *in view of* their existence in culture. This means they are not seen as isolated jewels, but as things always-already engaged, as interlocutors, within the larger culture from which they have emerged. It also means that 'analysis' looks to issues of cultural relevance, and aims to articulate how the object contributes to cultural debates. Hence the emphasis on the object's existence in the present. It is not the artist or the author but the objects they make and 'give' to the public domain that are the 'speakers' in analytic discussion. For now, I wish to insist on the participation of the object in the production of meaning that 'analysis' constitutes.

The most important consequence of this empowerment of the object is that it pleads for a qualified return to the practice of 'close reading' that has gone out of style. I wrote *Travelling Concepts* for this reason, as a whole it *is* that plea; it 'argues' it by demonstrating it (Bal, 2002). This is why all of the chapters – different as they are in the way they explore the possible relations between concept and object and the function they assign to the concepts – are *case studies* rather than systematic explanations of the concept concerned.

MS: For you, then, in the end how much of this has to do with method or methodology, critical theory and criticality, discursive and self-reflexive practice? (Here I'm thinking about your co-founding of the Amsterdam School of Cultural Analysis at the University of Amsterdam, and also about a cluster of your publications specifically on cultural theory and cultural analysis such as *The Point of Theory* [Bal and Boer, 1994], *Double Exposures*, [1996], and, as you've already mentioned, *Travelling Concepts in the Humanities* [2002]).

MB: As I've just said, methodology is always important. It's just too often misconceived of as a dogma. Methodological reflection leads inevitably to a move beyond disciplinary boundaries. This is so simply because disciplines have been created historically, at a particular time, and in the long run, rather arbitrarily. For me, without methodological reflection no scholarship can amount to much. But when methods are accepted as grids that automatically lead to understanding of the object, they are equally futile. Instead, methods are discourses that can and must be put into dialogue with the objects. This is why a renewed concept of close reading lies at the heart of all my work.

MS: More recently, you've been pursuing the notion of 'migratory aesthetics', an instance of this close reading for sure?

MB: Yes, that's my current passion. I first coined the phrase to explain the phenomenon in *GLUB (Hearts)* (2004), a multimedia/video installation I did with Entekhabi. *GLUB*, Arabic for 'hearts' names edible 'seeds' – the stuff of the future, growth and change, movement and sustenance. *Hearts* connote the beating heart of a live culture, survival, affection, and excitement. In this film, it is the excitement, overruling complaints and problems, anxieties and xenophobia.

The mixed societies that have emerged from migration have benefited from migrants arrival. Cities have become heterogeneous ('colourful'), music and cinema have been spectacularly enriched. On the streets of Berlin, e.g. in Kreuzberg, the shells of seeds testify to the presence of migrant culture in contemporary European urban centres. Those traces of passing gestures are the 'low' icons of migratory aesthetics. 'Low': inexpensive, modest, and thrown away as rubbish; 'low' as unspectacular, democratic because available to all, and lying around on the once immaculate pavements. Aesthetic, though, because they mark the look of the city that, through these shells and the sociability of the people who left them after eating outside and together, has donned a visible aspect of diversity.

GLUB was presented here as a modest, barely visible 'icon' of the aesthetic changes in everyday urban culture that I term migratory aesthetics. Arab youngsters are often seen hanging around eating seeds. These have rather little taste, provide little nourishment, and have no hallucinogenic qualities. One migrant said they eat them to pass the time that stretches out so endlessly for the unemployed. Then it became a habit, then an appreciated tradition, incorporating (literally) a sense of family and community. It now characterizes the visual sight of migrant young men in European cities. More so, however, when European youngsters began to imitate the cool-looking habit. Identity dissolves, while contact is being established, not necessarily between persons but surely within the 'look' of culture. *GLUB*-eating young men of Arabic *and* German backgrounds testify to the permeability of cultural boundaries, hence, identities.

My publisher at Chicago asked me to come up with a book on this concept, and I am trying to do it. Meanwhile, I initiated a short-term collaboration around it with University of Leeds (Griselda Pollock), and we got funding for a two-year workshop. After the term for this had expired, I continued to seek opportunities, and I am now doing the most exciting new thing. I am co-curating a travelling exhibition, boldly titled 'Migratory Aesthetics', to be held, first in Spain, then in the Netherlands, and hopefully, in many other places in Europe. The co-curator is a young Spanish scholar of modern and contemporary art, Miguel-Ángel Hernández-Navarro.

The starting point is that the aesthetic dimension of the social phenomenon of migration has not been foregrounded in its own right. This dimension moves in two directions: the influence of newcomers to the host countries' culture, especially the 'look' of public space (*GLUB* is a prime example); and the influence of host countries on the subjective relationships, primarily entertained through memory, of migrants to their homeland, whether they have personal memories of that homeland or not; whether this homeland is imaginary or the product of 'post-memory'. These relationships, in turn, also impact on the countries of residence, where they circulate among migrants and their interlocutors, like ghosts. We think it is time to also acknowledge, even celebrate, the enormous cultural benefits of migration for the so-called host societies, so as to strike a more positive note, an attention in which the absorption of the memories of the countries and departure communities of is fully integrated. This is what the qualifier 'migratory' denotes. It also indicates the doubly moving quality of video.

The exhibition seeks to foreground such a positive 'tone', and thus contribute to the enhancement of the artistic potential of the social fabric itself of the cities where the exhibition will be held. The thematic foci of the show, while not limited to or even concentrating on migration, stress the low-threshold accessibility of the medium of video as well as the artistic and intellectual accessibility of the fantasy-driven, imaginative images, and sounds that the works, together, generate. It is our firm conviction that no concessions to populism or didacticism are necessary to produce an exhibition that is artistically original and of a high-level, and will bring people into the gallery who would not ordinarily visit art venues. To give just one example: school children, used to television and other forms of moving images, will also recognize both the sophisticated play with forms and the friendly approach to cultural diversity with which they are familiar in their everyday lives. The aesthetic of many works is inspired by the accessibility of video; while art is often taken to be an inspiration for everyday culture, here the emphasis goes in the opposite direction. Thus, while many will recognize and consequently be fascinated by the way the artworks play with their own everyday culture, the level at which the works re-imagine these traditions will be an inspiration to look and think critically and imaginatively. This will help lessen the gap between urban populations.

But the most important means to attract visitors beyond the usual constituencies is the intensification of the bond between art and the city. The relation between the exhibition and the city will be enhanced in the mode of installing, the distribution of works through the space, and in the general 'feel' of the exhibition as a busy, buzzing, noisy space. In Murcia, where the show begins, the venue, an old church transformed into a space for contemporary art, is located across from the very international food market. In Enkhuizen, where the Zuiderzeemuseum will host the show, the location is at the waterfront, in a historic district still replete with the traces of older waves of migration. In both these sites, a film is commissioned that addresses the local situation and thus brings the city inside the gallery in yet another way. In other cities, we will seek to include a few works that also anchor the show locally.

We are envisioning an exhibition of video art as a terrain, or field, to explore the questions that emerge when we put migration and video together. In order to elaborate an alternative aesthetic able to enhance the aesthetic of migration as a *migratory aesthetic*, both more political and embodied than classical aesthetic, and more incorporative of 'aesthetic thinking' (Bennett and Frow, 2007) than usual reflections on migration, we concentrate the exhibition on that which is not easily visible because it is not ordinarily considered either 'aesthetic' or 'migratory'. We focus on the medium of video as a privileged one to grasp the connection between the two parts of the phrase. Video, is, we claim, eminently suitable to articulate and show the bond between Europeans and the recently arrived populations. We aim to conduct this reflection in ways that return to aesthetics its old meaning of *sense-based binding.*

Between 'moving' as a multiple quality of the image, and 'binding' as a specific conception of aesthetics, we wish to deploy video art as a body of thought that helps articulate the concept of 'migratory aesthetics'. In addition to being just the right tool to mobilize, so to speak, mobility at the heart of our reflection, video is also a recently arrived new inhabitant in the art world, so that migrancy and video can be considered conceptual metaphors of each other. On the art-sociological level, video is also the emblematic medium of generalized availability. Being, on the one hand, an instrument of recording, hence, posing the dual problem of documentary and realism, it is also the tool of manipulation and subsequent creation. Throughout the exhibition, this integration of movement and (emotional) moving with documentary and manipulative making will be present, and elaborated in relation to works that explore a limited number of sub-themes.

To make this a bit more concrete, here are some examples of themes around which we seek to organize the exhibition:

(1) the *ordinary*, banal, and sometimes abject 'look' of the urban everyday (e.g. Conce Codina's work);
(2) the *hetero-temporality* of a world that likes to think in progression – from modern to post-modern and beyond – thus considering cultures less obsessed with such narrowly linear temporality, 'under-developed' (e.g. Jesus Segura's three works);
(3) the *surface* or 'skin' that prevents us from seeing, as both racism and the opaqueness of the seemingly transparent medium of video elaborate together, like a blind corner (*ángulo ciego*) two examples are Célio Braga's exploration of the skin as access to the face and Roos Theuws' experiment with the skin of video;
(4) distance and closeness, or 'facing': the bond between speech – as in not just 'giving voice', but also listening, and answering, all in multiple meanings – and the face, turning the classical 'window of the soul' into an 'inter-face'; again, Braga's work, as well as my portraits of mothers of migrants;
(5) the cut, or severance, between mobility and sedentariness, embodied in the discrepancy between a dubious form of visibility of migrants in the West and the absence of those left behind, most poignantly embodied in mothers separated from their child; one example would be Mona Hatoum's *Measures of Distance*; another, Ballester's *Mimoune*, based on the aesthetic of home video.

These themes will not be treated in isolation, but will run through the exhibition like undercurrents. They constitute the knots that bind migration and video together, as well as art works and viewers.

The new area, for me, the 'discovery' if you like, is that bond between migratory culture and video culture. This project is growing so big – with academic discussion workshops in each city – that it may well occupy me for a long time.

MS: Do 'travelling concepts' continue to drive your current and forthcoming research, writing, and art making projects? And is this where you see the future of Visual Culture Studies, and of studies in the Humanities more generally?

MB: As you can gather from all this, my answer is yes. I will continue to push what has been so productive for myself, my students, and the Amsterdam School for Cultural Analysis (ASCA) I am fortunate enough to work in. I am especially privileged now that I have been awarded the Royal Dutch Academy of Arts and Sciences Professorship. In addition to being the greatest academic honour one can earn in this country, it comes with a very nice budget for teaching replacements and possibilities to travel. '*Nothing is Missing*', the project on mothers for which I must travel to the countries of origin, would not have been possible without that special support. It is funny how things come around: work on travelling concepts now earned me the means to do the actual travelling.

As for the future ... it is becoming a bit difficult to pronounce on that. The future is in the hands of the younger generations. I love to work with young people, benefit from their creativity and their technological literacy, the ease of taking nothing for granted. They will determine how the academy evolves. If they can overcome the burden of bureaucracy, I'd be ecstatic. I haven't managed that.

I don't know what the future of the visual environment will become. It's changing, rapidly, and well it should. A culture that fails to change dies.

Notes

1 This danger is real and potentially fatal for the humanities. I have had occasion to witness it while serving on evaluation committees of postgraduate programmes. This danger alone is enough to make us cautious about giving up discipline-based groupings too easily.

2 On this perceived ahistoricism, there is a very useful chapter in Hal Foster's book *Design and Crime* (2002) London: Verso, pp. 83–103, that helped me finally fully understand why at least one of the Editors of the 'Questionnaire' felt that if Visual Culture Studies organized itself on a model of Anthropology it was no longer organized around a model of history as were Art History, Film History, and so on, hence its ahistoricism. I discuss this at some length with Foster elsewhere in this collection.

3 The term is coined after Patricia Parkerm (1992) 'Preposterous Events', *Shakespeare Quarterly*, 43 (2): 186–213.

4 Naturally, Fabian means the epistemological requirement of 'shared time' much more literally than I can claim for a historical relationship. But heuristically, it makes sense to seek such a coevalness to understand how, precisely, the past is in the present. See Fabian, Johannes (1984) *Time and the Other: How Anthropology Makes Its Object.* New York: Columbia University Press/New Haven, CT: Yale University Press.

References

Bal, Mieke (1985 [1978]) *Narratology: Introduction to the Theory of Narrative.* Toronto: University of Toronto Press.

Bal, Mieke (1987) *Lethal Love: Literary Feminist Readings of Biblical Love Studies.* Bloomington: Indiana University Press.

Bal, Mieke (1988a) *Death and Dissymmetry: The Politics of Coherence in the Book of Judges.* Chicago: The University of Chicago Press.

Bal, Mieke (1988b) *Murder and Difference: Gender, Genre and Scholarship on Sisera's Death,* (Gumpert, Matthew *trans.*). Bloomington: Indiana University Press.

Bal, Mieke (ed.) (1989) *Anti-Covenant: Counter-Reading Women's Lives in the Hebrew Bible.* Sheffield: Sheffield Academic Press/The Almond Press.

Bal, Mieke (1991a) *On Story-telling: Essays in Narratology.* Santa Rosa, CA: Polebridge Press.

Bal, Mieke (1991b) *Reading 'Rembrandt': Beyond the Word-Image Opposition.* New York: Cambridge University Press.

Bal, Mieke and Boer, Inge E. (eds.) (1994) *The Point of Theory: Practices of Cultural Analysis.* Amsterdam: Amsterdam University Press.

Bal, Mieke (1996) *Double Exposures: The Subject of Cultural Analysis.* New York: Routledge.

Bal, Mieke (1997) *The Mottle Screen: Reading Proust Visually.* Stanford, CA: Stanford University Press.

Bal, Mieke (1999) *Quoting Caravaggio: Contemporary Art, Preposterous History.* Chicago: University of Chicago Press.

Bal, Mieke (2001) *Looking in: The Art of Viewing.* The Netherlands: G&B Arts International.

Bal, Mieke (2001) *Louise Bourgeois Spider: The Architecture of Art-writing.* Chicago: The University of Chicago Press.

Bal, Mieke Bal (ed.) (2002) *Travelling Concepts in the Humanities: A Rough Guide.* Toronto: University of Toronto Press.

Bal, Mieke (2003a) 'Visual essentalism and the object of visual culture', *Journal of Visual Culture,* 2 (1): 5–32.

Bal, Mieke (2003b) 'Reply', *Journal of Visual Culture,* 2(2): 260–68.

Bal, Mieke (2005) *The Artemisia Files.* Chicago: The University of Chicago Press.

Bal, Mieke (2006) *A Mieke Bal Reader.* Chicago: The University of Chicago Press.

Bennett, Tony and Frow, John (eds.) (2007) *Handbook of Cultural Analysis.* Oxford and Malden, MA: Blackwell.

Bleeker, Maaike (2002) *The Locus of Looking: Dissecting Visuality in the Theatre.* PhD thesis, University of Amsterdam.

Bryson, Norman (2003) 'Visual culture and the dearth of images', *Journal of Visual Culture,* 2(2): 229–32.

Culler, Jonathan (2000) 'Philosophy and Literature: The Fortunes of the Performative', *Poetics Today*, 21(3): 503–519.
Elkins, James (2003) 'Nine modes of interdisciplinary for visual studies', *Journal of Visual Culture*, 2(2): 232–37.
Fabian, Johannes (1984) *Time and the Other: How Anthropology Makes Its Object*. New York: Columbia University Press/New Haven, CT: Yale University Press.
Foster, Hal (2002) *Design and Crime*. London: Verso.
Holly, Michael Ann (2003) 'Now and Then', *Journal of Visual Culture*, 2(2): 238–42.
Hooper-Greenhill, Eilean (2001) *Museums and the Interpretation of Visual Culture*. London: Routledge.
Leech, Peter (2003) 'Visual culture and the ideology of the sublime', *Journal of Visual Culture*, 2(2): 242–46.
Mirzoeff, Nicholas (2003) 'Stuff and nonsense', *Journal of Visual Culture*, 2(2): 247–49.
Mitchell, W.J.T. (2003) 'The obscure object of visual culture', *Journal of Visual Culture*, 2(2): 249–52.
Naficy, Hamid (2001) *An Accented Cinema: Exilic and Diasporic Filmmaking*. Princeton: Princeton University Press.
Parkerm, Patricia (1992) 'Preposterous Events', *Shakespeare Quarterly*, 43(2): 186–213.
Pollock, Griselda (2003) 'Visual Culture and its discontents: joining in the debate', *Journal of Visual Culture*, 2(2): 253–60.
Rifkin, Adrian (2003) 'Waiting and Seeing', *Journal of Visual Culture*, 2 (3): 325–39.
'Visual Culture Questionnaire' (1996) *October*, no.77, summer, 25–70.
Wolff, Janet (2002) 'Mixing Metaphors and Talking about Art', in Michael Ann Holly and Keith Moxey (eds.) *Art History, Aesthetics, Visual Studies*. Williamstown, MA: Sterling and Francine Clark Art Institute, pp. 260–68.

INDEX